C0-FZK-146

WordPerfect for Windows

Timothy J. O'Leary
Linda I. O'Leary

Copyright © 1993 by McGraw-Hill, Inc. All rights reserved. Printed in the United States of America. Except as permitted under the United States Copyright Act of 1976, no part of this publication may be reproduced or distributed in any form or by any means, or stored in a database or retrieval system, without the prior written permission of the publisher.

4 5 6 7 8 9 0 BAN BAN 9 0 9 8 7 6 5 4

ISBN 0-07-048878-9

Library of Congress Card Number 92-82700

Information has been obtained by Mitchell McGraw-Hill from sources believed to be reliable. However, because of the possibility of human or mechanical error by our sources, Mitchell McGraw-Hill, or others, Mitchell McGraw-Hill does not guarantee the accuracy, adequacy, or completeness of any information and is not responsible for any errors or omissions or the results obtained from use of such information.

CONTENTS

Overview Word Processing WP3
Definition of Word Processing WP3
Advantages of Using a Word Processor WP3
Word Processing Terminology WP5
Case Study WP5
Before You Begin WP6

Lab1 Editing a Document WP7
Loading the WordPerfect for Windows Program WP7
Exploring the WordPerfect Window WP8
Entering WordPerfect Commands WP9
The Button Bar WP11
Opening a File WP12
Moving Around the Document Window WP15
Moving Through the Document WP18
Editing a Document WP22
Closing a File WP33
Saving and Replacing an Existing File WP34
Printing a Document WP35
Exiting WordPerfect for Windows WP36
Key Terms WP37
Command Summary WP37
Lab Review WP38
Matching WP38
Fill-In Questions WP38
Practice Exercises WP39

Lab 2 Creating and Formatting a Document WP40
Creating a Document WP40
Spell-Checking WP42
Saving a New File WP46
Copying Text Between Documents WP46
Moving Text WP49
Replacing Selected Text WP50
Using the Date Command WP52
Aligning Text Flush with the Right Margin WP54
Displaying Hidden Codes WP55
Setting Margins WP57
Using and Setting Tabs WP59
Using the Indent Command WP61
Using the Replace Command WP64
Deleting Codes WP67
Setting Justification WP68
Saving the Document in a New File WP69
Printing the Document WP70
Key Terms WP71
Command Summary WP71
Lab Review WP72
Matching WP72
Practice Exercises WP72

Lab 3 Merging Documents and Creating Tables WP77
The Merge Feature WP77
Entering Merge Codes in the Primary File WP78
Creating the Secondary File WP83
Merging the Primary and Secondary Files WP89
Creating a Table WP91
Entering Text in a Table WP93
Entering a Formula WP94
Selecting Cells WP95
Setting Cell Display WP96
Copying a Formula WP96
Bolding and Centering Table Text WP98
Changing the Column Width WP99
Changing the Table Line Style WP100
Inserting a Row WP101
Key Terms WP103
Command Summary WP104
Lab Review WP104
Matching WP104
Practice Exercises WP105

Lab 4 Creating a Report and a Newsletter WP111
Changing Case WP111
Creating a Table of Contents WP112
Creating Footnotes WP118
Editing a Footnote WP121
Numbering Pages WP122
Suppressing Page Numbers WP123
Preventing Widows and Orphans WP124
Using Block Protection WP125
Changing Fonts WP127
Creating Graphic Lines WP128
Defining Columns WP130
Using Hyphenation WP135
Adding Graphics WP136
Adding a Text Box WP141
Key Terms WP145
Command Summary WP146
Lab Review WP147
Matching WP147
Practice Exercises WP147

Case Project WP151

Summary WordPerfect 5.1 for Windows WP155
Glossary of Key Terms WP155
Summary of Selected WordPerfect 5.1 for Windows Commands WP157

Index WP161

OVERVIEW
Word Processing

One of the most widely used applications software programs is a word processor. To put your thoughts in writing, from the simplest note to the most complex book, is a time-consuming process. Even more time-consuming is the task of editing and retyping the document to make it perfect. There was a time when perfection in written communication was difficult, if not impossible, to achieve. With the introduction of word processing, errors should be nearly nonexistent—not because they are not made, but because they are easy to correct. Word processors let you throw away the correction fluid, scissors, paste, and erasers. Now, with a few keystrokes, you can correct errors, move paragraphs, and reprint your document easily.

Definition of Word Processing

Word processing applications software is a program that helps you create any type of written communication via a keyboard. A word processor can be used to manipulate text data to produce a letter, a report, a memo, or any other type of correspondence. Text data is any letter, number, or symbol that you can type on a keyboard. The grouping of the text data to form words, sentences, paragraphs, and pages of text results in the creation of a document. Through a word processor you can create, modify, store, retrieve, and print part or all of a document.

Advantages of Using a Word Processor

The speed of entering text data into the computer depends on the skill of the user. If you cannot type fast, a word processor will not improve your typing speed. However, a word processor will make it easier to correct and change your document. Consequently, your completed document will take less time to create.

Another timesaver is word wrap; as you enter text you do not need to decide where to end each line, as you do on a typewriter. When a line is full, the program automatically wraps the text down to the next line.

Where a word processor excels is in its ability to change, modify, or *edit* a document. Editing involves correcting spelling, grammar, and sentence-structure errors. As you enter characters using the keyboard, they are displayed on the screen and stored electronically in the computer's main memory. As you find errors, you can electronically delete and correct them. Once the document is the way you want it to appear, it can be permanently saved on a disk and printed on paper. Goodbye, correction fluid!

In addition to editing a document, you can easily revise or update it by inserting or deleting text. For example, a document that lists prices can easily be updated to reflect new prices. A document that details procedures can be revised by deleting, or cutting, old procedures and inserting new ones. This is especially helpful when a document is used repeatedly. Rather than recreating the whole document, you change only the parts that need to be revised.

Revision also includes the rearrangement of pieces, or blocks, of text. For example, while writing a report, you may decide to change the location of a single word or several paragraphs or pages of text. You can do it easily by cutting, or removing selected text from one location, then pasting, or placing, the selected text in another location. Blocks of text can also be copied from one area of the document to another. This is a real advantage when the text includes many recurring phrases or words.

Combining text in another file with text in your document is another advantage of word processors. An example of this is a group term paper. Each person is responsible for writing a section of the paper. Before printing the document, the text for all sections, which is stored in different files, is combined to create the complete paper. The opposite is also true. Text that may not be appropriate in your document can easily be put in another file for later use.

Many word processors include additional support features to further help you produce a perfect document. A spelling checker checks the spelling in a document by comparing each word to a dictionary of words. If an error is found, the program suggests the correct spelling. A syntax checker electronically checks grammar, phrasing, capitalization, and other types of syntax errors in a document. A thesaurus displays alternative words that have a meaning similar or opposite to the word you entered.

You can also easily control the appearance or format of the document. Formatting includes such operations as changing the line spacing and margin widths, adding page numbers, and displaying page headers and footers. You can also quickly change how your text is aligned with the left or right margin. For example, text can be centered between the margins, or justified—evenly aligned on both the left and right margins. Perhaps the most noticeable formatting feature is the ability to apply different fonts (type styles and sizes) and text appearance changes such as bold and italics to all or selected portions of the document. Some word processing programs also have the ability to produce and display graphics lines and boxes. Graphic boxes can then be used to hold text or graphic images that you place into the document.

Many word processing programs also include the WYSIWYG (What You See Is What You Get) feature. This feature allows you to see on screen exactly (or as close as possible) how your document will appear when printed. This means that the effects of your format changes are immediately displayed on the screen.

If, after reading the printed copy, you find other errors or want to revise or reformat the document, it is easy to do. Simply reload the document file, make your changes, and reprint the text! Now that saves time!

Word Processing Terminology

The following list of terms and definitions are generic in nature and are associated with most word processing programs.

Block: Any group of characters, words, lines, paragraphs, or pages of text.

Bold: Produces dark or heavy print.

Center: Centers a line of text evenly between the margins.

Copy: To duplicate selected text in another location in the document.

Cut: To remove or delete selected text from an area in the document.

Document: Text-based output created by a word processing program.

Edit: To change or modify the content of the document.

Font: Type styles and sizes.

Format: Defines how the printed document will appear; includes settings for underline, boldface, print size, margin settings, line spacing, and so on.

Insert: To enter new text into a document between existing text.

Justified: Text that is evenly aligned on both the left and right margins.

Paste: To place selected text in another location in the document.

Spelling checker: A support feature that checks words or the entire document for correct spelling.

Text data: Any number, letter, or symbol you can type on a keyboard.

Thesaurus: A support feature that displays synonyms and antonyms for words in your document.

Word wrap: The automatic adjustment of the number of characters or words on a line that eliminates the need to press the ↵ (Return) key at the end of each line.

WYSIWYG: The feature that displays a document on screen as close as possible to how it will appear when printed.

Case Study

As a recent college graduate, you have accepted your first job as a management trainee for The Sports Company. The Sports Company is a chain of discount sporting goods shops located in large metropolitan areas throughout the United States. The program emphasis is on computer applications in the area of retail management and requires that you work in several areas of the company.

In this series of labs, you are working in the Southwest Region office and are responsible for setting up the credit card enrollment program and for assisting with the monthly newsletter.

In Labs 1 and 2, you will create a letter to be sent to all new credit card recipients. You will learn how to use the word processing program to edit and format the letter.

Lab 3 demonstrates how to personalize the letter by creating a form letter and merging the recipients' personal information such as their name into the form letter. You will also prepare a table that summarizes the gross sales for the regional stores.

In Lab 4, the regional office has decided to send a monthly newsletter to credit card customers. You have been asked to design and prepare several articles for inclusion in the newsletter.

Before You Begin

The following assumptions have been made:

- WordPerfect 5.1 for Windows has been properly installed on the hard disk of your computer system.
- The default program settings are in effect except for the following:
  1. The Format Retrieved Documents for the Default Printer initial setting has been changed to Off.
  2. The Prompt for Hyphenation setting is Never.

The File/Preference/Environment command can be used to change these settings. These exceptions are necessary to ensure that the procedures and figures in the text are the same for all students.

- The WorkBook printer appears in the Select Printer dialog box when Select Printers from the File menu is used.
- The data disk contains the data files needed to complete the series of WordPerfect 5.1 for Windows labs and practice exercises. These files are supplied by your instructor.
- You have completed the Windows labs or you are already familiar with how to use Windows.

LAB

1 Editing a Document

CASE STUDY

The Sports Company is a chain of sporting goods shops located in large metropolitan areas across the United States. The stores are warehouse oriented, discounting the retail price of most items 15 percent. They stock sporting goods products for the major sports: team sports, racquet sports, aerobics, golf, and winter sports.

As a recent college graduate, you have accepted a job in a management training program for The Sports Company. The training program emphasis is on computer applications in the area of retail management. The program requires that you work in several areas of the company. You have been assigned to work in the Southwest Regional Office. You will be responsible for getting the credit card program set up and for assisting with the monthly newsletter.

During the next four labs you will be using WordPerfect for Windows to create a letter to be sent to the new credit card recipients, and to work on the monthly newsletter.

Competencies

In this lab you will learn how to:

1. Load the WordPerfect for Windows program.
2. Issue commands.
3. Move around a document.
4. Delete characters, words, and lines of text.
5. Undelete text.
6. Insert text in Insert and Typeover modes.
7. Insert and delete blank lines.
8. Clear the display.
9. Save and print a document.
10. Exit WordPerfect for Windows.

Loading the WordPerfect for Windows Program

Start Windows. (If you need help, refer to Windows Lab 1 or consult your instructor for details.)

The Windows Program Manager should display the WordPerfect Applications window icon.

Note: If your system is set up differently, your instructor will provide alternative instructions.

Open the WordPerfect Applications window. The WordPerfect Applications window contains four program icons: WordPerfect, File Manager, Speller, and Thesaurus. File Manager, Speller, and Thesaurus are stand-alone applications that can be run under Windows without starting the WordPerfect program. Choose the WordPerfect for Windows application icon.

WP 5.2 note: The WordPerfect applications window contains two additional icons, Quick Finder File Indexer and WPWin Installation.

Put your data disk in drive A (or the appropriate drive for your system). A title screen is displayed while the computer loads the WordPerfect for Windows program into memory.

Exploring the WordPerfect Window

Your screen should be similar to Figure 1-1.

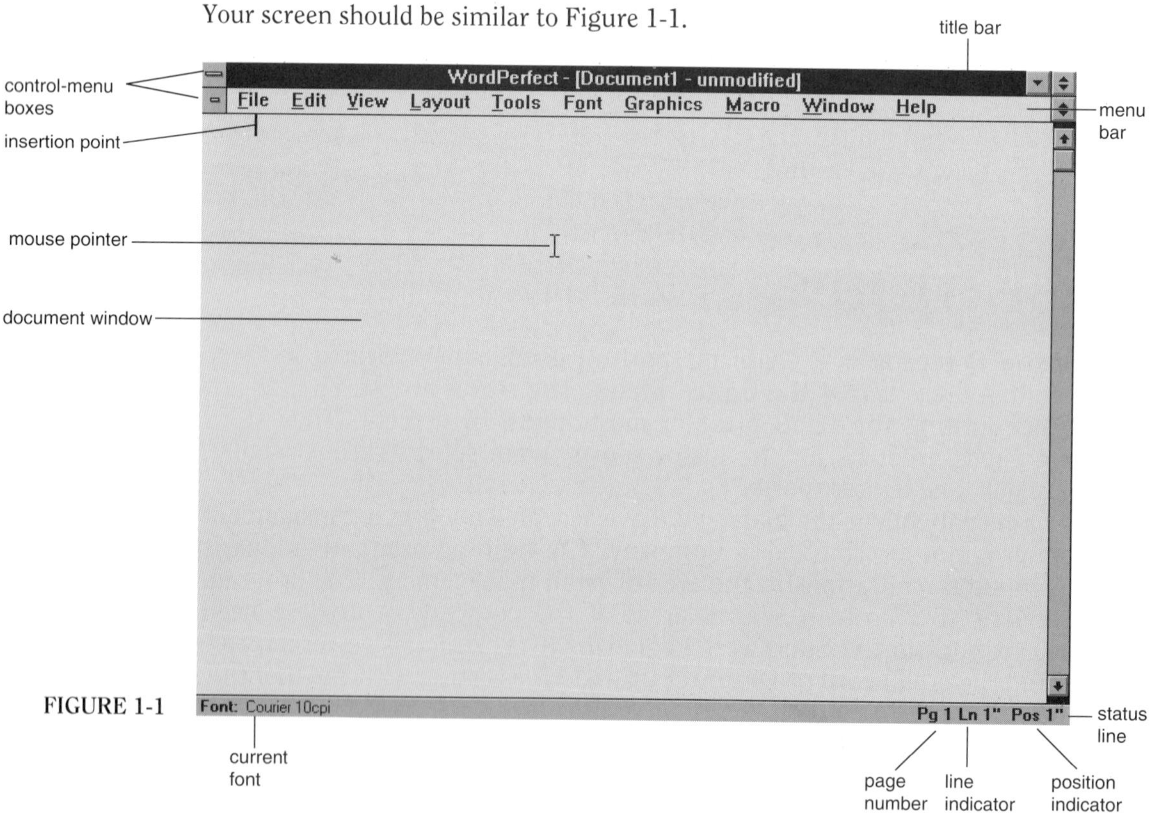

FIGURE 1-1

The WordPerfect for Windows application window is displayed. As you can see, many of the features on the WordPerfect application window are the same as in the Windows applications. Among those features are a title bar, a menu bar, control-menu boxes, Minimize and Maximize buttons, icons, and mouse compatibility. You can move and size WordPerfect windows, select commands, use Help, and switch between files and programs just like in Windows. Your knowledge of Windows makes learning and using WordPerfect for Windows much easier.

The large blank area below the menu bar is the WordPerfect for Windows document window. The WordPerfect word processing program is similar to the Write application you used in Windows, except it is much more powerful. The document window is currently empty and is like a blank sheet of paper waiting for you to type on it. The insertion point shows you where the next character you type will appear. If you have a mouse, the mouse pointer appears as an I-beam when it is in the document window area, or as an arrow when it is moved to the application parts of the window.

The line of information at the bottom of the screen is the **status line**. It tells you four pieces of information:

Font The currently selected **font** (typeface and size). The font on your screen may be different than in Figure 1-1.

Pg 1 The number of the **page** where the insertion point is located. It is currently on page 1.

Ln 1" The vertical distance in inches between the insertion point and the top of the page. This is the **line** on which the insertion point rests. The insertion point is currently 1 inch from the top of the page.

Pos 1" The horizontal location or **position** of the insertion point on the line. This is displayed in inches from the left edge of the paper. The insertion point is currently 1 inch from the left edge of the paper.

The font, line, and position settings on your screen are the default or initial WordPerfect for Windows settings. WordPerfect for Windows comes with many default settings, which are generally the most commonly used settings. For example, the current position of the insertion point at 1 inch from the left edge of the paper is the default left margin setting. The right margin default setting is 1 inch from the right edge of the paper. Other default settings include a standard paper-size setting of 8½ by 11 inches, tab settings every half inch, and single line spacing. If you do not specify different settings, WordPerfect uses the default settings.

Entering WordPerfect Commands

As in other Windows applications, you communicate with WordPerfect by choosing a menu item from the menu bar. When chosen, the selected menu bar item displays a drop-down menu of commands from which you must choose. The procedure to operate the menu is the same as in Windows. Commands can be chosen by clicking on the menu item or command with the mouse or by using the keyboard. If you are using the keyboard, you must activate the menu bar first by pressing (ALT) or (F10). Then a menu item or command can be chosen by typing the underlined letter or by moving the highlight to the command and pressing (↵). The command to open a file is in the File menu. To open this menu,

Press: (ALT) + F

or

Click on: File

The File drop-down menu of commands is displayed. The highlighted bar called the selection cursor appears over the first command in the drop-down menu and in the menu bar over the chosen command. The status line displays a brief description of the New command, the command the selection cursor is on in the drop-down menu.

Many of the features in the drop-down menu should be familiar to you. If a shortcut key is available, it is displayed to the right of the command. The ellipses (...)

indicate that a dialog box will be displayed for you to specify additional information needed to carry out the command. A dimmed command indicates the command is not available for selection until certain other conditions are met. A check mark means that a command is on.

A new feature on the menu is the (▶) arrowhead symbol. This symbol means that a **cascading menu** will be displayed when this command is selected. To see an example of a cascading menu,

Choose: Preferences

Your screen should be similar to Figure 1-2.

FIGURE 1-2

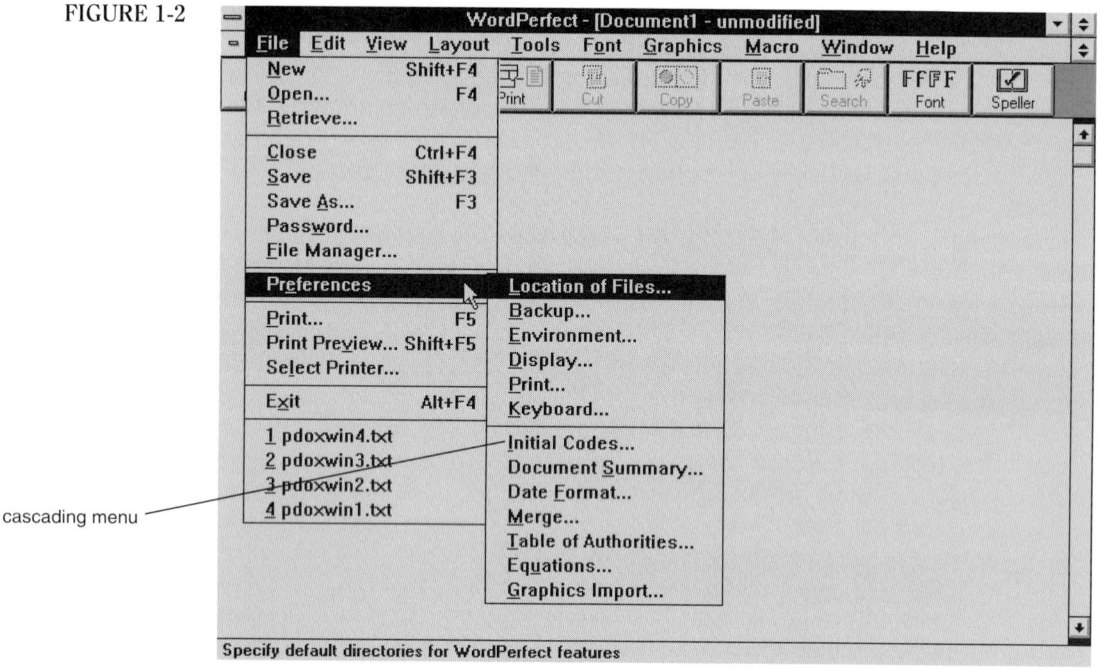

The cascading menu displays options associated with the Preferences command in the File menu. To cancel the cascading menu,

Press: ESC

At the bottom of the File menu, a list of the most recently used files may be displayed. If they are not displayed, this is because the setup at your school has turned this feature off.

WP 5.2 note: The File menu contains an additional command, Find File.

To preview the commands associated with each menu, display the drop-down menu for each of the other menu bar items.

Open the Help drop-down menu. The WordPerfect Help menu is similar to the Windows Help menu.

To select the Index command,

Choose: Index

WP procedure: The Help menu contains the Contents command in place of the Index command. Choose Contents. Then to display the index, choose the Index button or Index from the Contents topic list.

The Help Index window provides the means to access an alphabetical list of all the topics in the Help files. The screen tells you how to use the Help Index. The Help buttons and other Help features operate just like the Windows Help system.

The Help window can be closed by choosing Exit from the Help File menu, by choosing Close from the Help control menu ((ALT) + (F4)), or by double-clicking on the Help control-menu box. Using any of these methods, close the Help Index window.

You can also quickly open the Help Index by pressing the (F1) shortcut key (this shortcut key, however, is not displayed on the menu). When no other command is in use, the (F1) key accesses the Help system as if you had selected Help from the menu bar and then Index from the drop-down menu of commands.

The Button Bar

WordPerfect has several additional features that you can display on the screen. These features are listed in the View menu.

Choose: View

For the most part, the commands in this menu are toggle commands. This means that when you choose the command, it turns the feature either on or off. Those options with a check mark are options that are on by default. The feature you would like to display on the screen is the **Button Bar**. This feature is used with the mouse as a shortcut to commands on the menu. One predefined Button Bar comes with the WordPerfect for Windows program. You can also create your own customized Button Bars. Even if you do not have a mouse, you can display the Button Bar; however, you must have a mouse to use it.

To display the predefined Button Bar,

Choose: Button Bar

Your screen should be similar to Figure 1-3.

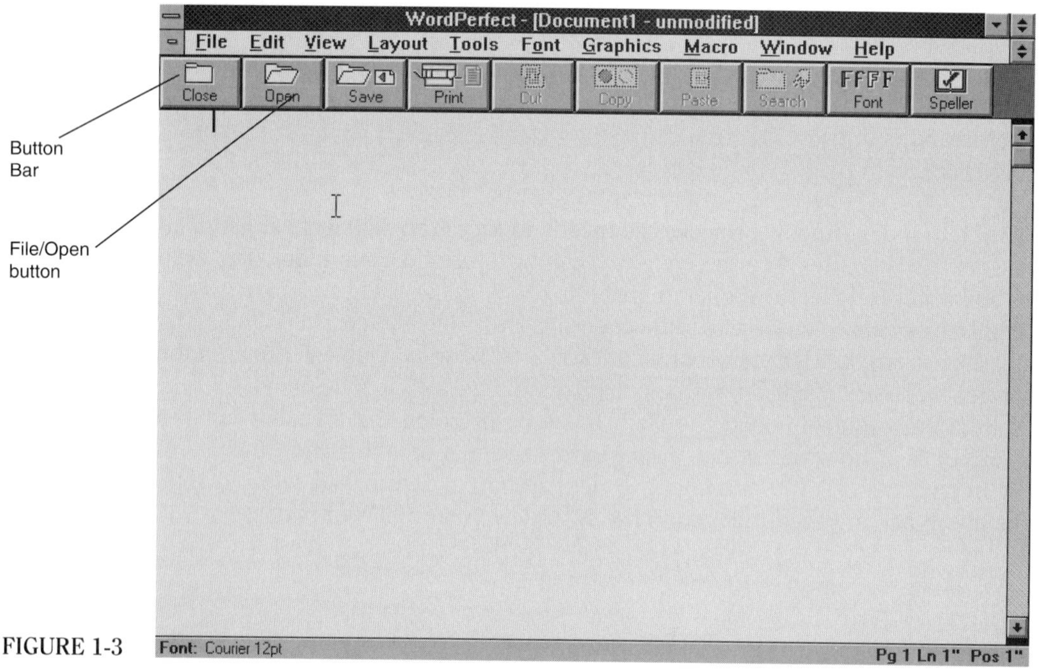

FIGURE 1-3

The Button Bar is displayed below the menu bar. It contains 10 icon buttons that represent many of the menu bar commands. The label below each icon tells you the command the button will perform. As in the menu bar, if the button appears dim, it is not available for selection. If you have a mouse, you can click on the appropriate button to choose a command. You will learn how to use the Button Bar in the next section.

WP 5.2 note: The Paste button displays a graphic of paper and a paste jar. Additionally, when the pointer is on the Button Bar, the status line displays the message, "Use right mouse button to display Button Bar menu." This menu lets you move and modify the Button Bar or select from among 10 other button bars that are available in this release.

Opening a File

The first draft of the credit card letter has already been created for you and saved on your data disk in a file named LETTER. To open this file, you need to choose Open from the File menu. This command can be chosen by using the drop-down menu, by using the shortcut key, F4, or if you have a mouse, by clicking on the Open button on the Button Bar. Using any of these methods,

Choose: File/Open

Your screen should be similar to Figure 1-4.

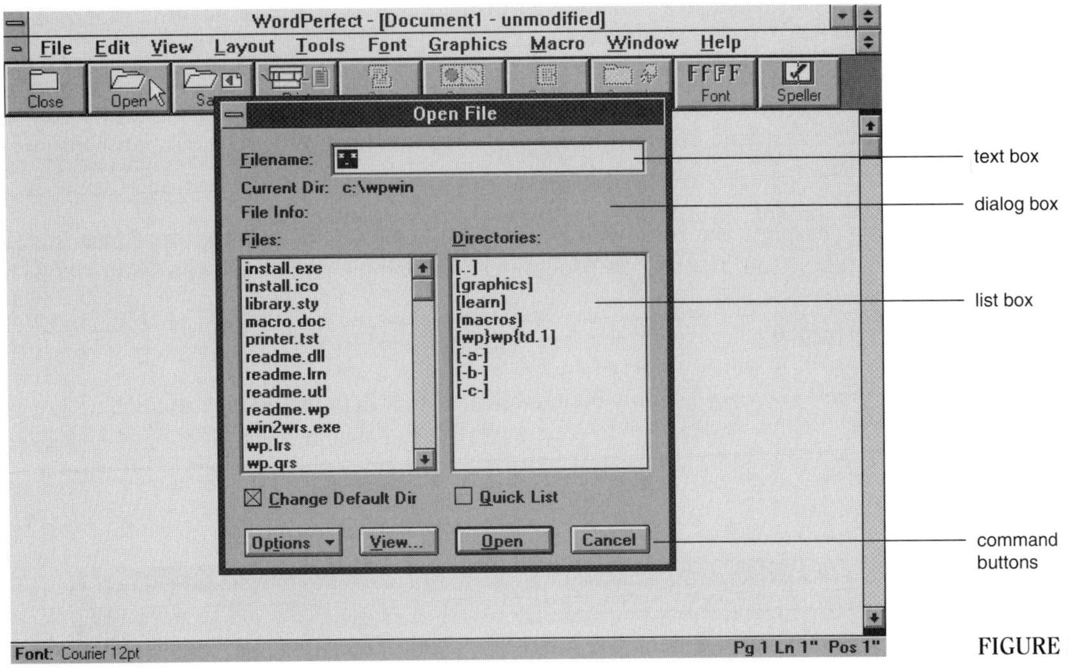

FIGURE 1-4

Note: The files and directories displayed on your screen will be different than those in Figure 1-4.

The Open File dialog box is displayed. It contains the same dialog box features as dialog boxes in Windows: a text box, list boxes, and command buttons. It also operates just like Windows dialog boxes. If you have a mouse, simply click on the area you want to use, or if the option you want to select is visible, double-click directly on it to select it. To move from one area to another using the keyboard, press (ALT) and the underlined letter of the box name or press (TAB) until the area you want to use is selected. Then select the option from the list or type the text in the text box.

You need to enter the path and filename of the file you want to open. As in Windows, you can type the path and name of the file in the text box or you can choose the path and file from the list boxes. You will choose the drive and filename from the list boxes. The filename will then be automatically entered into the filename text box. First you need to change the drive from the default drive to the drive containing your data disk by selecting the appropriate drive from the Directories list box.

Select: a (or the appropriate drive)

Now the filenames and directories displayed in the Files list box are those on your data disk in the selected drive.

Note: If you get a system error message, check that your disk is properly inserted in the drive and that the disk-drive door is completely closed. Reselect the option.

The file you want to open is LETTER. If necessary, scroll the Files list box until the filename is displayed.

Select: LETTER

Note: If the filename LETTER is not displayed in the Files list box, ask your instructor for help.

To complete the command, you need to choose the Open button. Since this is the default button, you can choose it if you are using a keyboard by pressing ↵.

Choose: Open

Mouse note: You could simply double-click on the filename to open the file.

Your screen should be similar to Figure 1-5.

FIGURE 1-5

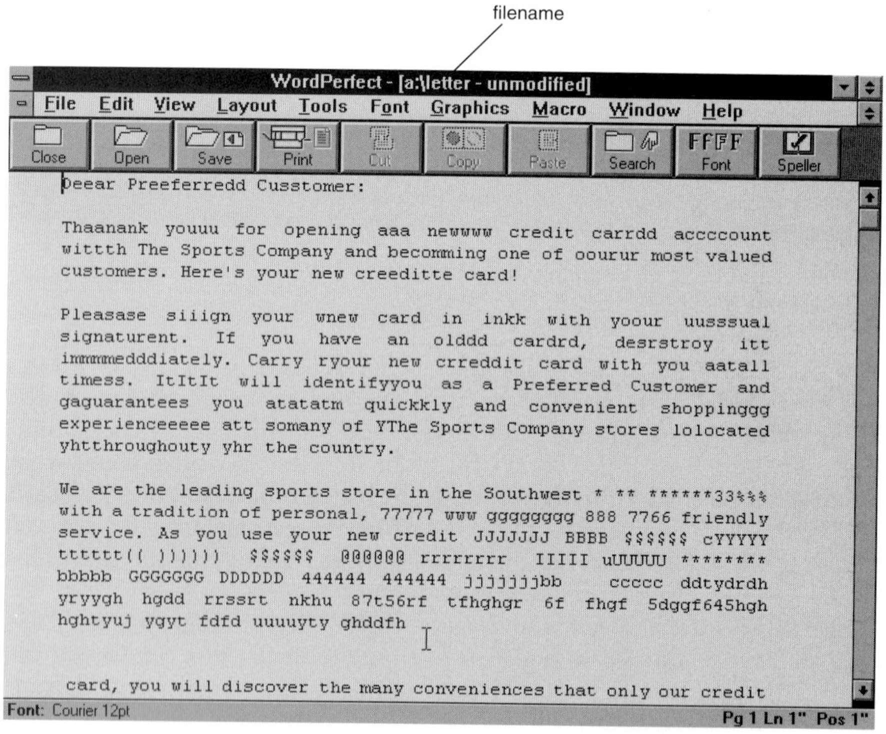

The file is loaded and displayed in the document window. This file contains a first draft of the letter to new credit card customers. As you can see, it contains many errors. You will learn how to correct these errors in this lab.

Also notice, in addition to the program name in the title bar, the filename is also displayed. The "unmodified" indicator following the filename tells you that no changes have been made to this file since it was opened or since it was last saved. As soon as a change is made to the file, this indicator disappears.

Moving Around the Document Window

The mouse or the keyboard can be used to move through the text in the document window. Depending upon what you are doing, the mouse is not always the quickest means of moving; therefore, if you are using the mouse, you will learn how to move through the document using both methods. If you do not have a mouse, follow the keyboard directions only. If you have a mouse, follow the instructions in *both* sections.

You use the mouse to move the insertion point to a specific location in a document. To do this, position the I-beam at the location in the text where you want to move the insertion point to and click the left button.

Move to: "y" of "you" (first line of first paragraph)

Notice the insertion point has not moved and the status line information has not changed.

Click: left button

The insertion point should now be positioned on the right or left side of the "y."

If it is positioned to the left of the "y," this means the I-beam was positioned more to the left side of the character when you pressed the mouse button. The letter to the right of the insertion point is the selected character, in this case the "y."

If it is positioned to the right of the "y," this means the I-beam was positioned more to the right side of the character when you pressed the mouse button. The letter to the right of the insertion point is the selected character, in this case the "o."

Throughout the labs you will be instructed to move to a specific letter in the text. This means to move the insertion point to the *left* side of the character so that the character to the right is selected.

Practice using the mouse to move the insertion point to the left side of a character by moving it to the following locations on the screen:

Move to: "I" in "If" (second line of second paragraph)
Move to: "c" in "country" (last word of second paragraph)
Move to: "D" in "Deear" (first line of document)

The insertion point can also be moved around the screen using the arrow keys. The arrow keys move the insertion point one character space in the direction indicated by the arrow.

Note: Be careful to only use the keys specified as you are following the directions in this section. If you do, the instructions and figures in the text should be the same as what you see on your screen. Also, make sure the (NUM LOCK) (number lock) key is not on when using the numeric keypad area. If it is, numbers will be entered on the screen rather than the insertion point moving through the text.

Press: (→) (6 times)

Your screen should be similar to Figure 1-6.

FIGURE 1-6

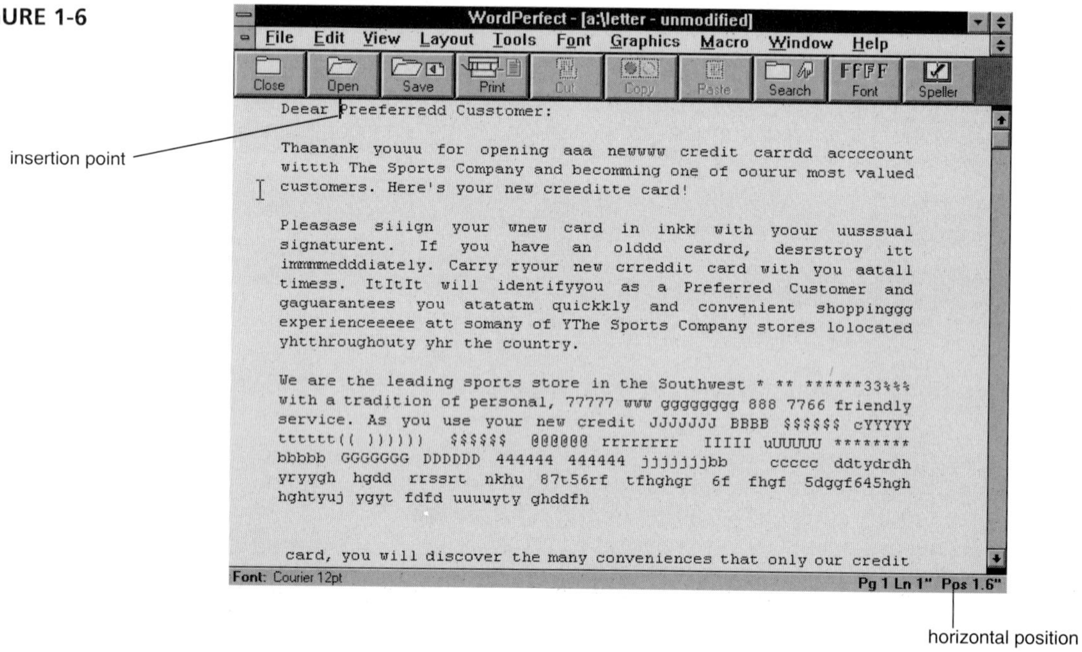

The insertion point moved six character spaces to the right and should be positioned to the left of the "P" in "Preeferredd." When the insertion point is positioned to the left of a character, the character to the right is the selected character. In this case, "P" is selected. Notice how the Pos number in the status line has increased to 1.6", reflecting the change in the horizontal location of the insertion point on the line.

Press: (↓)

The insertion point moved down one line. Since this is a blank line, the insertion point moves back to the left margin on the line. The number in the Ln indicator on the status line has increased to 1.17", reflecting the change in the location of the insertion point by telling you its new vertical or line location.

Press: (↓)

The insertion point moved down to the next line and to the second "n" in "Thaanank." It moved to that position because it was last located in a line containing text at that position (1.6"). The insertion point will attempt to maintain its position in a line of text as you move up or down through the document.

By holding down either ← or →, the insertion point will move quickly character by character along the line.

To see how this works, hold down → until the insertion point is positioned on the "a" in the word "acccount."

If you moved too far to the right along the line of text, use ← to move back to the correct position.

This saves multiple presses of the arrow key. Many of the WordPerfect insertion point movement keys can be held down to execute multiple moves.

Using the arrow keys and the status line for insertion point location reference,

Move to: "d" in "lolocated" (last sentence of second paragraph, Ln 2.83" Pos 7.4")

Note: Throughout the WordPerfect labs, you will be instructed to move the insertion point to specific locations in the text. To confirm the insertion point position, a brief description of where the text is located and/or the line and position location follows in parentheses. If your insertion point is not at the described location, move it there before continuing.

The default right margin setting is one inch from the right side of the paper (Pos 7.5".) To see what happens when the insertion point reaches the right margin,

Press: → (2 times)

The insertion point automatically moved to the beginning of the next line. Unlike a typewriter, you did not need to press Return to move from the end of one line to the beginning of the next. It is done automatically for you.

You can also move the insertion point word by word in either direction on a line using CTRL in combination with → or ←.

Press: CTRL + → (2 times)

The insertion point moved two words to the right along the line. It should be positioned on the "t" in the word "the." To move back to the first word in this line,

Press: CTRL + ← (2 times)

The HOME and END keys can be used to quickly move the insertion point to the beginning or end of a line of text respectively. To move to the end of this line,

Press: END

To move back to the beginning of the line,

Press: HOME

The insertion point should be back on the "y."

Moving Through the Document

The document window space is not large enough to display the entire document. To bring additional text into view in the window you can scroll the text using either the mouse or the keyboard.

The scroll bar on the right border of the document window operates just like the scroll bar in Windows. The ↑ and ↓ scroll arrows in the vertical scroll bar will scroll the document window vertically. Just as in Windows, to scroll continuously, hold down the mouse button while pointing to a scroll arrow. Again, if you are using a mouse, complete both the mouse and keyboard directions in this section.

Click: ↓ scroll arrow (3 times)

The text at the top of the window has scrolled off the screen, and the bottom of the letter is now displayed. Notice that the insertion point is no longer displayed on the screen. It is still located next to the "y" (Ln 3" Pos 1"). To actually move the insertion point, you must click on a location on the screen. Dragging the scroll box moves multiple screens forward or backward through the document. Clicking above or below the scroll box moves backward or forward one full window on the document. The location of the scroll box reflects your position in a file.

Move to: "T" in "The" (Ln 6.83" Pos 1")

The insertion point is now displayed in the document window.

Drag the scroll box to the top of the scroll bar and move the insertion point to the "D" in "Deear" (Ln 1" Pos 1").

Using the ↓,

Move to: last line of text on the screen (Ln 4.83" Pos 1")

If the insertion point is positioned on either the top or bottom line of the screen, using ↑ or ↓ will scroll more lines of the document onto the screen. As you scroll up or down through the document, the lines at the top or bottom of the screen move out of view to allow more text to be displayed.

To scroll the rest of the letter into view on the screen,

Press: ↓ (12 times)

The insertion point should be at the beginning of the word "The."

Your screen should be similar to Figure 1-7.

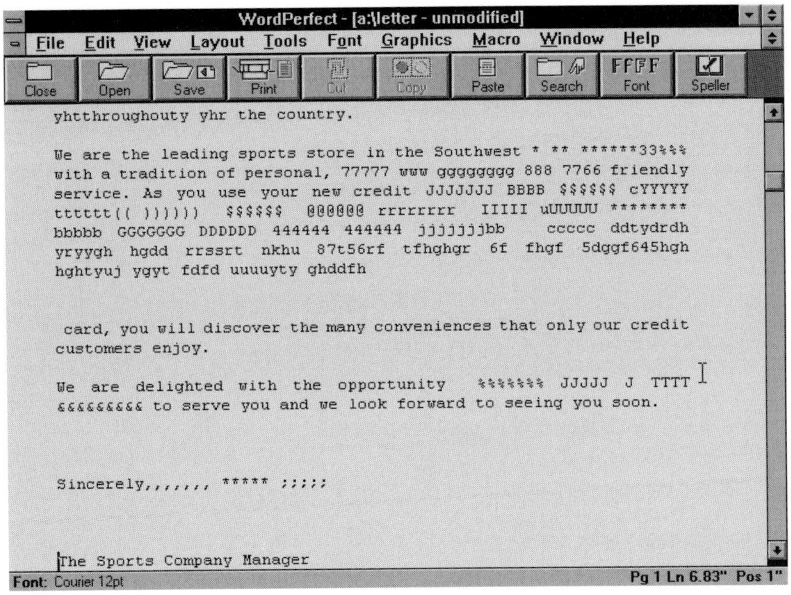

FIGURE 1-7

The lines of text at the beginning of the letter are no longer visible in the window. They scrolled off the top of the window to allow the new lines at the bottom of the window to be displayed.

You can also move in large jumps quickly through a document by moving a window or a page at a time, moving to a specific page, or moving to the end or beginning of the document.

To move up or down a full window of text on the document, use the (PGUP) or (PGDN) keys.

Press: (PGUP) (2 times)

The insertion point moved to the top line of the current window and then to the top line of the previous window of text.

If you have a mouse you can click above or below the scroll box to move a window at a time on the document.

The insertion point can be moved to the top line of a page using the (ALT) + (PGUP) or (ALT) + (PGDN) key combination. A page refers to the physical printed page. To move to the top of the next page,

Press: (ALT) + (PGDN)

The insertion point is positioned on the first line of page 2. Notice the status line displays Pg 2 Ln 1". To show where one page ends and another begins, WordPerfect displays a solid line to mark the page break. To see this line,

Press: (↑)

Your screen should be similar to Figure 1-8.

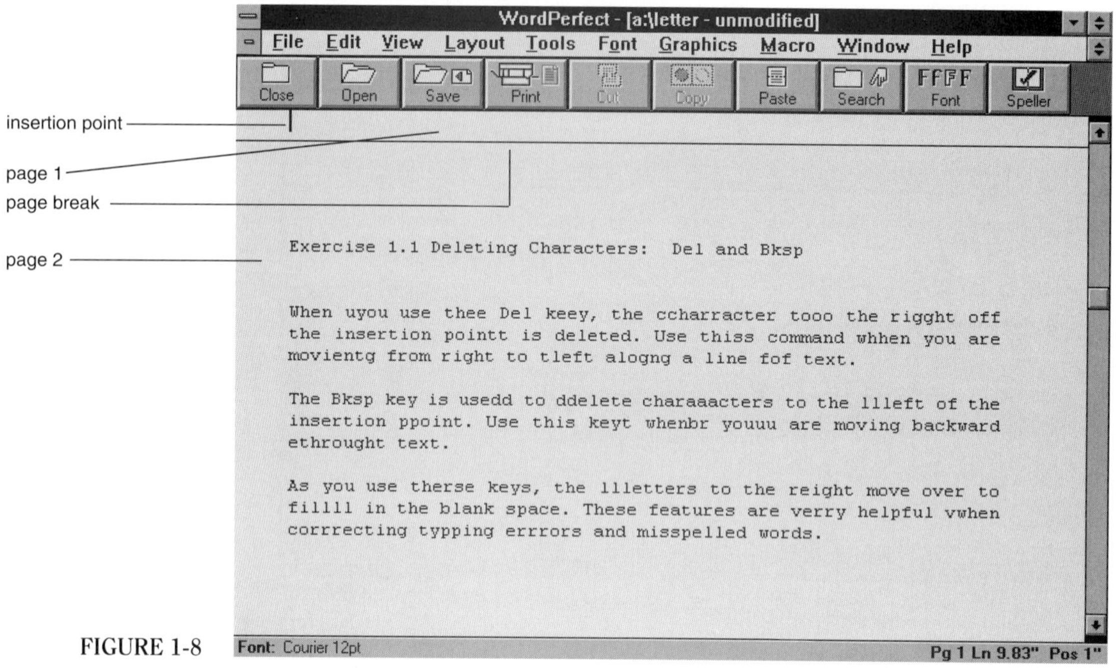

FIGURE 1-8

The insertion point is positioned on the last line of page 1, and the status line displays Pg 1 Ln 9.83". To move to the top of page 1,

Press: ALT + PGUP

The insertion point should be on the first line of page 1.

To move through several pages of the document at once, you could press ALT + PGDN or ALT + PGUP multiple times. Or you can use the Go To command in the Edit menu.

Note: Throughout the WordPerfect for Windows labs, command sequences will appear following the word "Choose:". The keyboard shortcut will appear below the command sequence following the symbol ➢. The mouse alternative will appear following the word "Click." You can use either the mouse or the keyboard to enter the command.

Choose: Edit/Go To
➢ CTRL + **G**

Your screen should be similar to Figure 1-9.

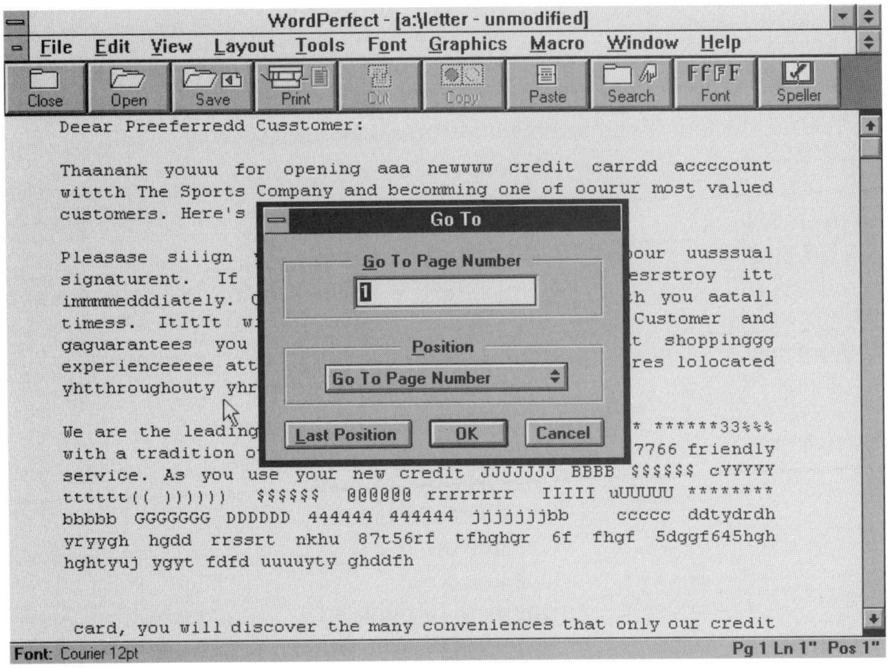

FIGURE 1-9

The Go To dialog box is displayed. To learn more about the Go To command, you will use the Help system.

Press: (F1) Help

By pressing (F1) after selecting a command from a menu, the Help system displays information directly related to the procedure you are trying to perform. This is called **context-sensitive Help**. Read the information in the Help window about the Go To command. Close the Help window.

The Go To Page Number text box is selected. To enter the page number you want to move to,

Type: 5
Choose: OK

Reminder: You can press (↵) to choose OK.

The insertion point is positioned on the first line of page 5.

The biggest jump the insertion point can make is to move to the beginning or end of a document. To move to the end of this document,

Press: (CTRL) + (END)

The insertion point should be positioned on a blank line on page 9 of this document. This is the last line in the file.

To move quickly back to the first line of text in the document,

Press: CTRL + HOME

The insertion point should be positioned on the first line of page 1 of this document.
To review, the following movement features have been covered:

Mouse	Action
Point to the new location and click left button	Positions insertion point
Click scroll arrow	Scrolls the text line by line in the direction of the arrow
Click above/below scroll box	Scrolls the document window by window
Drag scroll box	Moves multiple windows up/down

Key	Action
→	One character to right
←	One character to left
↑	One line up
↓	One line down
CTRL + →	One word to right
CTRL + ←	One word to left
HOME	Left end of line
END	Right end of line
ALT + PGUP	Top of previous page
ALT + PGDN	Top of next page
PGUP	Top of window
PGDN	Bottom of window
CTRL + HOME	Beginning of document
CTRL + END	End of document
Edit/Go To<page #>OK	Moves to top of specified page

Editing a Document

Now that you have learned how to move around the document, you are ready to learn how to correct errors in or **edit** a document.

The next part of this lab contains a series of exercises. Each exercise will show you a WordPerfect editing feature and allow you to practice using the feature. As you read the text in the book, you will be directed to use the editing feature to correct the exercise on your screen. When you have completed the exercise, a figure in the book will show you how your screen should appear. After completing each exercise, press ALT + PGDN to go to the next exercise. To begin the exercise,

Press: ALT + PGDN

Exercise 1.1: Deleting Characters—DEL and BKSP

The first exercise, "Exercise 1.1 Deleting Characters: DEL and BKSP," should be on your screen.

The paragraphs in this exercise contain many errors that you will correct using the (DEL) and (BKSP) keys. The (DEL) key removes the selected character and the (BKSP) key removes the character to the left of the insertion point.

The first error is in the second word, "uyou." The character "u" preceding the word "you" needs to be deleted. To position the insertion point on the "u,"

Move to: "u" in "uyou" (Ln 2.17" Pos 1.5")

As you delete text on a line, WordPerfect examines the line to see whether the word beginning on the next line can be moved up to fill in the extra space without exceeding the margin setting. This process of filling in the spaces is called **reformatting**. If there is not enough space, WordPerfect adjusts the size of the blank spaces between the words to keep the right and left margins even. When text is displayed with even right and left margins, it is called **full justification**. This is the default setting in WordPerfect. Watch your screen carefully as you,

Press: (DEL)

Your screen should be similar to Figure 1-10.

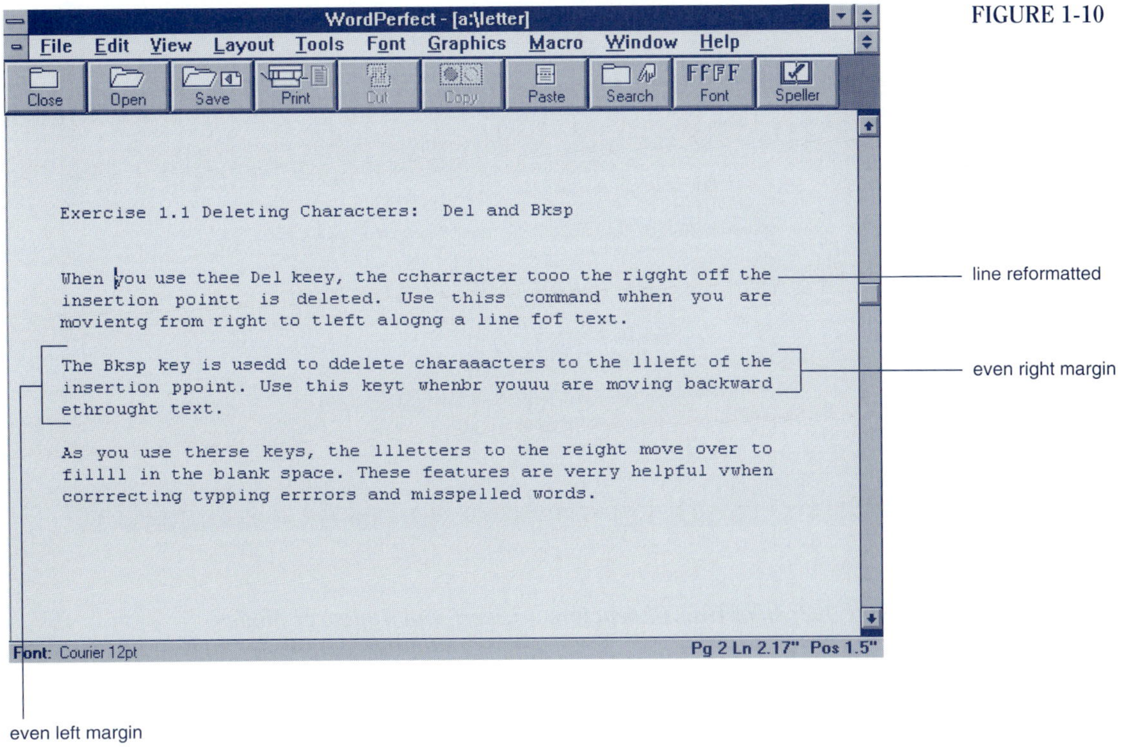

FIGURE 1-10

The selected character, in this case the "u," is deleted. The text to the right moved over one space to fill in the space left by the deleted character. Additionally, because there was enough space on the line, the first word on the second line, "the," moved up to the end of the first line.

Also notice that because you made a change to the file, the indicator "unmodified" is no longer displayed in the title bar. Continue to correct the first paragraph using the (DEL) key.

A second way to delete a character is with (BKSP). This key will delete the character to the left of the insertion point. Therefore it is particularly useful when you are moving from left to right along a line of text.

The first word in the last line of the second paragraph should be "through." You will remove the "t" at the end of this word.

Move to: space after "t" in "ethrought" (Ln 3.17" Pos 1.9")
Press: (BKSP)

The character to the left of the insertion point, in this case the "t," was removed and the text to the right moved over to fill in the blank space.

Complete the exercise by using (BKSP) to correct the text in the second paragraph as you move backward through the text.

Practice using the (DEL) and (BKSP) keys to correct the third paragraph.

When you are done, your screen should be similar to Figure 1-11.

FIGURE 1-11

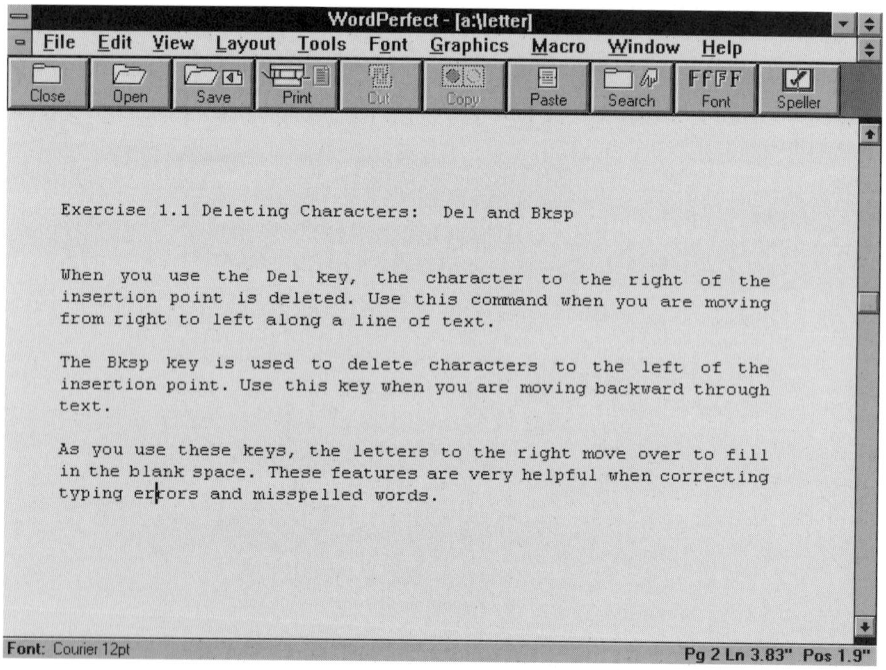

Exercise 1.2: Inserting Characters—Insert and Typeover Modes

Press: (ALT) + (PGDN)

Text can be entered into a document in either the Insert or Typeover modes. The default setting for WordPerfect is the **Insert mode**. As you type in Insert mode, new characters are inserted into the existing text. The existing text moves to the right to make space for the new characters, and the text on the line is reformatted as necessary.

The first sentence on the screen should read: "The insert mode allows new text to be entered into a document." The three missing words, "insert," "to," and "a," can be easily entered into the sentence without retyping it. To enter the word "insert" before the word "mode" in the first sentence,

Move to: "m" in "mode" (Ln 2.17" Pos 1.4")
Type: **insert**
Press: Spacebar

The word "insert" has been entered into the sentence by moving everything to the right to make space as each letter is typed.

Continue to correct the sentence by entering the word "to" before the word "be" and the word "a" before the word "document."

The second method of entering text in a document is the **Typeover mode**. In this mode, the new text types over the existing characters. The (INS) (Insert) key changes the mode from Insert to Typeover.

Press: (INS)

To tell you that the Typeover mode is on, the word "Typeover" appears on the left side of the status line.

The next sentence should read: "The typeover mode allows you to type over existing text." To correct this sentence,

Move to: "o" of "overtype" (Ln 2.67" Pos 1.4")
Type: **typeover**

As each character was typed, the character (or space) under it was replaced with the character being typed.

Next, to replace the word "under" with "over,"

Move to: "u" of "under" (Ln 2.67" Pos 4.7")
Type: **over**

Notice there is still one extra character. To remove the extra "r,"

Press: (DEL)

To turn off the Typeover mode,

Press: (INS)

Your screen should be similar to Figure 1-12.

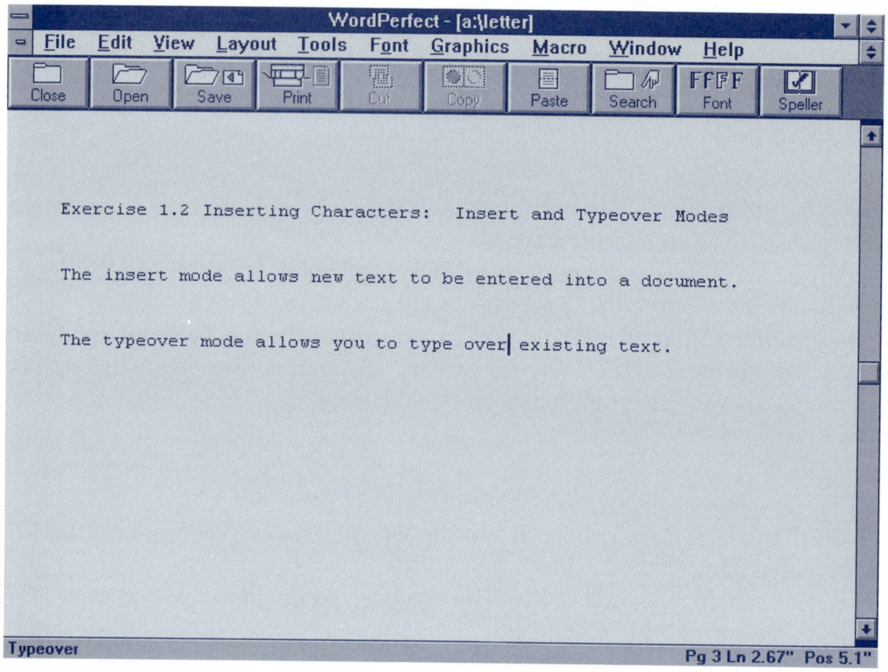

FIGURE 1-12

Exercise 1.3: Deleting Words—CTRL + BKSP

Press: ALT + PGDN

The CTRL + BKSP key combination is used to delete entire words. The insertion point can be positioned on any character of the word to be deleted. Any punctuation following a word is considered part of the word and is deleted also.

The first line on the screen contains several duplicate words. To remove the first duplicate word, "command,"

Move to: "c" of "command" (Ln 2.17" Pos 1.5")
Press: CTRL + BKSP

The word the insertion point is positioned on is deleted. Notice also that the blank space following the word was deleted, leaving the correct number of spaces between words. The text to the right filled in the blank space from the deleted word.

If the insertion point is placed on a blank space between words, then using CTRL + BKSP deletes the word to the left of the insertion point and the blank space the insertion point is on.

Use CTRL + BKSP to delete the other unnecessary words in the sentences on the screen.

After completing the exercise, your screen should be similar to Figure 1-13.

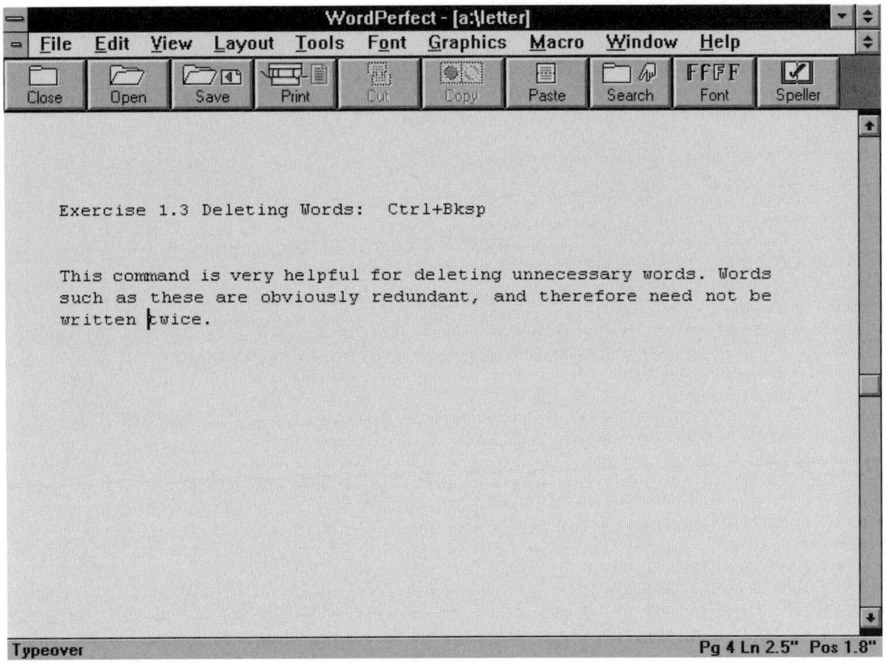

FIGURE 1-13

Exercise 1.4: Deleting to End of Line—(CTRL) + (DEL)

Press: (ALT) + (PGDN)

The (CTRL) + (DEL) key combination will delete everything on a line from the insertion point to the right. If the insertion point is placed at the beginning of a line, all the text on the line will be deleted.

You will delete the unnecessary text following the word "insertion point" in the first line of this exercise.

Move to: "8" immediately following "point" (Ln 2.17" Pos 5.4")
Press: (CTRL) + (DEL)

The text from the insertion point and to the right of the insertion point is deleted.

Continue this exercise by deleting the unnecessary characters at the end of the next two lines.

Next, delete the entire contents of the fourth line by placing the insertion point on the first character in the line.

Your screen should be similar to Figure 1-14.

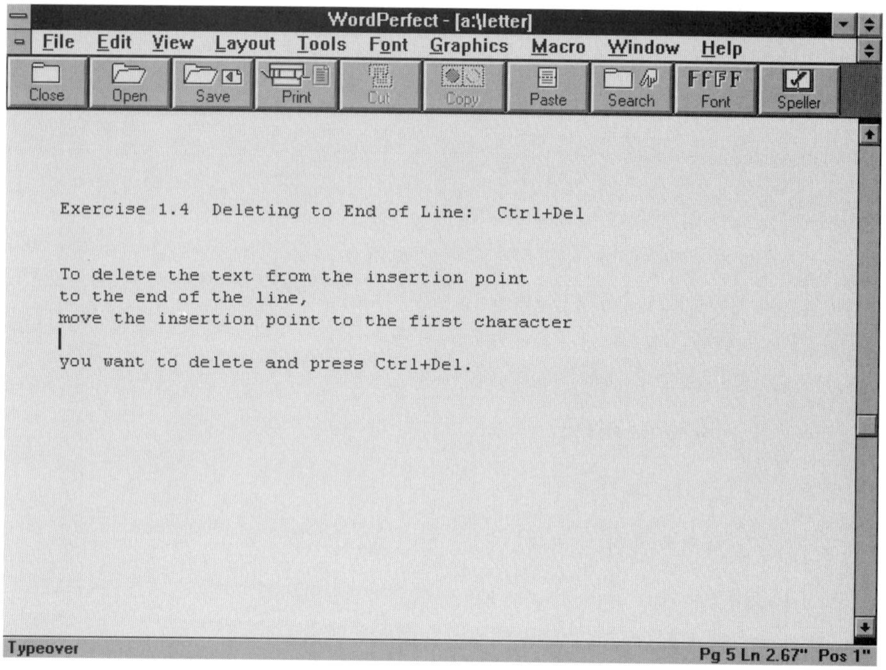

FIGURE 1-14

Exercise 1.5: Deleting Selected Text

Press: (ALT) + (PGDN)

Several characters, words, or lines of text can be deleted at once by first selecting the text and then pressing (DEL). Selecting text is done the same way as you learned in Windows. To select text, first move the insertion point to the beginning of the text to be deleted. Then select the text by expanding the highlight using the mouse or the keyboard.

You will erase the lines labeled 1, 2, and 3 in the exercise. First, to select these lines,

Move to: "Y" of "You" (Ln 2.67" Pos 1")

A word, sentence, or paragraph can be selected as follows:

Double-click	Selects a word
Triple-click	Selects a sentence
Quadruple-click	Selects a paragraph

To select portions of text, simply drag the mouse to expand the highlight to cover the portion of text you want to select.

Drag the mouse until lines 1 through 3 are highlighted.

If you needed to cancel a selection, you would simply click the mouse.

Text is selected by holding down SHIFT and using the → or ← keys to expand the highlight character by character in the direction indicated. You can also use the ↑ or ↓ keys to expand the highlight to the same position on the line above or below.

Additionally, there are many keystroke combinations that can be used to select blocks of text. For example, you can use SHIFT + CTRL + → or ← to select a word to the right or left, or SHIFT + CTRL + ↑ or ↓ to select from the insertion point to the beginning or end of a paragraph. Alternatively, you could press the Select function key, F8, to turn on Select mode, and then expand the highlight using the arrow keys. Using F8 eliminates the need to hold down SHIFT.

Hold down SHIFT or press F8.

Press: ↓ (3 times)

Release the SHIFT key.

If you needed to cancel a selection, you could simply move the insertion point without holding down SHIFT, or you could press F8 again.

Your screen should be similar to Figure 1-15.

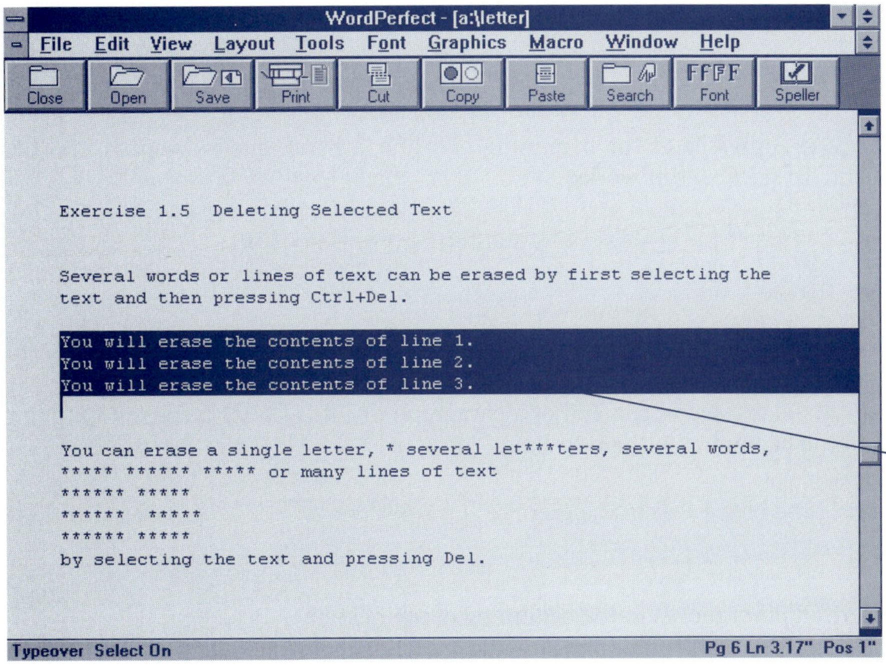

selected text

FIGURE 1-15

The highlight covers lines 1 through 3, indicating they have been selected. Next, to erase the selected lines of text,

Press: DEL

The contents of lines 1, 2, and 3 have been deleted.

In a similar manner, select and erase all the asterisks (*) from the remaining lines of text in this exercise.

Exercise 1.6: Inserting and Deleting Blank Lines

Press: (ALT) + (PGDN)

The (↵) key is used to insert a blank line into text or to end a paragraph. This is the same as if you pressed Return on a typewriter. This is called a **hard carriage return.** When (↵) is pressed, WordPerfect automatically enters a hidden **code** at that location in the document. Codes are used by the program to control the display of text. The codes are hidden so that the screen does not get cluttered. You will learn in the next lab more about these codes and how to display the codes on the screen.

If (↵) is pressed in the middle of a line of text, all text to the right of the insertion point moves to the beginning of the next line. For example,

Move to: "m" of "middle" (Ln 2.17" Pos 5.3")
Press: (↵)

A hard carriage return code is entered at the end of the first line, and the text from the insertion point to the right moves down to the beginning of the next line.

If you press (BKSP), the hard carriage return code at the end of the first line is deleted and the text returns to its original location.

Press: (BKSP)

If (↵) is pressed at the beginning of a line, a blank line is inserted into the document. To see how this works,

Move to: "I" of "If" in the second sentence (Ln 2.67" Pos 1")
Press: (↵)

A blank line is inserted into the text, forcing the line the insertion point is on to move down one line.

If (↵) is pressed at the end of a paragraph or line of text, the insertion point moves to the beginning of the next line.

Move to: end of last line in the exercise (Ln 3.67" Pos 2")
Press: (↵)

The insertion point moves to the beginning of the next line.

To delete a blank line, position the insertion point at the beginning of the blank line and press (DEL). To try this,

Move to: beginning of blank line between second and third sentence (Ln 3.17" Pos 1")
Press: (DEL)

Your screen should be similar to Figure 1-16.

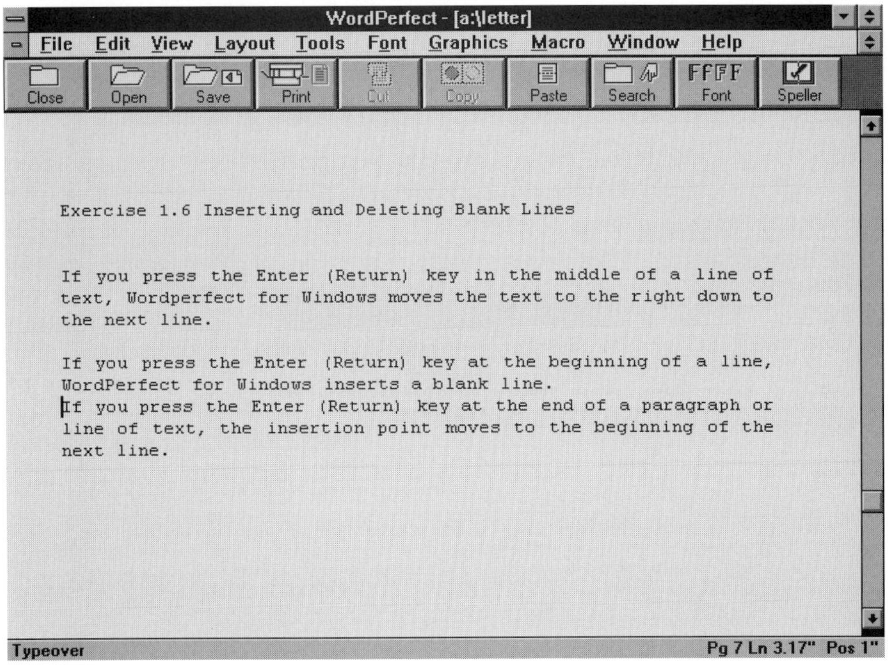

FIGURE 1-16

The blank line is deleted and the text below moves up one line.

Exercise 1.7: Undeleting Text— ALT + SHIFT + BKSP

Press: ALT + PGDN

It is easy to accidentally delete text you did not intend to delete. Fortunately, the Edit/Undelete command lets you restore your deletions. The shortcut key for this command is ALT + SHIFT + BKSP. To do this, each time text is deleted WordPerfect stores it in a special file called a **buffer**. Only the last three deletions are stored.

To see how this works, delete the three sentences numbered 1, 2, and 3 by moving to the beginning of each line and pressing CTRL + DEL.

To restore the deleted text,

Choose: Edit/Undelete

➢ ALT + SHIFT + BKSP

Your screen should be similar to Figure 1-17.

deleted text

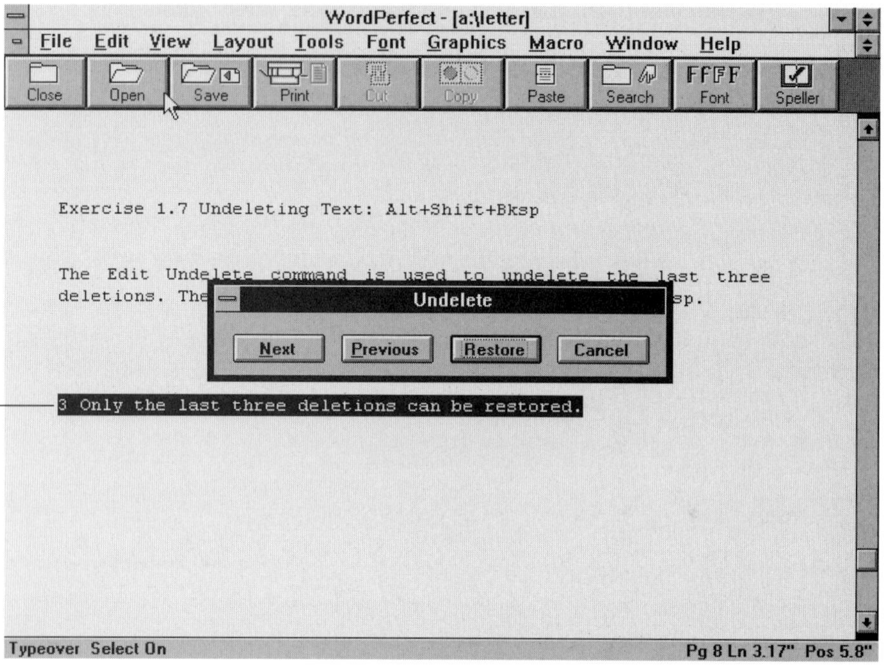

FIGURE 1-17

The most recently deleted text (sentence 3) appears highlighted in the document at the location of the insertion point. The Undelete dialog box is displayed. It lets you restore the highlighted text or see the previous deletions. To see the previous deletion,

Choose: Previous

The second deletion is displayed. To see the third deletion again,

Choose: Next

The third deletion is displayed again. To restore the highlighted text,

Choose: Restore

The third deletion is reentered at the insertion point position.

Next you will restore the first and second deletions in numerical order above sentence 3. To do this, first position the insertion point in the location where you want the text displayed. Then issue the Undelete command, display the deleted text, and choose Restore. If you forget to move the insertion point first, you can press (ESC) or choose Cancel to clear the dialog box and begin again.

Restore sentences 1 and 2. When you are done, the screen should appear as it did before you deleted the sentences.

To review, the following editing keys have been covered:

Key	Action
BKSP	Deletes character to left of insertion point
DEL	Deletes character at insertion point
INS on	Inserts character into text
INS off	Uses Typeover mode to insert text
CTRL + BKSP	Deletes word the insertion point is on
CTRL + DEL	Deletes line of text from insertion point to right
↵	Moves insertion point to next line or inserts a blank line
ALT + SHIFT + BKSP *or* Edit/Undelete	Restores the last three deletions

Closing a File

Now that you know how to move around a document and how to use several different types of editing keys, you will correct the rough draft of the credit card letter. A copy of the rough draft is in another file named LETTER2.

Before opening another file, you will close the current document file using the File/Close command. CTRL + F4 or the Close button are the shortcuts for this command. As you become more familiar with the program, you will probably rely less on the drop-down menus to issue commands and more on the shortcut keys and the Button Bar. This is because the shortcut keys and Button Bar accomplish the same procedure with fewer keystrokes.

To clear the current document from the screen,

Choose: File/Close
Shortcut: CTRL + F4 or Close button

The prompt in the prompt box, "Save changes to a:\Letter?", is asking whether you want to save the changes you made to the active document file, LETTER, to the disk. In most cases, before you close a document, you will want to save the work you have done onto a disk. In this way you would be able to open the file again and resume work on it if needed. Therefore, WordPerfect's default response to this prompt is "Yes."

However, you will not save the edited version of this file. This way, if you want to you can repeat the exercises for practice. By responding "N" (No) to the prompt, the changes you made to the document file LETTER will not be saved. The original version of the file LETTER will remain on the disk unchanged. To indicate that you do not want to save the document as it appears on the screen,

Choose: No

The document LETTER is cleared from the display, and a blank WordPerfect document window is displayed. The file you want to edit is named LETTER2.

Choose: File/Open
➢ F4 or Open button

The directory you last selected is still the current directory. The file you want to open, LETTER2, should be displayed in the Files list box.

Select: LETTER2
Choose: Open

The rough draft of the credit card letter is displayed on the screen. Using the editing features you have learned, correct the letter on your screen. Use Figure 1-18 as a guide for missing words and how your screen should appear when you are done.

FIGURE 1-18

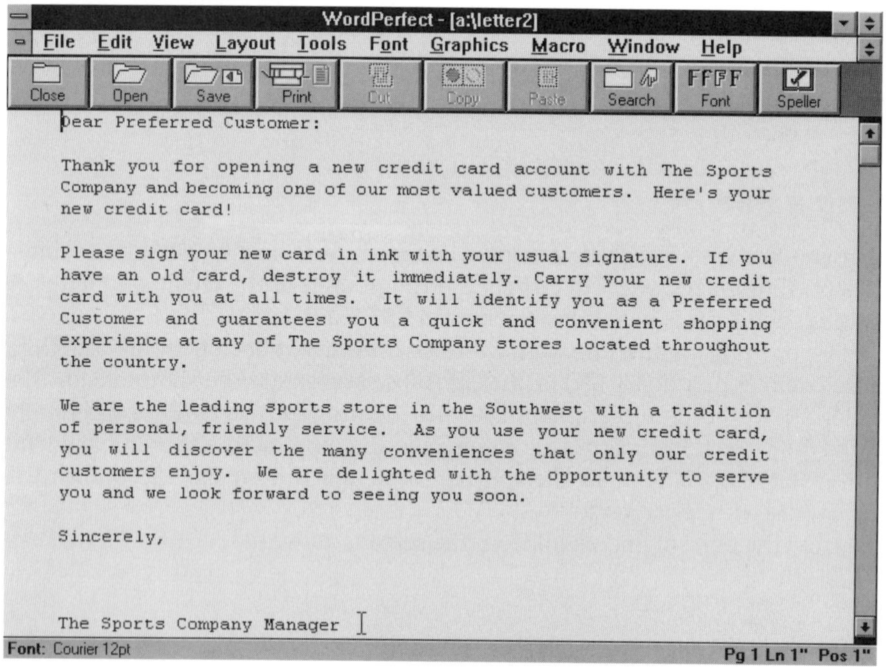

Enter your name immediately above the last line of the letter.

Saving and Replacing an Existing File

Now that you have corrected the letter, you need to save the corrections to a disk file. There are two commands on the File menu that can be used to save a file, Save and Save As. The Save command saves the edited document using the same path and filename by replacing the contents of the existing disk file with the changes you have made. The (SHIFT) + (F3) key or the Save button on the Button Bar are the shortcuts for this command. The Save As command saves the edited document to the disk by prompting you for a new filename. This command lets you save both the original version of the document and the revised document as two separate files.

Since you do not need to keep the original version of LETTER2, you will use the Save command to replace the disk copy with the edited document.

Choose: File/Save
➢ (SHIFT) + (F3) or Save button

The edited document replaces the contents of the disk file, and you are returned to the edited document.

Printing a Document

Finally, you need to print a copy of the credit card letter to give to the Regional Manager. If you have printer capability, you can print a copy of the edited document. The Print command is on the File menu.

Note: Please consult your instructor for printing procedures that may differ from the directions below.

Choose: File/Print

➢ F5

or

Click: Print button

Your screen should be similar to Figure 1-19.

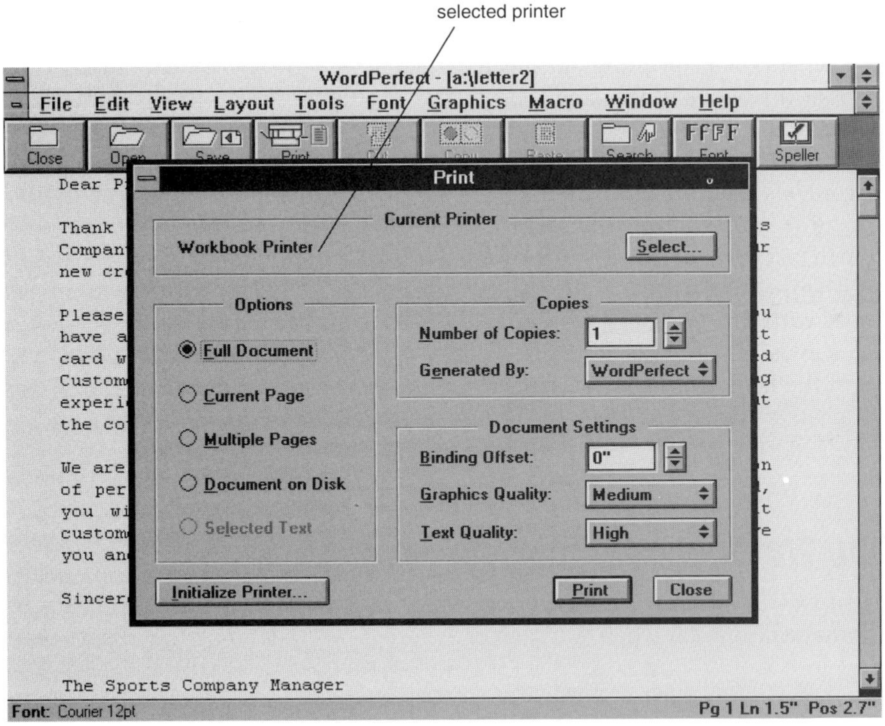

FIGURE 1-19

From the Print dialog box, you need to specify the printer you will be using and the document settings. The printer that is currently selected, Workbook Printer, is displayed in the Current Printer box. This is the printer that was selected when the file was saved originally. You need to change the selected printer to a printer that your computer system can support. The Select button lets you select a different printer. You cannot print the file using the Workbook Printer.

Choose: Select

The Select Printers dialog box is displayed. The list box displays a list of printers your school has defined. The currently selected printer is highlighted.

From the list of printers, select the appropriate printer for your computer system.

Choose: Select

You are returned to the Print dialog box, and the printer you selected should be displayed as the current printer.

The Options area of the Print dialog box lets you specify how much of the document you want printed: the full document, the current page, multiple pages, or a document on disk. Full document is the default setting. The other two areas of the dialog box, Copies and Document Settings, let you specify the number of copies and document features such as binding offset and text quality. Unless otherwise instructed, the default settings are appropriate.

Now you are ready to instruct WordPerfect to print the letter. First turn the printer on. If necessary, adjust the paper so that the perforation is just above the printer scale. To print a copy of the entire document,

Choose: Print

Your printer should be printing out the document.

The printed copy of the credit card letter should be similar to Figure 1-18. It may not match exactly if the printer you selected prints using a different font size than the one used to print the document in the text. The font size of the selected printer controls the number of characters that can be printed on a line. The display of the document also reflects this change in font size.

When a document is saved, the selected printer and print settings you specified are saved with the document. All the document files supplied with the labs have been saved with the Workbook Printer as the selected printer. This was necessary in order to standardize the display of text on the screen so that the instructions and screens in the book would be the same for all users. To print any of these files, you need to change the selected printer to one appropriate for your particular microcomputer system.

Exiting WordPerfect for Windows

When you exit the WordPerfect program, if you do not turn off the Button Bar, it will automatically appear when you reopen the program. To turn off the Button Bar,

Choose: View/Button Bar

The Button Bar is no longer displayed on the screen.

The Exit command on the File menu is used to quit the WordPerfect program.

Choose: File/Exit

➢ (ALT) + (F4)

or

Double-click: WordPerfect control-menu box

A prompt appears asking if you want to save the changes you have made to the edited document. Whenever you try to exit the program or close a document that has been modified, this prompt will appear as a safeguard against accidentally losing your work. In this case, the only change you made was to select a different printer. To save the new printer settings,

Choose: Yes

The edited document is saved to disk using the same filename. You are returned to the Windows program. Exit Windows.

Always exit the WordPerfect program using the File/Exit command. Never turn off your computer until you exit properly, or you may lose data.

Key Terms

status line	edit
font	reformatting
page	full justification
line	Insert mode
position	Typeover mode
cascading menu	hard carriage return
Button Bar	code
context-sensitive Help	buffer

Command Summary

Command	Shortcut	Button Bar	Action
Help/Index	F1		Displays alphabetical list of Help topics
View/Button Bar			Displays Button Bar
File/Open	F4		Opens selected file
Edit/Go To	CTRL + G		Moves to specified page
Edit/Undelete	ALT + SHIFT + BKSP		Restores deleted text
File/Close	CTRL + F4		Closes file
File/Save	SHIFT + F3		Saves file using same filename
File/Print	F5		Prints file using selected printer
File/Exit	ALT + F4		Exits WordPerfect program

LAB REVIEW

Matching

1. status line	______	**a.**	new text writes over existing text
2. CTRL + G	______	**b.**	deletes text on line to the right of the insertion point
3. Typeover	______	**c.**	moves to the top of the document
4. font	______	**d.**	inserts a blank line or ends a paragraph
5. ALT + F4	______	**e.**	moves to the end of a line
6. CTRL + HOME	______	**f.**	line of information below the document window
7. END	______	**g.**	shortcut for File/Exit
8. CTRL + Bksp	______	**h.**	deletes word the insertion point is on
9. ↵	______	**i.**	character style and size
10. CTRL + DEL	______	**j.**	shortcut for the Edit/Go To command

Fill-In Questions

1. In the following WordPerfect for Windows screen, several items are identified by letters. Enter the correct term for each item in the space provided.

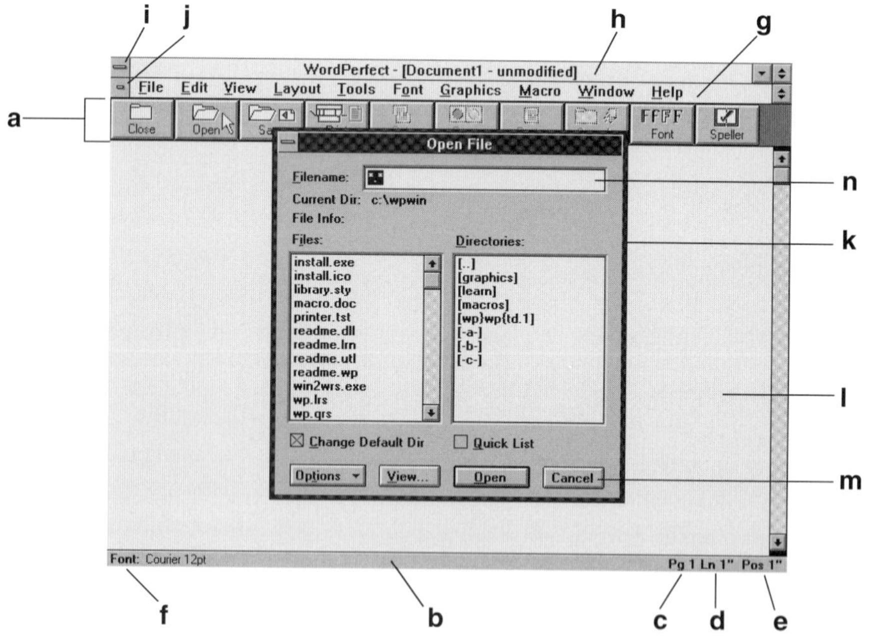

a. ______________________ **h.** ______________________
b. ______________________ **i.** ______________________
c. ______________________ **j.** ______________________
d. ______________________ **k.** ______________________
e. ______________________ **l.** ______________________
f. ______________________ **m.** ______________________
g. ______________________ **n.** ______________________

2. Complete the following statements by filling in the blanks with the correct term.

a. The ____________________ occupies the largest area of the WordPerfect for Windows screen.

b. The ________________________ is located at the bottom of the screen.

c. Name the three ways you can enter a command: ______________, ______________________, ______________________.

d. Text can be entered in a document in either the ______________ or ______________ modes.

e. The _____________ key erases the character to the left of the insertion point.

f. The process of adjusting the size of the spaces between words is called ____________________.

g. When text has even right and left margins it is called _____ ____________________.

h. WordPerfect saves your last _______________ deletions in a special file called a _______________.

i. WordPerfect inserts hidden _______________ into a document to control the display of text.

j. The selected ______________ determines the default font size of your document.

Practice Exercises

Note: Whenever you print a file that was provided on your data disk, you must first change the selected printer to an appropriate printer for your computer system.

1. Open the file PRACTICE. Follow the directions in the file to correct the sentences. Print the file. Save the corrected file using the same filename.

2. Open the file CROCS and correct the errors using the editing features you learned in this lab. Enter your name as the last line in the document. Print the file. Save the corrected file using the same filename.

3. Open the file FLASH and correct the errors using the editing features you learned in this lab. Enter your name as the last line in the document. Print the file. Save the corrected file using the same filename.

4. Open the file PARTY and correct the errors using the editing features you learned in this lab. Enter your name as the last line in the document. Print the file. Save the corrected file using the same filename.

LAB

Creating and Formatting a Document 2

Competencies

In this lab you will learn how to:

1. Create and save a new document.
2. Spell-check the document.
3. Copy and move text.
4. Enter the system date.
5. Align text flush with the right margin.
6. Display and delete hidden codes.
7. Set margins, tabs, and indents.
8. Search and replace text.
9. Set justification.

CASE STUDY

After editing the rough draft of the credit card letter, you showed it to The Sports Company Regional Manager. The manager would like the letter to include information about The Sports Company newsletter and a discount on the first purchase made with the new credit card. You will enter the new information into a new file, copy it to the credit card letter, and then add some finishing touches to the letter.

Creating a Document

Start Windows. Open the WordPerfect Applications window. Choose the WordPerfect for Windows application icon. Turn on the Button Bar.

Put your data disk in drive A.

A blank WordPerfect screen is like a blank piece of paper you put into the typewriter. To create a new document, simply begin typing the text. When the insertion point reaches the end of a line, however, do not press ↵. WordPerfect will automatically **word wrap** the text on a line based on the margin settings. The only time you need to press ↵ is at the end of a paragraph or to insert blank lines.

As you type the text shown below, do not press ↵ until you are directed to at the end of the paragraph. Include two spaces following a period at the end of a sentence.

Type: **Additionally, each month you will receive The Sports Company News, a newsletter about new products, sports trends, sports safety tips, and upcoming events. The newsletter will also include announcements of special pre-sale days for our preferred customers only. If you have questions about an event, call or come in and speak to the Customer Service representative.**

Press: ↵

Your screen should be similar to Figure 2-1.

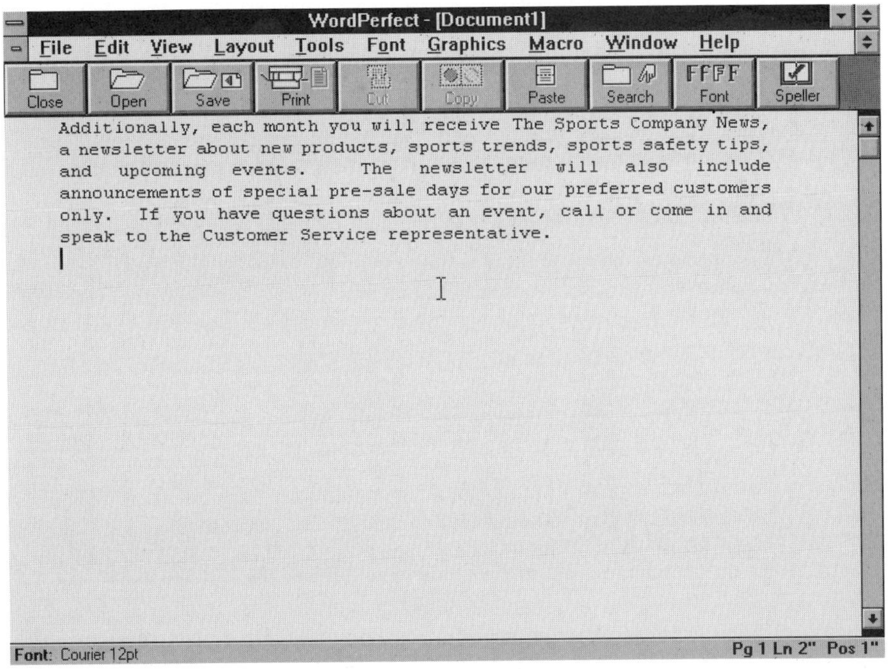

FIGURE 2-1

The text on your screen may not exactly match the text in Figure 2-1. This is because the selected printer your WordPerfect program is using controls the font (print) size, which affects the number of characters WordPerfect can display on a line. This in turn affects where WordPerfect word wraps the line of text.

As you can see, the automatic word wrap feature makes entering text in a document much faster than typing. This is because a carriage return does not need to be pressed at the end of every line.

To insert a blank line to separate the paragraphs,

Press: ↵

To enter the second paragraph,

Type: **You can begin using your new credit card with your very next purchase. In appreciation for becoming a new credit card customer, you will receive 10% off the first purchase you make with your new card. Please turn in this letter at the time the discount is given.**

To end the second paragraph,

Press: ↵

Your screen should be similar to Figure 2-2.

FIGURE 2-2

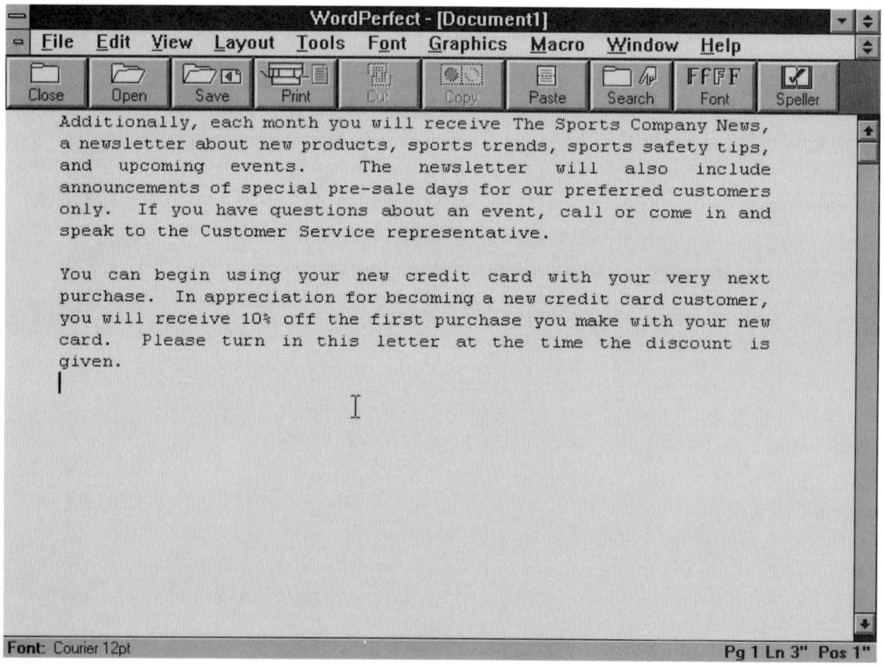

Check that you have entered the two paragraphs correctly. Do not be concerned if there is a difference in where WordPerfect decided to word wrap. If you find any errors, correct them using the editing features you learned in Lab 1.

Spell-Checking

It is always a good idea to check your spelling in a document when you are finished working on it. To help you do this quickly, WordPerfect has a built-in dictionary which checks for spelling errors. Additionally, it will look for words that are incorrectly capitalized, words with numbers, and duplicate words.

To enter several intentional errors in the first sentence of this document,

- Change the spelling of "Sports" to "Sprots."
- Enter a second "new" after the word "new."
- Change the word "products" to "prOducts."

To begin spell-checking,

Choose: Tools/Speller

➢ CTRL + F1

or

Click: Speller button

Your screen should be similar to Figure 2-3.

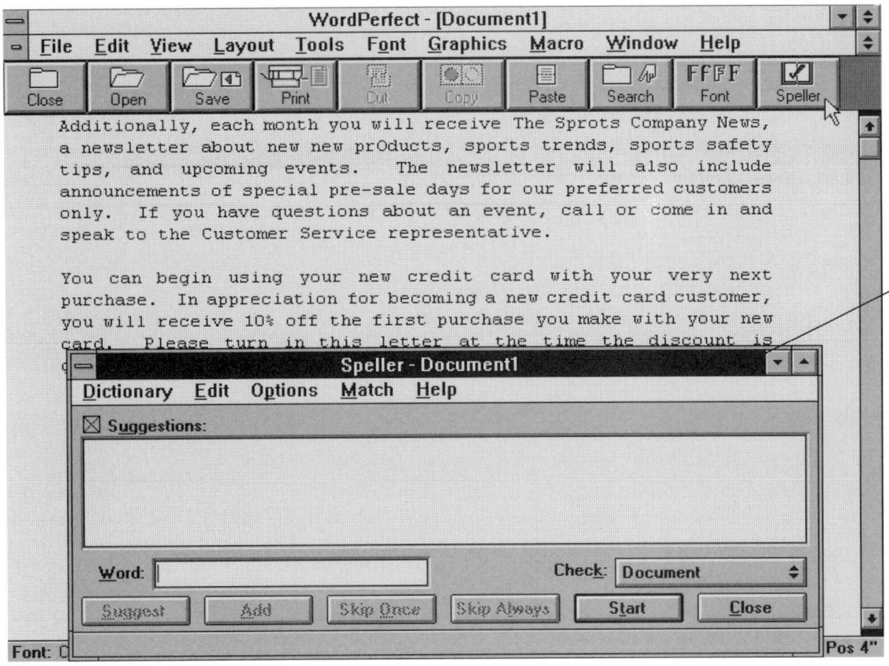

FIGURE 2-3

Speller application window

The Speller is a separate application program. Therefore it is displayed in an application window. You can tell Speller is an application because it has its own title bar, menu bar, and Maximize and Minimize buttons. Because Speller is an application, it can be used to check words in other non–word-processor applications.

WP 5.2 note: The Speller window appears slightly different; however, it contains the same options as in version 5.1.

The Check drop-down list box lets you specify how much of the document you want to check. You can spell-check a word, a document, to end of document, a page, to end of page, selected text, or to end of selection. The default setting, Document, will spell-check the entire file starting from the top of the file.

WP 5.2 note: The options in the Check drop-down list box are displayed when the Check menu is opened.

To start the Speller,

Choose: Start

Your screen should be similar to Figure 2-4.

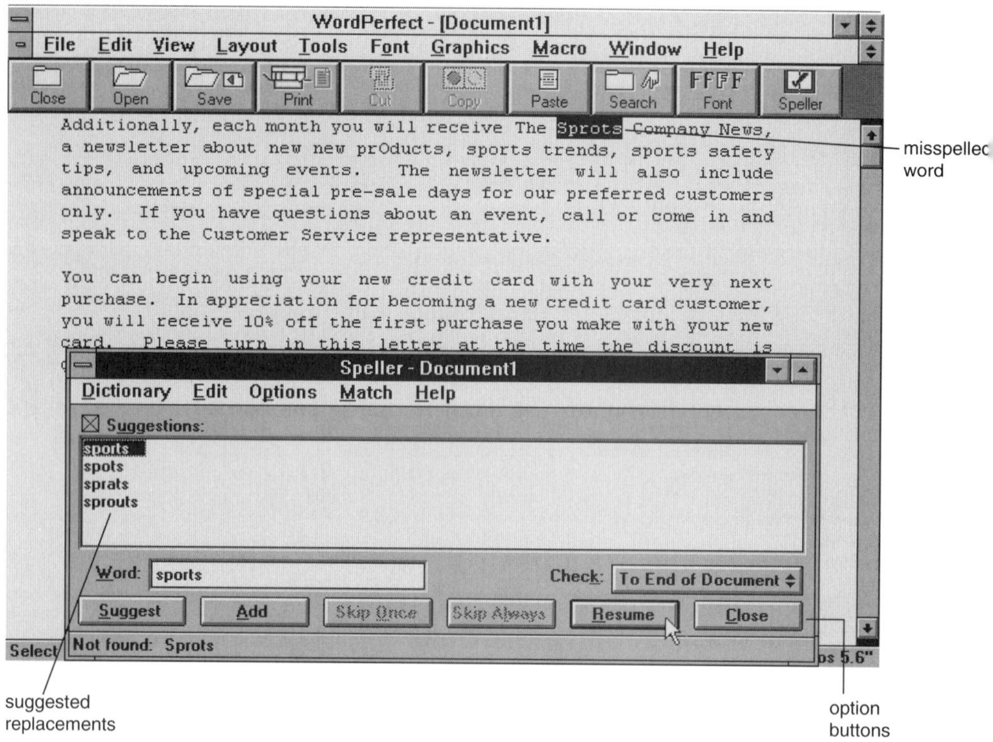

FIGURE 2-4

The Speller has encountered the first word that is not in its dictionary. The word "Sprots" is highlighted in the document window. The Suggestions box lists four possible replacements. Sometimes the Speller does not display any suggested replacements. This is because it cannot locate any words in its dictionary that are similar in spelling. The Word text box displays the highlighted word in the Suggestions box, or if there are no suggestions, it displays the highlighted word in the text.

WP 5.2 note: The Replace With text box is the same as the Word text box in version 5.1.

To tell Speller what to do, you need to choose from the option buttons. They have the following effects:

Suggest	Suggests words if the Suggestions check box is turned off.
Add	Adds the word to the **supplementary dictionary**. The Speller uses the supplementary dictionary as a secondary dictionary whenever it does not encounter the word in the main dictionary. When a word is added to the supplementary dictionary, the Speller will always accept the added word as correct.
Skip Once	Accepts the word in the document as correct for this occurrence only.
Skip Always	Accepts the word in the document as correct throughout the spell-check of this document.
Replace	Enters the word displayed in the Word text box in place of the highlighted word.
Close	Exits the Speller.

To change the spelling of the word to one of the suggested spellings, highlight the correct word in the list and then choose Replace. Since Sports is already highlighted,

Choose: Replace

The Speller replaces the misspelled word with the selected suggested replacement and moves on to locate the next error. If there were no suggested replacements, and you did not want to use any of the option buttons, you could edit the word yourself by typing the correction in the Word text box and then choosing Replace. If you have a mouse, you can edit the word directly in the document and then choose one of the Skip option buttons to continue spell-checking the document.

The double-word error has been located, and the Speller dialog box is displayed. The option Disable Checking will ignore all double-occurring words for the rest of the document if you turn it on. The dialog box contains two command buttons,

Continue	Leaves the words as they are
Delete 2nd	Deletes the second occurrence of the word

To delete the second of the duplicate words,

Choose: Delete 2nd

The next error the Speller locates is the capitalization error. WordPerfect uses a set of predefined capitalization patterns to check for inconsistent capitalization in words. Predefined capitalization patterns are based on the first three characters only. If the first two characters are uppercase or the second character is uppercase, speller will change the word so that only the first letter is uppercase. If the third character is uppercase, Speller will change the whole word to lowercase. When the second and third characters are uppercase, Speller changes the whole word to uppercase.

To edit the word,

Choose: Replace

Mouse note: To replace, you can double-click on the word with the correct spelling in the replacement list.

The word "products" is corrected.

There should be no other misspelled words. However, if the Speller encounters others in your file, correct them as needed. When no others are located, the Speller will display a prompt box telling you that spell check has been completed. To exit the Speller,

Choose: OK/Close

WP 5.2 procedure: Choose Yes

Return to the top of the document.

Saving a New File

Next you want to save the two paragraphs as a new file. Since this document has never been saved before, you can use either the Save or Save As command. Both commands will display the Save As dialog box.

Choose: File/Save

➢ SHIFT + F3

or

Click: Save button

You need to specify where you want the file saved and a filename. You will save the file on your data disk using the filename CREDITCD.W51. You can select the drive containing your data disk from the Directories list box and then enter the name in the Filename text box. Alternatively, you can specify the path as part of the filename in the Filename text box. For example, if your data disk is in the A drive you would enter A:CREDITCD.W51. Using either method, enter the path and filename.

To complete the command,

Choose: Save

After a few moments, the document is saved on the disk.

Next you will open the credit card letter. A complete, corrected copy of the credit card letter is saved for you on your data disk in a file named LETTER3. Open the file LETTER3.

You now have two documents open in two separate document windows. The LETTER3 document window is the **active window** and completely covers the CREDITCD.W51 document window. The active document is the document you can work in. You can have up to nine document windows open at one time, but only one can be active. To make the CREDITCD.W51 document window active,

Choose: Window/1 a:\creditcd.w51-unmodified

The CREDITCD document window is now active and covers the LETTER3 window. Using the Window menu, you can select a specific document window that you want to make active. You can also press CTRL + F6 to cycle forward through all open documents, or CTRL + SHIFT + F6 to cycle backward. When there are only two windows open, CTRL + F6 will switch from one document window to the other. To make the LETTER3 document window active,

Press: CTRL + F6

Copying Text Between Documents

After looking at the letter, you decide you want the two new paragraphs from the CREDITCD.W51 file to be entered following the first paragraph of the credit card letter.

Just like in the Windows Write and Cardfile applications, you can copy text from one file to another easily by selecting the text, copying it to Clipboard, and then pasting the text from the Clipboard into another document file.

To make it easier to view the document windows, you can tile them.

Choose: Window/Tile

Your screen should be similar to Figure 2-5.

FIGURE 2-5

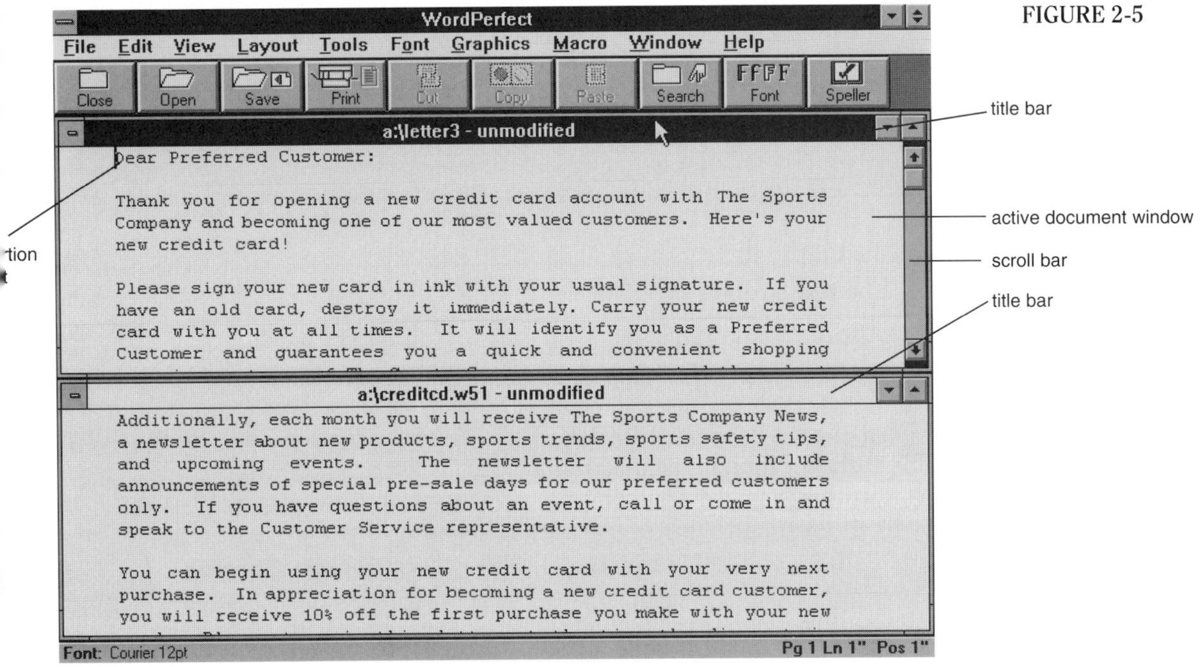

The application window now displays two document windows one above the other. The active document window is LETTER3, in the upper half of the screen. You can tell it is the active window because the title bar is a different color or highlighted, it contains the insertion point, and the scroll bar is displayed. Any text you type or commands you choose affect only the active document. The status line provides information for the active document. Now that the windows are visible, if you are using a mouse you can click anywhere on a document window to make it active. Make the CREDITCD.W51 document window active.

Now you are ready to copy the two paragraphs from the CREDITCD.W51 file.

Select the two paragraphs in the CREDITCD.W51 file. Once text is selected, the Edit menu can be used to Cut, Copy, Paste, or Append the selected text to the same document or another. The options have the following meanings:

Option	Shortcut	Action
Cut	SHIFT + DEL *or* Cut	Removes the text from its present location so it can be moved to another location
Copy	CTRL + INS *or* Copy	Leaves the original text and moves a duplicate to another location
Paste	SHIFT + INS *or* Paste	Inserts the selected text after one of the other options has been selected
Append		Adds the text to the end of a file on the disk

You want to copy the selected text to the LETTER3 document window.

Choose: **E**dit/**C**opy
➢ (CTRL) + (INS)
or
Click: Copy button

Make the LETTER3 window active.

Move to: blank line separating the second and third paragraphs (Ln 3")

To paste the text stored in the Clipboard into the active document,

Choose: **E**dit/**P**aste
➢ (SHIFT) + (INS)
or
Click: Paste button

The two paragraphs from the CREDITCD.W51 file have been inserted into the LETTER3 file at the location of the insertion point.

You no longer need to view both document windows. To make it easier to work with the LETTER3 document window, maximize the window. (Click on the Maximize button or choose Ma**x**imize from the document control menu.)

Move to the top of the document. The spacing between the paragraphs needs to be adjusted. To separate the second and third paragraphs with a blank line,

Move to: "A" in "Additionally" (Ln 3" Pos 1")
Press: (↵)

Your screen should be similar to Figure 2-6.

FIGURE 2-6

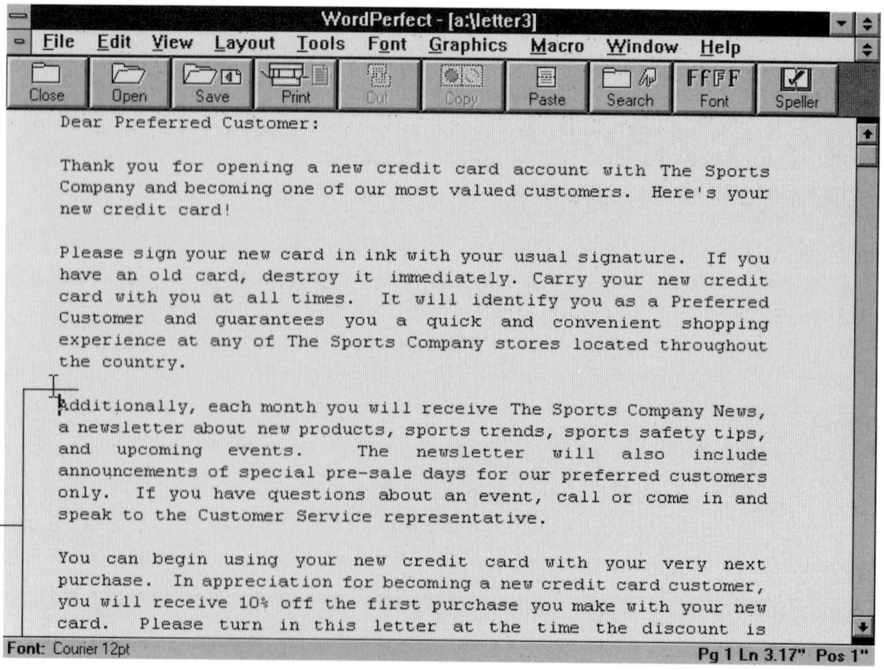

View the entire letter. When you finish viewing the letter, move to the top of the letter.

Moving Text

After looking over the credit card letter, you decide to change the order of the paragraphs in the letter. You want the paragraph about the 10 percent discount (fourth paragraph) to follow the second paragraph. To position the text in the window so that the entire paragraph is visible,

Press: (PGDN)
Press: (↓)

A complete sentence or paragraph can be selected by choosing Edit/Select from the menu or with the mouse.

To select a sentence or a paragraph, move the I-beam anywhere within the text to be selected. Then click the mouse quickly three times to select a sentence or four times to select a paragraph.

Move the I-beam anywhere in the fourth paragraph.

Click the mouse quickly four times.

To select a sentence or a paragraph, first move the insertion point anywhere within the sentence or paragraph.

Place the insertion point anywhere in the fourth paragraph.

Choose: Edit/Select

The two options on the cascade menu allow you to specify the area of text to be selected (sentence or paragraph). To specify a paragraph,

Choose: Paragraph

Select mode is on.

The entire paragraph is highlighted including the blank line below the paragraph.

The Cut command will remove the selected text and store it in the Clipboard. The contents of the Clipboard can then be pasted into a new location. To cut the selected text,

Choose: Edit/Cut
➢ (SHIFT) + (DEL)

or

Click: Cut button

The selected paragraph is removed from the document.

Next you need to move the insertion point to the location where the text will be inserted.

Move to: "A" in "Additionally" (Ln 3.17" Pos 1")

To paste the text into the document from the Clipboard,

Choose: Edit/Paste

➢ (SHIFT) + (INS)

or

Click: Paste button

Your screen should be similar to Figure 2-7.

FIGURE 2-7

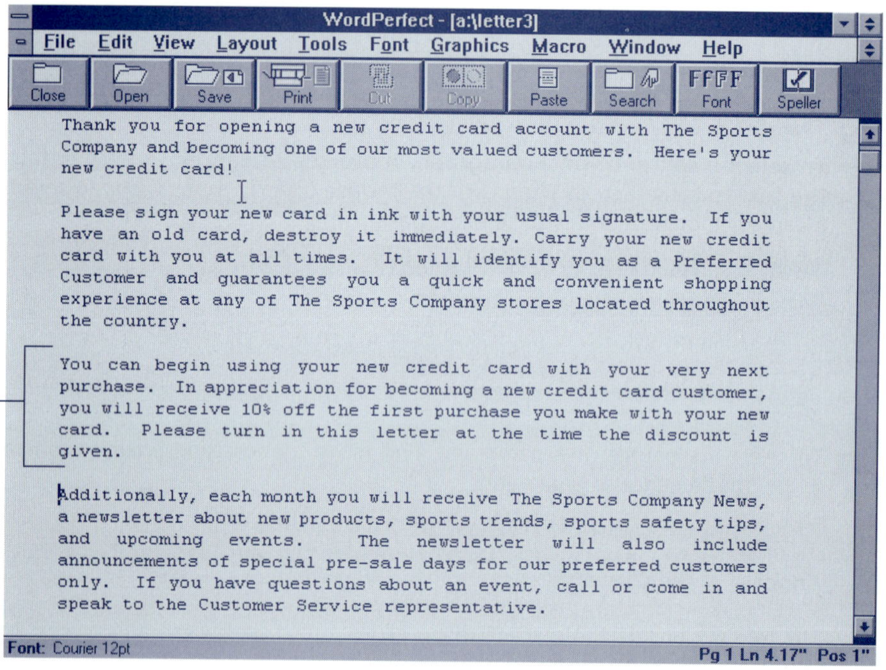

cut and pasted paragraph

The marked paragraph is reentered into the document beginning at the insertion point location. That was a lot quicker than retyping the whole paragraph!

Replacing Selected Text

Text can be selected for reasons other than cutting and copying. You can also select text to be deleted and replaced with new text you type.

You would like to reword the last sentence of the second paragraph. Instead of "It will identify you as a..." you would like it to say "Your new credit card identifies you as a...". Since the part you want to replace is shorter than the new text, Typeover mode will cut off some of the text you want to keep. By selecting the text you want to remove and then typing in the new text, the part you want to keep will not be affected.

Move to: "I" in "It" (Ln 2.33" Pos 3.9")
Select: "It will identify" (through Pos 5.5"; do not include the blank space after the "y")
Type: **Y**

The "Y" is entered on the line and the selected text has been deleted. You can also press DEL before typing the new text. However, as you just saw, this is unnecessary if you want to enter new text at the current location.

To continue entering the new text,

Type: **our new credit card identifies**

The new text is inserted into the sentence and the text following has been reformatted.

Next you want to add the telephone number of the Customer Service Department to the letter. You want it to follow the reference to the Customer Service representative in the last sentence of the fourth paragraph.

Move to: period of the last sentence of fourth paragraph (Ln 5" Pos 5.4")
Press: Spacebar
Type: **(1-800-555-9838)**

After looking at the sentence, you decide you would like to move the telephone number to follow the word "call" in the same sentence. Select the telephone number including the parentheses.

Interim releases of WordPerfect for Windows dated April 1992 or later and release 5.2 include a drag and drop feature. You can use this feature instead of selecting Cut and Paste or Copy and Paste from the menu. You can tell if your release has this feature by moving the I-beam to the selected text. If the I-beam does not change to an arrow, this feature is not available. In this case, follow the instructions in the keyboard section below.

To use the drag and drop feature to cut and paste the selected text, move the I-beam to the selected text. When it changes to an arrow, drag the pointer to the location where you want text inserted. A box outline appears at the bottom of the arrow, and a thin I-beam appears where the arrow is pointing to show you were the text will be placed. When correctly positioned, release the mouse button.

Drag the telephone number to the space after "call" in the same sentence. Click anywhere outside the selected text to clear the highlight.

To use the drag and drop feature to copy and paste selected text, follow the same procedure except hold down CTRL while dragging.

As you learned above, cut the selected text and then paste the telephone number after the word "call" in the same sentence.

Delete the parentheses surrounding the number and correct the spacing as necessary. Delete the extra space before the period at the end of the sentence.

Your screen should be similar to Figure 2-8.

FIGURE 2-8

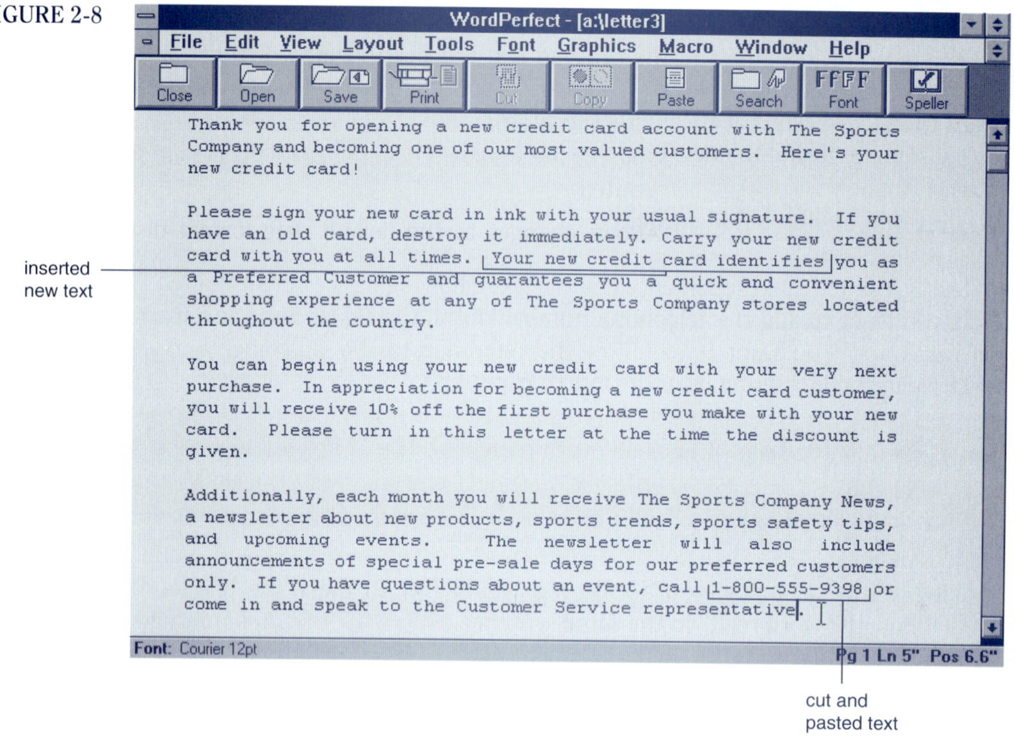

After looking over the letter, you decide you want to make the following changes:

- enter the current date above the salutation
- increase the margin width
- indent the paragraphs
- divide up the first paragraph by indenting the text
- replace the words "new credit card" with "new Sports Company credit card"
- change the right margin to print ragged

Next, you will make these changes to the credit card letter.

Using the Date Command

You want the date to be entered on the first line of the letter. Move to the top of the letter (Ln1" Pos1"). To insert a blank line and move to it,

Press: ↵

Press: ↑

A blank line has been inserted at the top of the letter where the date will be entered.

The Tools/Date command inserts the current date as maintained by your computer system into your document.

Choose: Tools/Date

The three date options in the Tools cascade menu are:

Text (CTRL + F5)	Inserts the current date as text into your document
Code (CTRL + SHIFT + F5)	Inserts a WordPerfect code which automatically updates the date whenever the file is opened or printed
Format	Allows changes to the default date format display

Because the credit card letter will be mailed to new customers, you want the current date to be entered whenever the letter is printed. To do this, the Code option is used.

Choose: Code

Your screen should be similar to Figure 2-9.

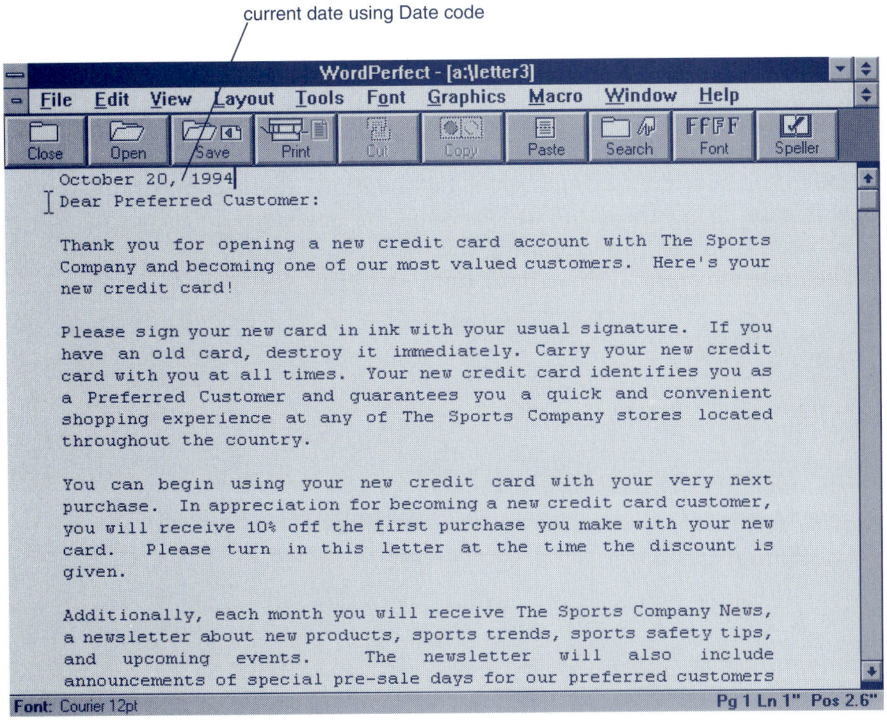

FIGURE 2-9

The current date is entered into the letter at the location of the insertion point. Although it appears as text, it is a WordPerfect code. Whenever this file is opened or printed, WordPerfect will display the current system date using this format. You will see shortly how the date is stored as a WordPerfect code.

Note: The date in Figure 2-9 will be different from the date that appears on your screen. If you did not enter the current date at the DOS prompt, then the default system date is used.

Aligning Text Flush with the Right Margin

Next you want the date to end flush against the right margin. The Layout/Line/Flush Right command or the shortcut (ALT) + (F7) is used to do this. The insertion point must first be positioned on the first character of the text to be aligned and there must be a hard carriage return at the end of the existing line of text for this command to work correctly.

To position the insertion point at the beginning of the date,

Press: (←)

Because the date is a WordPerfect code rather than text entered character by character, the program considers the date a single character and the insertion point jumps quickly to the beginning of the line.

To move the date flush with the right margin and reformat the screen,

Select: Layout

The Layout menu options affect the design of the document. You will be using many of these options shortly. The Line option controls the placement of text on a line.

Choose: Line

There are two options that affect the placement of text on a line, Center and Flush Right. Notice the shortcut key equivalent for the Flush Right command is (ALT) + (F7). In this case, using the shortcut key would be quicker than using the menu. However, because you are already using the menu, to align the text located to the right of the insertion point flush with the right margin,

Choose: Flush Right

Your screen should be similar to Figure 2-10.

FIGURE 2-10

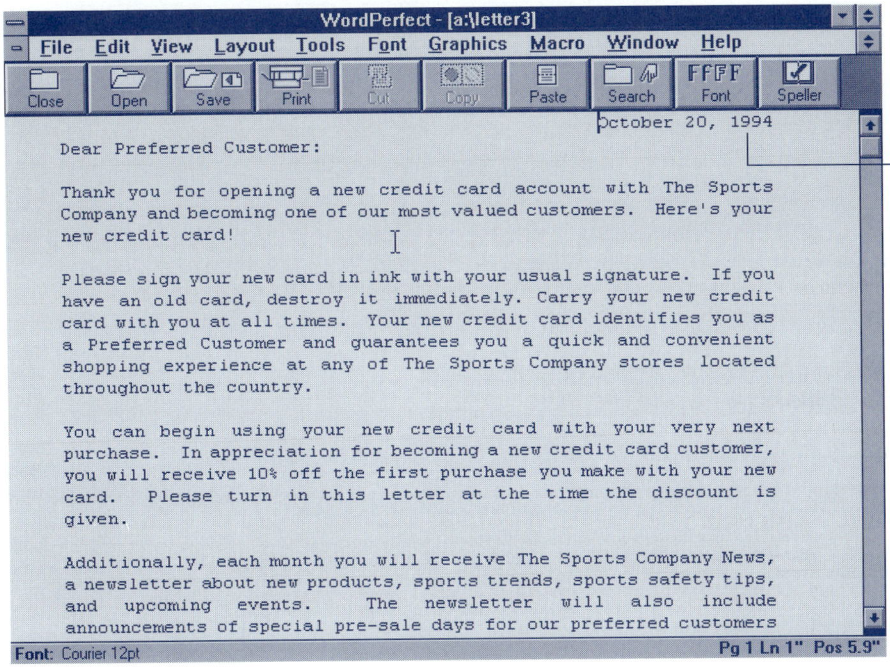

The date has moved so that it ends flush with the right margin.

The Flush Right command can also be used before typing in new text that you want aligned with the right margin. As you type the text, it is entered so that the last character in the line is even with the right margin.

Next you want the date separated from the salutation by four blank lines. Move to the beginning of line 2 and insert four blank lines between the date line and the salutation.

Displaying Hidden Codes

As discussed in Lab 1, WordPerfect places hidden codes in the document whenever a feature is used that controls the format and display of the document. The codes consist of symbols that tell WordPerfect and the printer what to do. When the program reads the code, it reformats the text as appropriate in the document from that point on to the new setting. The codes are hidden so that your document on the screen looks as close as possible to the text as it will appear when printed. Because the codes are hidden, your screen is not cluttered.

Depending upon the code, it is entered into the document at the beginning of a page or paragraph or at the location of the insertion point when the command is issued. WordPerfect lets you see the hidden codes in the document so that you can remove the codes you no longer want or need. To see the hidden codes, use the View/Reveal Codes or the shortcut command (ALT) + (F3).

Choose: View/Reveal Codes

➢ (ALT) + (F3)

Your screen should be similar to Figure 2-11.

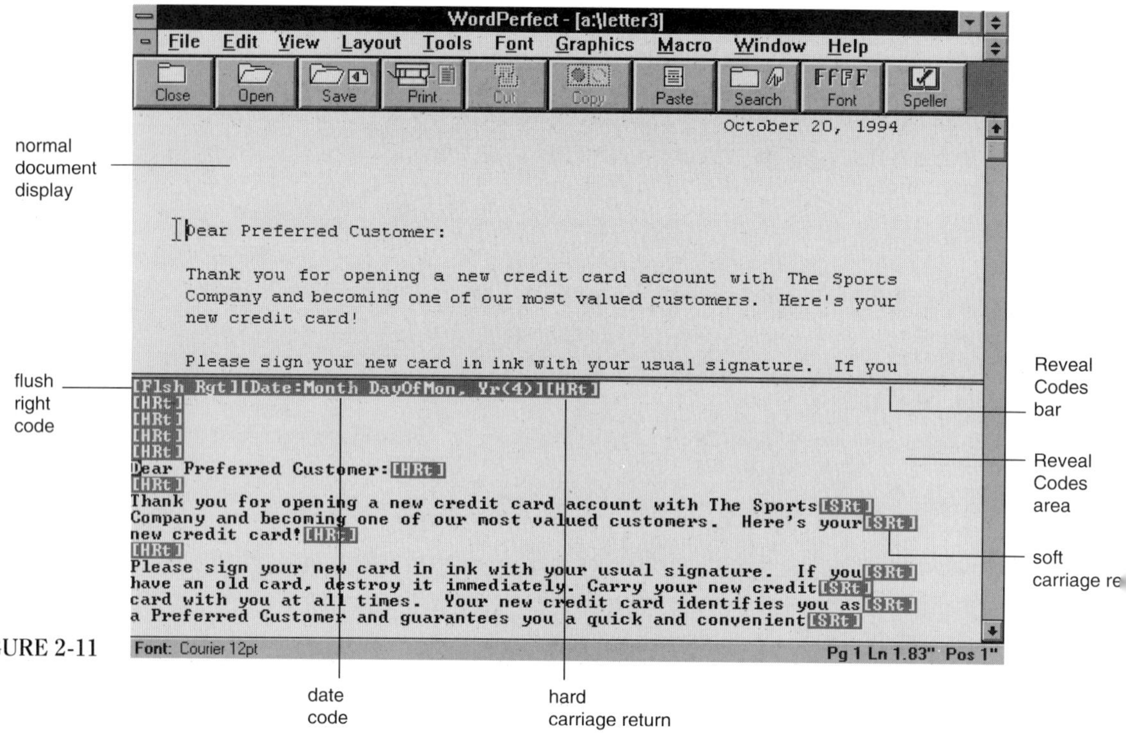

FIGURE 2-11

The document window is divided into two areas by the Reveal Codes bar. The upper area displays the document as it normally appears. The lower area displays the same text with the hidden codes revealed. This is the Reveal Codes area. The codes are always displayed in brackets ([]).

The first code displayed in the Reveal Codes area of the window is [Flsh Rgt]. This code instructs WordPerfect to align all text on a line following the code (in this case the date) flush with the right margin. The next code enters the date. The [HRt] code represents a hard carriage return. At the end of the first two lines of the first paragraph, a [SRt] code is displayed. This code identifies the location of a **soft carriage return**. As WordPerfect reformats the text on the screen, it enters a [SRt] code at the end of a line. This code shows the location where WordPerfect decided to automatically word wrap to the next line.

When Reveal Codes is on, you can type characters or use any WordPerfect features. The text in the Reveal codes portion of the window may not wrap the same as the text in the normal text display portion, however. This is because it contains the format codes.

To return to the normal document display and hide the codes again, you must reselect the Reveal Codes command. To do this quickly using the shortcut key command,

Press: ALT + F3

You can also open Reveal Codes by dragging on the reveal codes bar on the scroll bar. The reveal codes bars are located above the upper scroll arrow and below the lower scroll arrow. It is a small solid rectangle (see Figure 2-12). Point to the reveal codes bar and, when the pointer changes to a double arrow, drag it to the middle of the window. You can make the Reveal Codes area any size you want by positioning the bar appropriately on the window. To close Reveal Codes, point to the bar and drag the bar to the top or bottom of the window.

Try this by opening and then closing the Reveal Codes area.

Setting Margins

Next you would like to see how the letter would look if you changed the right and left margin widths from the default setting of 1 inch to $1\frac{1}{2}$ inches. To change the left and right margin widths of a document, the Layout/Margins (CTRL + F8) command is used. The new margin setting must be entered at the beginning of the document so that the entire document below the setting will be formatted to the new margin specifications.

To position the insertion point at the top of the document,

Press: CTRL + HOME

You will use the shortcut key command to open the Margins dialog box.

Press: CTRL + F8

The Margins dialog box displays the four margin settings that can be changed: Left, Right, Top, and Bottom. The default margin settings are currently displayed in the text boxes. The Left Margin text box is highlighted. The margin setting can be entered as a decimal or as a fraction. To change the left margin setting to $1\frac{1}{2}$ inches, you could enter either 1.5 or $1\frac{1}{2}$. The program always displays the setting as a decimal. When the current setting is highlighted (selected), typing new information will replace the old setting.

Type: 1.5
Press: TAB

Your screen should be similar to Figure 2-12.

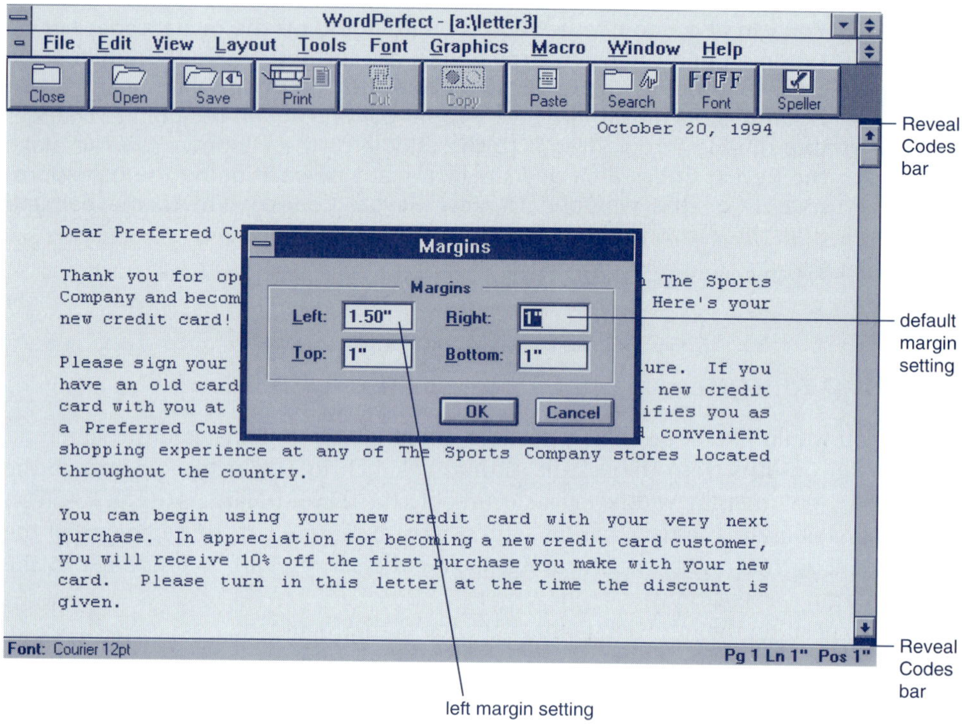

FIGURE 2-12

The highlight moved to the Right Margin settings text box. In a similar manner, change the right margin setting to 1.5.

If you wanted, you could continue to select other options. However, first you want to see how the document has changed with the new margin settings. To execute the command,

Choose: OK

The letter has been reformatted to fit within the new margin settings. The left margin now begins at Pos 1.5" and the right margin is set at Pos 7.0".

To see the code that was inserted into the document, open the Reveal Codes area. The code [L/R Mar:1.5",1.5"] is displayed. Close the Reveal Codes area.

It is easy to see that the left margin is positioned on 1.5" by looking at the status line; but without moving to the end of a full line of text, it is hard to tell where the right margin is positioned. The WordPerfect Ruler will tell you where the margins are set and also where the tabs are set. The display of the Ruler can be turned on and off using the View menu. To display the Ruler,

Choose: View/Ruler

➢ ALT + SHIFT + F3

Your screen should be similar to Figure 2-13.

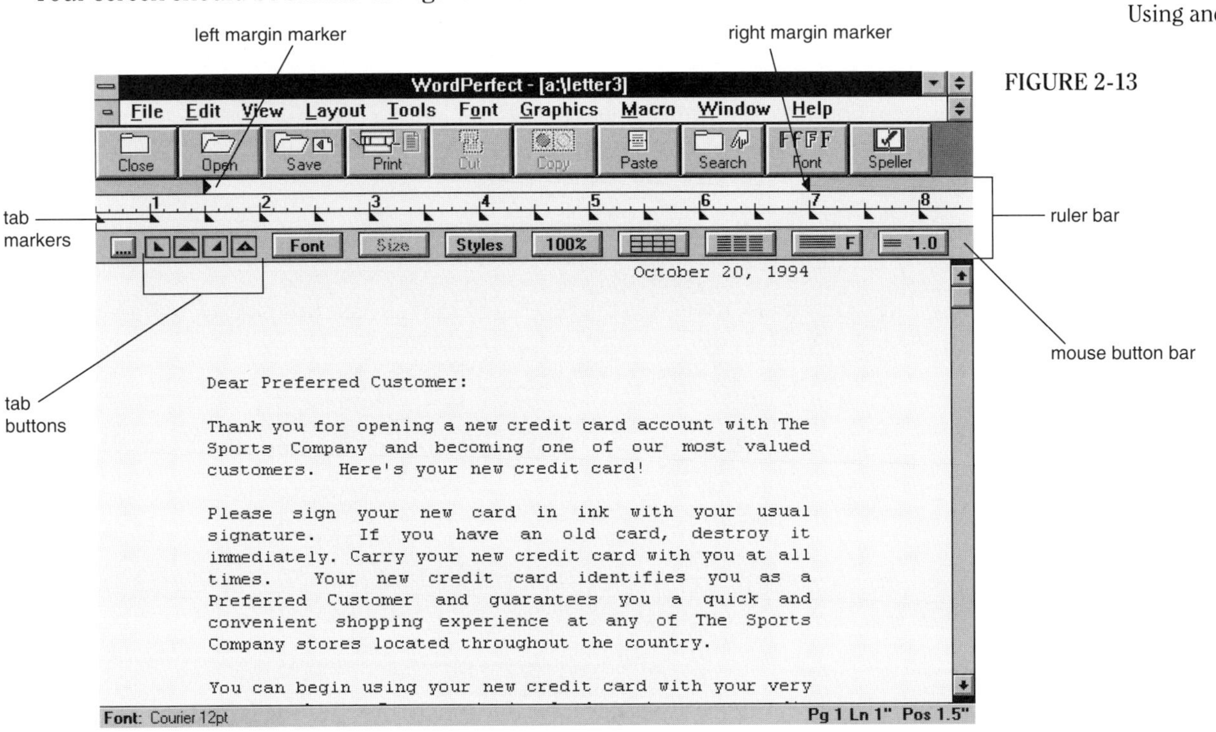

FIGURE 2-13

The first line of the Ruler shows the margin settings. The arrowhead symbols (▶ ◀) mark the location of the left and right margins on the Ruler. The right margin marker is positioned at the 7" mark on the Ruler. The third line of the Ruler shows the location of each tab stop as identified by the tab markers (◣). The buttons below the Ruler contain mouse shortcuts for several of the Layout menu commands.

Using and Setting Tabs

Next you want to change the letter style from block to indented. To do this you will indent the first line of each paragraph and the closing.

WordPerfect has set the default tab setting at every half inch. As with other default settings, the tab settings can also be changed. The tab settings can be changed using the mouse or the menu command Layout/Line/Tab Set.

To clear or change a tab setting, click on the tab marker and drag it to a new location on the Ruler or below the Ruler to remove it. To add a tab setting, drag a Tab button to the location on the ruler. The Tab buttons let you add left (◣), center (▲), right (◢), or decimal (△) style tabs. As you drag a tab button, a vertical line appears to show you the location of the tab in the document.

Remove the 3" tab marker by dragging it off the ruler bar.

Note: Mouse users, also follow the procedures in the keyboard section.

To clear or change a tab setting, the Layout/Line/Tab Set command is used.

Choose: Layout/Line/Tab Set

Your screen should be similar to Figure 2-14.

FIGURE 2-14

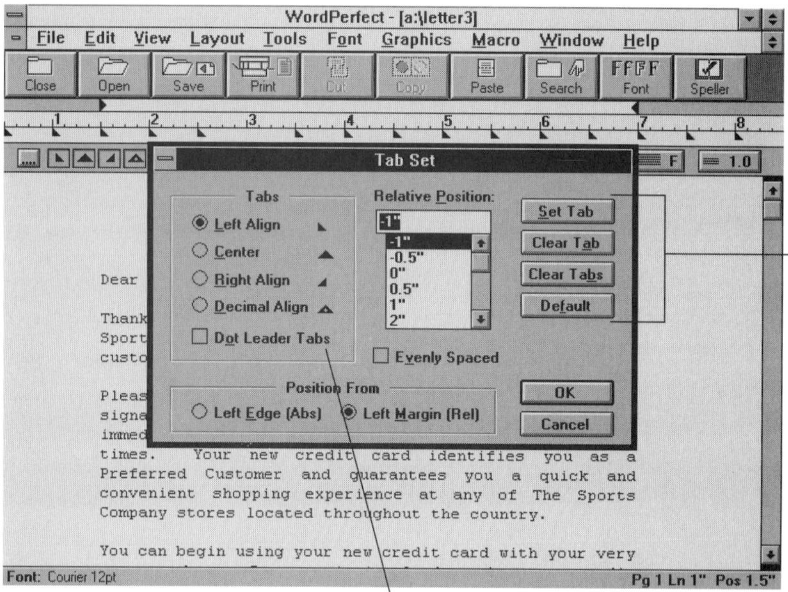

The Tab Set dialog box lets you select special tab styles (displayed in the Tabs group box), add or change tabs, clear a tab, clear all tabs, and set the tabs back to default. To use Help for information about setting tabs,

Press: F1

Read this Help screen and any other related Help screens for information on this topic. When you are done, close Help (double-click Help control menu box or choose Close from Help control menu).

Practice using the dialog box by clearing all tabs (Choose: Clear Tabs). Notice that the tabs are cleared from the Ruler and from the Relative Position list box.

Return the tab settings back to the default (Choose: Default).

The default tab settings are displayed on the Ruler again. You do not need to make any changes to the default settings. To exit the dialog box,

Choose: Cancel

Now you want to indent the first line of the first paragraph one tab stop.

Move to: "T" in "Thank" (Ln 2.17" Pos 1.5")
Press: TAB

Your screen should be similar to Figure 2-15.

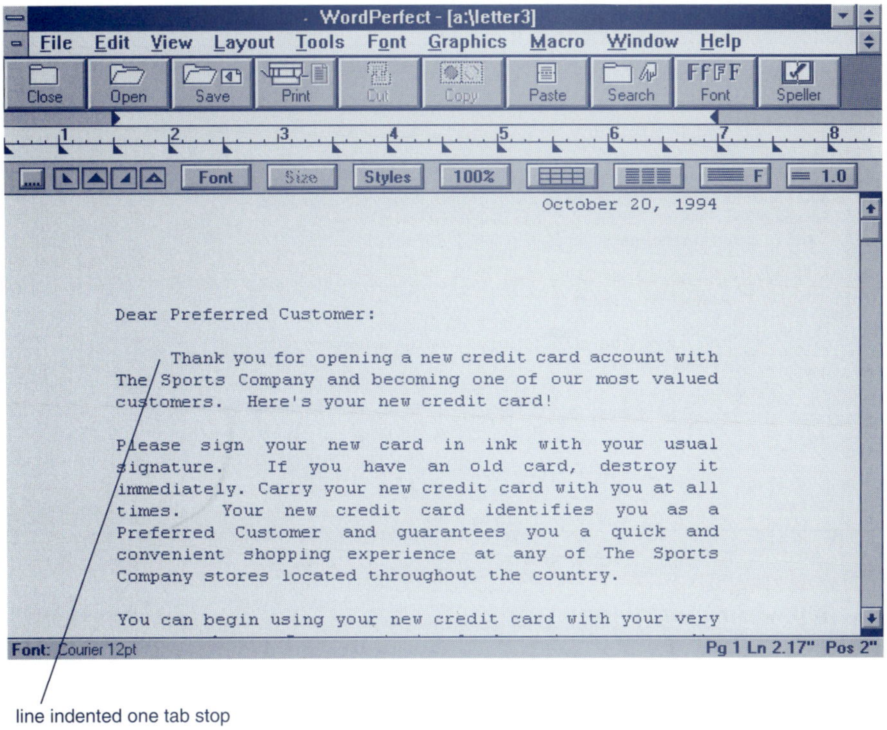

FIGURE 2-15

Pressing (TAB) indents the first line of text five spaces. The text on the following line begins at the left margin.

In a similar manner, indent the first line of the other four paragraphs. Notice as you move down through the text that each paragraph is automatically reformatted.

To indent the closing lines,

Move to: "S" in "Sincerely" (Ln 7.67" Pos 1.5")
Press: (TAB) (5 times)
Move to: "T" of "The" (Ln 8.33" Pos 1.5")
Press: (TAB) (5 times)

Move to the top of the document.

Using the Indent Command

Next you want to add a new sentence to the first paragraph and then itemize and indent several lines. To add the new sentence,

Move to: end of first paragraph (Ln 2.5" Pos 5.5")
Press: Spacebar (2 times)
Type: **Using your new credit card is as easy as 1-2-3.**

Now you want to number and indent the first three sentences in the second paragraph. When you complete the adjustment of the paragraph, it will look like Figure 2-16.

FIGURE 2-16

Dear Preferred Customer:

Thank you for opening a new credit card account with The Sports Company and becoming one of our most valued customers. Here's your new credit card! Using your new credit card is as easy as 1-2-3.

1. Please sign your new card in ink with your usual signature.

2. If you have an old card, destroy it immediately.

3. Carry your new credit card with you at all times.

Move to: "P" of "Please" (Ln 3" Pos 2")

You also want the numbers to appear darker or **bold** when printed. The command to change the appearance of text to bold is Font/Bold. The shortcut for this command is CTRL + B. You will turn on this feature before typing the text. Then everything you type until you turn it off again will appear bold.

Choose: Font/Bold
➢ CTRL + **B**

To enter the number,

Type: **1.**

The number and period appear in bold on the screen, and when printed will be printed bold.

To turn off the bold feature,

Choose: Font/Bold
➢ CTRL + **B**

Another way you can change text to bold is to select the text and then use the command to add bold. The selected text will change to bold.

Next, to indent the text following the number,

Choose: Layout/Paragraph/Indent
➢ F7

Your screen should be similar to Figure 2-17.

FIGURE 2-17

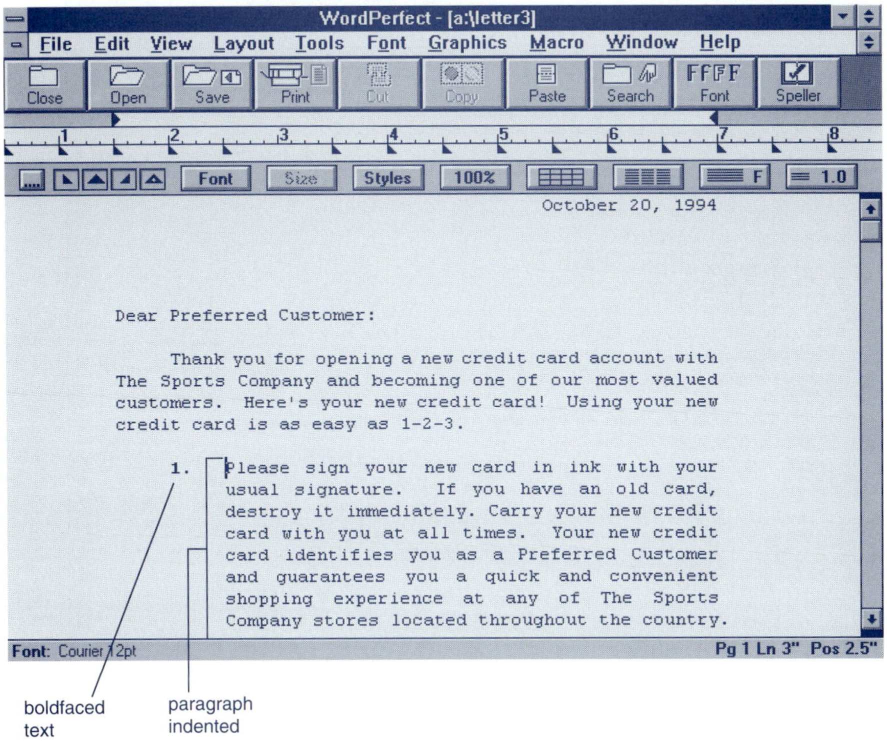

As you can see, using Indent is different from tabbing. It causes all the text that follows the indent to be adjusted to a temporary left margin until WordPerfect reaches a hard carriage return code.

To itemize the next two sentences,

Move to:	"I" of "If" (Ln 3.17" Pos 4.3")
Press:	↵ (2 times)

The text following the hard carriage return has moved back to the original margin setting. To tab and number the second sentence,

Press:	TAB
Press:	CTRL + **B**
Type:	**2.**
Press:	CTRL + **B**

The shortcut key F7 is much quicker than using the Layout menu. To indent the sentence,

Press:	F7

Number and indent the third sentence using the same procedure as above.

Make the last sentence beginning with "Your new..." a new paragraph. (Do not forget to indent the first line of the paragraph.)

When completed, your screen should be similar to Figure 2-18.

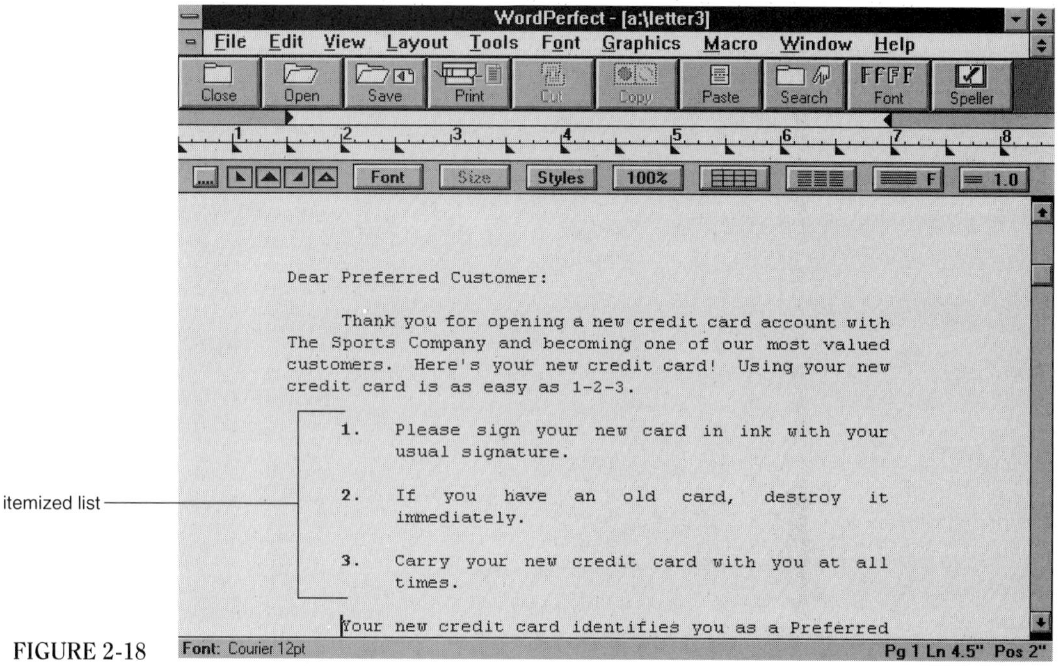

FIGURE 2-18

Using the Replace Command

Next you want to find all occurrences of the words "new credit card" in the letter and change them to "new Sports Company credit card" where appropriate. The Edit/Replace ((CTRL) + (F2)) command will help do this quickly. WordPerfect will begin the search for all occurrences of words beginning at the insertion point. To search the whole letter,

Press: (CTRL) + (HOME)

You will use the menu to perform this task.

Choose: Edit

The Edit menu contains four commands that can be used to search through text for matching text. The four search commands have the following uses:

Search	(F2)	Moves to specified text in the document
Search Next	(SHIFT) + (F2)	Moves to the next occurrence of the text you last searched for
Search Previous	(ALT) + (F2)	Moves to the previous occurrence of the text you last searched for
Replace	(CTRL) + (F2)	Locates specified text and replaces it with the specified replacement text

Since you want to locate and replace text,

Choose: Replace

The Search and Replace dialog box is displayed. The Search For text box is used to enter the text you want to locate. When entering the search text, lowercase letters will match both upper- and lowercase letters in the text. However, if you enter the search text in uppercase letters, only uppercase matches will be found. After entering the search text, do not press (↵).

Type: **new credit card**

Your screen should be similar to Figure 2-19.

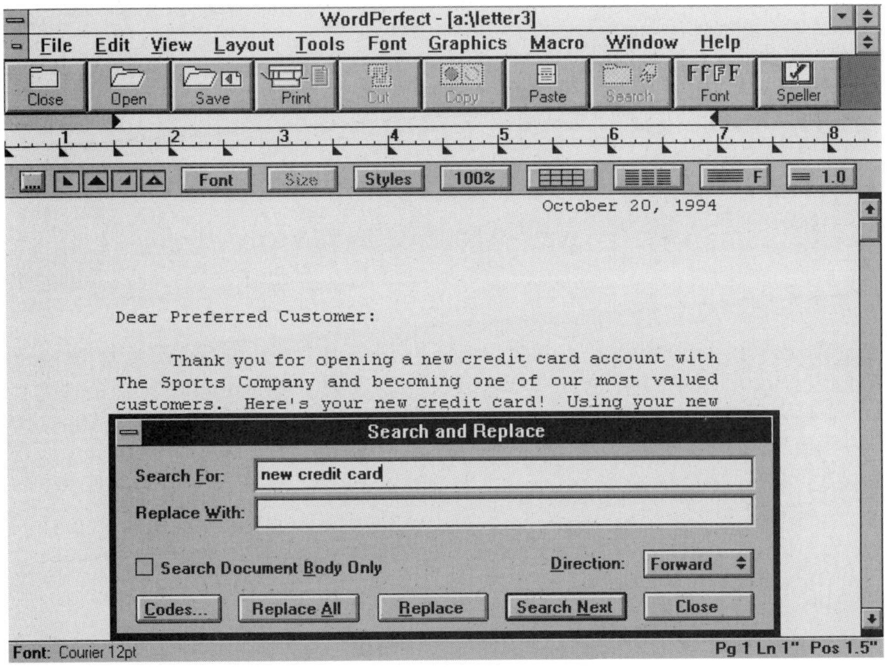

FIGURE 2-19

You want to replace "new credit card" with "new Sports Company credit card." The replacement text must be entered exactly as you want it to appear in your document. To enter the replacement text,

Press: (TAB)
Type: **new Sports Company credit card**

You can search either forward or backward from the insertion point through the document. The Direction list box displays Forward. This is the default setting and, because the insertion point is at the beginning of the document, it is the appropriate setting.

To begin the search,

Choose: Search Next

Your screen should be similar to Figure 2-20.

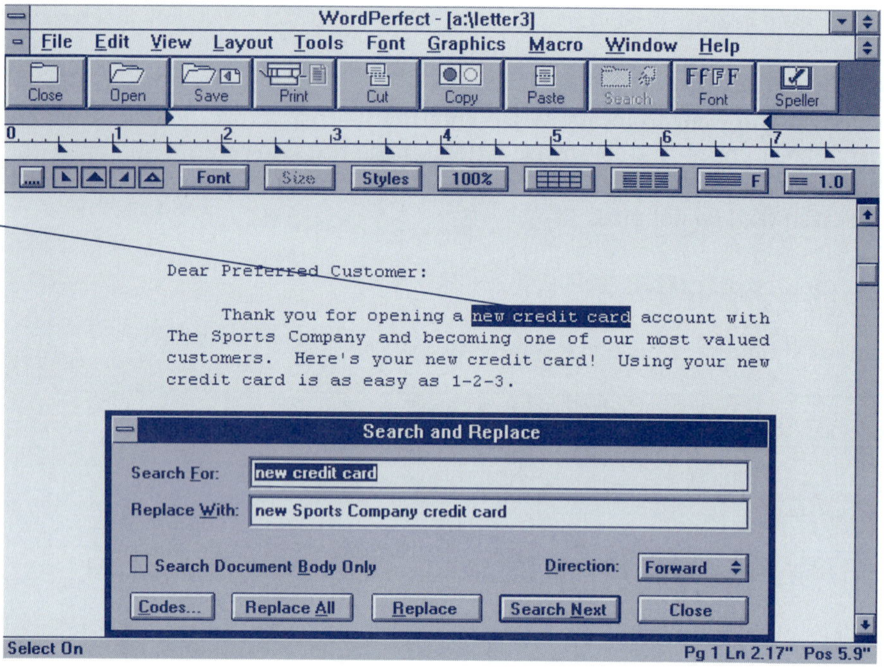

FIGURE 2-20

Immediately the insertion point moves to the first occurrence of the search text and highlights it. You do not, however, want to replace this text. To tell the program to continue the search without replacing the highlighted text,

Choose: Search Next

WordPerfect immediately continues searching and locates a second occurrence of the search text. You do want to replace this text with the replacement text. To do this,

Choose: Replace

The highlighted text has been replaced, and the third occurrence of matching text is located. You want to replace this and all other occurrences of the search text. To do this,

Choose: Replace All

Using Replace All is much faster than confirming each match separately. However, care should be exercised when using Replace All, because the search text you specified might be part of another word and you may accidentally replace text you did not intend.

When WordPerfect has completed the search, the message "no more matches found" is briefly displayed in the status line and there are no matches highlighted in the document. Close the Search dialog box.

Deleting Codes

After the search is completed, you are at the end of the document. You notice that the last line of the letter is very close to the bottom of the page and the page break mark is displayed. You feel the letter would look better if the margins were reset back to the default setting of 1 inch.

Move to the top of the letter. To remove the code that controls the margin setting, you will view the Reveal Codes area. Turn on Reveal Codes.

The code [L/R Mar:1.5,1.5] controls the left and right margin settings. The first part of the code is an abbreviation of the command used. The selected settings are displayed next. If you are using the mouse, the [Tab Set] code is also displayed because you removed the 3" tab setting earlier in the lab.

To delete a code, the (BKSP) or (DEL) key is used. The (BKSP) key will delete codes to the left of the insertion point, and the (DEL) key will delete codes the insertion point is highlighting. You want to delete the margin code. The insertion point must be moved to the code before it can be deleted. Codes are highlighted or displayed in a different color when the insertion point is on them. If necessary, move the insertion point to the margin code. The margin code should be highlighted.

To remove the code,

Press: (DEL)

Your screen should be similar to Figure 2-21.

FIGURE 2-21

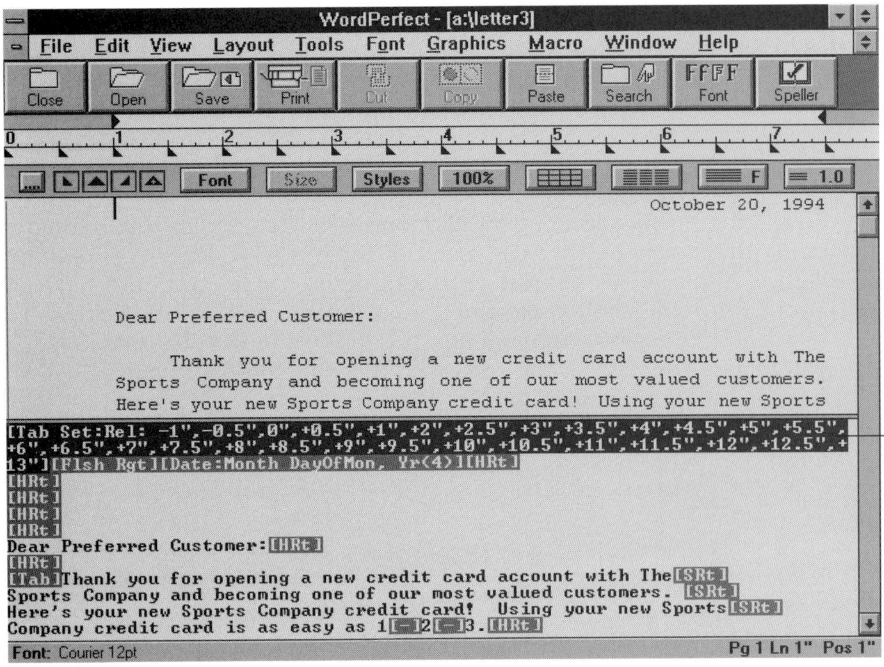

The code is deleted from the document. When a code is deleted, the document acts as if the code had never been entered. The removal of the margin code causes the margin settings to return to the default settings of 1 inch. By looking in the normal document display area and at the Ruler, you can see that the text is now displayed using the default margin settings of 1 inch. If your document contains the tab set code, delete it. Clear the Reveal Codes area.

Many codes can also be deleted from the document while you are in normal document display mode if you know where the code is located. If you do not know where the code was entered in the text, then it is best to use Reveal Codes while deleting codes. In either display mode, first move the insertion point to the location of the code in the document. Then use BKSP to delete codes to the left of the insertion point or DEL to delete codes to the right.

Now, to see where the letter ends on the page,

Press: CTRL + END

As you can see, because the margin widths were decreased, more text can be displayed on a line. Consequently the last line of the letter is no longer at the bottom of the page, and the page break line is no longer displayed.

Setting Justification

On the screen and when printed, the credit card letter has even left and right (full justification). You want the credit card letter to be printed with a ragged or uneven right margin. The command to change justification is Layout/Justification or the Justification button (F) on the ruler bar. Using this command inserts a code in the document to control the printing of the text. The code should be entered at the beginning of the document so that the entire letter will be printed with the selected justification. If it is not entered at the beginning of the document, the new justification setting will begin at the line the insertion point is on and will continue until you insert another code that changes the setting.

Move to the top of the document.

To use the Justification button, click on the button and continue to hold down the mouse button. The menu of options (Left, Right, Center, and Full) is displayed as long as you hold down the mouse button. Read about the four menu choices in the keyboard section that follows. To select an option, drag the highlight to the setting of your choice. When you release the button, the command is completed. To change the justification to left alignment,

Click: F

Select: Left

To open the Justification menu,

Choose: Layout/Justification

The Justification cascade menu displays four justification settings and their shortcuts. They have the following effects:

Left ((CTRL) + L)	Aligns text against left margin, leaving right margin ragged.
Right ((CTRL) + R)	Aligns text against right margin, leaving left margin ragged.
Center ((CTRL) + J)	Centers each line of text between the left and right margins.
Full ((CTRL) + F)	Aligns text against the right and left margins. This is the default setting.

To change justification to have even left and ragged right margins,

Choose: Left

Your screen should be similar to Figure 2-22.

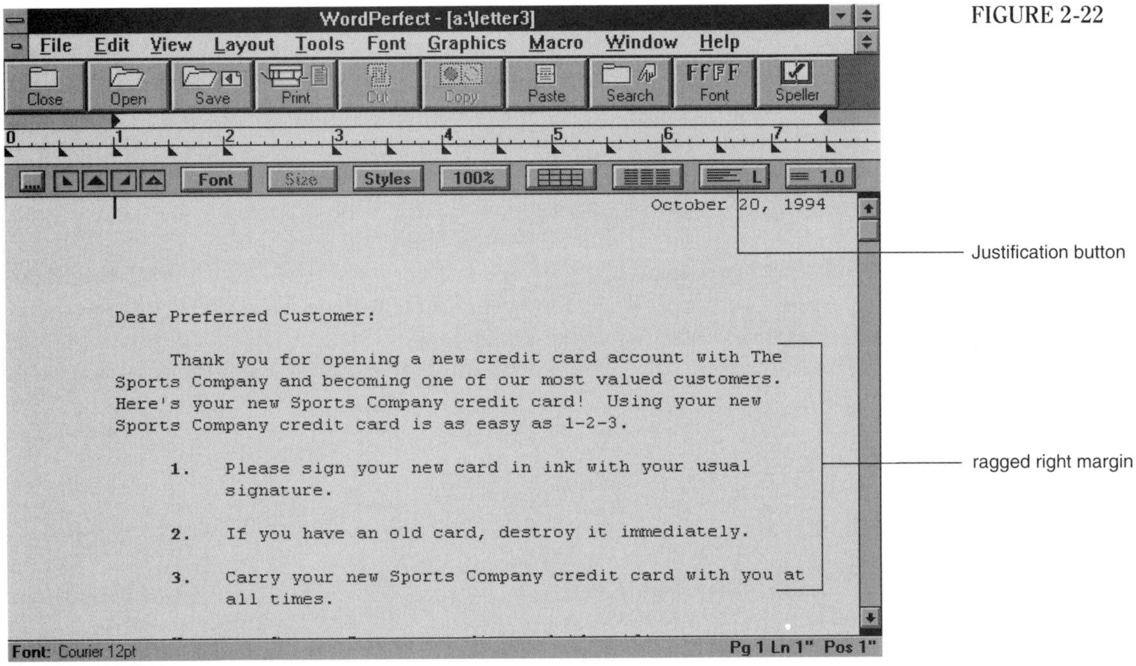

FIGURE 2-22

Notice that the Justification button now appears as [L], indicating that the new justification is left alignment.

Scroll through the letter to see the changes. The letter no longer has uneven spaces between words that were necessary to create full justification.

Turn off the display of the Ruler (View/Ruler) and return to the top of the document.

Saving the Document in a New File

You would like to save the edited version of the credit card letter that is displayed on the screen in a new file named LETTER4. This will allow the original file, LETTER3, to remain unchanged on the disk in case you would like to repeat the lab for practice.

Select: File/Save As (Shortcut: (F3))

To enter the new filename in the Save As text box,

Type: **LETTER4**
Choose: Save

The revised letter has been saved on the disk as LETTER4.

Printing the Document

To print a copy of the credit card letter,

Choose: File/Print
➢ (F5) or Print button

The Print dialog box is displayed.

Let's take a moment to look at the other Print options. The Binding Offset option allows you to move the printed document to the right or left side of the paper to allow space for binding. The current setting of 0" is the default. Number of Copies allows you to print multiple copies of a document. The default is to print one copy. Generated By is an option used to change between documents generated by WordPerfect and by the printer. The other two options, Graphics Quality and Text Quality, allow you to set the quality level at which the graphics or text are printed. The lower quality settings produce a "rough" copy and print faster.

Select the appropriate printer for your computer system. To print the letter, you could select either Full Document or Current Page from the Print dialog box since the credit card letter is only one page long. If the text were longer than a single page, selecting Current Page would print only the page on which the insertion point is positioned.

Select: Current Page
Select: Text Quality/Draft
Choose: Print

Your letter should be printing out. It has been reformatted to the printer settings associated with the printer you selected.

If you are ready to exit the WordPerfect program, turn off the Button Bar display.

Choose: File/Exit

A prompt box is displayed. The prompt "Save changes to a:letter4?" wants you to save the printer specifications to the file. To save the printer selection,

Choose: Yes

The printer specifications that were active when the file was saved were also saved with this file. If you were to open this file again, the printer you made active would appear on the Print screen as the selected printer.

Next you will be prompted to save CREDITCD. This time it is not necessary to save the file again.

Choose: No

Key Terms

word wrap
supplementary dictionary
active window
soft carriage return
bold

Command Summary

Command	Shortcut	Button Bar	Action
Tools/Speller	CTRL + F1	Speller	Turns on Speller application
Window/#<filename>			Makes selected window active
Window/Tile			Displays windows in tile style (without overlapping)
Edit/Copy	CTRL + INS	Copy	Copies selected text to Clipboard
Edit/Paste	SHIFT + INS	Paste	Pastes text from Clipboard
Edit/Select			Selects a complete sentence or paragraph
Edit/Cut	SHIFT + DEL	Cut	Cuts selected text
Tools/Date/Text	CTRL + F5		Inserts current date as text
Tools/Date/Code	CTRL + SHIFT + F5		Inserts current date maintained by computer system as code
Tools/Date/Format			Changes how dates you insert will appear in the document
Layout/Line/Flush Right	ALT + F7		Aligns text flush with right margin
View/Reveal Codes	ALT + F3		Displays hidden codes on split screen
Layout/Margins	CTRL + F8		Changes left, right, top, and bottom margins
View/Ruler	ALT + SHIFT + F3		Displays margin and tab settings
Layout/Line/Tab Set			Specifies types and position of tab stops
Font/Bold	CTRL + B		Changes selected text to bold font
Layout/Paragraph/Indent	F7		Indents text to first tab stop until a hard carriage return is reached
Edit/Search	F2		Locates specified text or codes
Edit/Search Next	SHIFT + F2		Looks for next occurence of search text
Edit/Search Previous	ALT + F2		Looks for previous occurence of search text
Edit/Replace	CTRL + F2		Searches for matching text and replaces it with new text
Layout/Justification/Left	CTRL + L	L	Aligns text on left margin
Layout/Justification/Right	CTRL + R	R	Aligns text on right margin
Layout/Justification/Center	CTRL + J		Centers text between margins
Layout/Justification/Full	CTRL + F	F	Aligns text on left and right margins
File/Save As	F3		Saves file with new filename
File/Print/Current Page/Print			Prints only the page on which insertion point is positioned

LAB REVIEW

Matching

1. [Tab]	_____	a.	places text from Clipboard into a document
2. margins	_____	b.	allows you to select an entire sentence or paragraph
3. Edit/Select	_____	c.	hidden code for a tab
4. SHIFT + INS	_____	d.	displays two windows one above the other
5. F7	_____	e.	indicates the left margin setting on the ruler bar
6. ALT + F3	_____	f.	blank area around printed text
7. Tile	_____	g.	removes text from document and stores it in Clipboard
8. ▶	_____	h.	quickly locates specified text
9. Edit/Cut	_____	i.	shortcut key for Reveal Codes
10. Search	_____	j.	Indent key

Practice Exercises

1. This problem will give you practice in creating, combining, and rearranging text.

   a. Enter the following text into a blank document window.

      It Happened at the zoo

      The first anteater ever born at the zoo arrived on February 10, 1992. The sex of the baby has not yet been determined because it clings tightly to its mother's fur. There it will stay until it is almost half her size.

      More than one hundred visitors and zoo employees witnessed the birth of Frisco, an African giraffe. Because the birth took place in an area partially hidden, one question went unanswered: was the calf male or female? After receiving a kick in the shins the Curator of Mammals announced the new cafe was female.

   b. Save the file as ZOO.DOC.

   c. Copy the text in the file ZOO2.DOC (on your data disk) into your file ZOO.DOC. The text in the file ZOO2.DOC should be entered at the end of the text in ZOO.DOC.

   d. Rearrange the paragraphs so that the first paragraph is about the tiger, the second paragraph is about the tapir, the third paragraph is about the giraffe, the fourth paragraph is about the anteater, and the fifth is about the birds.

   e. Set justification to have a ragged right margin. Center the title.

- **f.** Search the document for the word "zoo" and replace it with the word "Zoo."
- **g.** Enter your name and the current date on the last line of the document.
- **h.** Save and print the document.

2. As editor of the children's section of the local newspaper, you have received several short stories on animals that you would like to include in the next special edition.

- **a.** Enter the text below. Save the file as STORIES. Spell-check the file.

  The Sumatran Tiger

  The tiger is a big, strong, orange cat with black stripes. It is the largest member of the cat family. Adult tigers are powerful, but a baby is helpless at birth.

  The Sumatran tiger is an endangered species. There are fewer than 600 left in the wild.

  Gorillas

  To most people, gorillas are scary. But this is unfair. Once you get to know them, gorillas are actually gentle giants.

  Gorillas are plant-eaters. They eat juicy stems, leaves and tree bark. They use their large canine teeth to rip the bark right off the trees.

- **b.** Combine the text in the file STORIES2.DOC (on your data disk) with your STORIES file.
- **c.** Rearrange the document so that the first topic is about the gorillas, the second is about the tiger, the third is about the spider, and the fourth is about the wren.
- **d.** Set justification to have a ragged right margin. Center all titles.
- **e.** Enter your name and the current date on the last line of the document.
- **f.** Save and print the document.

3. As Vice-President of the Careers Club, you invited several professionals to present information to club members about preparing employment resumes. In this problem you will create and format a letter to thank the guests.

- **a.** Turn on the Ruler and set justification to left-aligned. Set the left margin to 2" and the right to 1.5".
- **b.** Clear all the tab settings after 2.5". Enter a new tab setting of 5.0".
- **c.** Enter the current date using the Date/Code command.

d. Enter the following letter:

Ms. Elizabeth Ramage
Human Resources Manager
JBS Services
34 W. University Dr.
Tempe, AZ 85257

Dear Ms. Ramage:

Thank you for taking the time to speak with the Career Club at our school last week. The information you presented on how to write resumes and other employment related documents was very helpful.

In addition, the personal attention you gave to many of the club members by reviewing resumes they had prepared was greatly appreciated.

I have received many very favorable comments from the members about this presentation and plan to arrange a similar presentation again next year. I hope you will consider participating again at that time.

Sincerely,

(Your name)

e. Display the date flush with the right margin.

f. Indent each paragraph five spaces.

g. Change the left margin setting to 1.5".

h. Indent the closing to the 5.0" tab position.

i. Save the letter as THANKS. Print the letter.

4. As Assistant Editor of the Travel Arizona magazine, you are responsible for researching "out of the way" places to visit in the state. Quarterly you send a memo to the Managing Editor that describes the ones you like best.

a. Enter the memo below using left and right margin settings of 1.5" and a tab setting of 2.2" only.

From: (Your name), Assistant Editor

To: Jane Walker, Managing Editor

Date: (Enter current date using the Date/Code command)

After reviewing the many interesting places we could write about I have chosen the following three:

Snowflake, the "Home of the Pioneers," was founded in 1878. It is located 27 miles south of Holbrook in Navajo County. This town has an array of old houses, a school house built in 1891, and a library that contains 36,500 books. Snowflake was founded in 1878 and is named for two Mormon pioneers, Erastus Snow and William J. Flake.

Ramsey Canyon is known as "Where you are Nature's guest!" It was established as a preserve in 1975. Fifteen species of hummingbirds, flycatchers, warblers, wrens, and woodpeckers, to name a few, are the birds that can be seen in the canyon. Birds and nature get highest priority in the Mile Hi/Ramsey Canyon Preserve.

Williams, the "Gateway to the Grand Canyon," is named for William Sherley Williams, a colorful mountaineer, trapper, and guide who died in 1849. According to the memorial, a bronze statue displayed in the city park, Williams first visited the area in 1826.

b. Delete the last sentence in the second paragraph ("Snowflake was founded...") using the Cut command.

c. Switch the order of the third and fourth sentences in the Ramsey Canyon paragraph.

d. Spell-check the document.

e. Save the document as TRAVEL and print the document.

5. You work for a large pet shop and are working on an article for the company newsletter on feeding wild birds. You want to make several changes to the article. Open the file BIRDS on your data disk.

- **a.** Spell-check the document.
- **b.** Indent the four items under "Equipment."
- **c.** Center the title at the top of the article.
- **d.** Under the Feeders heading, switch the third and fourth paragraphs.
- **e.** Search and replace the word "bird" with "wild bird" where appropriate.
- **f.** Enter your name and the current date on the last line of the document. Save and print the document.

6. Create a cover letter that could be included with your resume. Set the margins so that the letter is on one page and is balanced on the page. Set justification to left and spell-check the letter. Save and print the letter.

LAB

3 Merging Documents and Creating Tables

Competencies

In this lab you will learn how to:

1. Use the merge feature.
2. Enter merge codes in the primary file.
3. Create the secondary file.
4. Merge the primary and secondary files.
5. Create and modify a table.
6. Use formulas.
7. Bold and center table text.

CASE STUDY

You submitted the final copy of the credit card letter to the Regional Manager. The manager is very pleased with the content and form of the credit card letter, but would like it to be more personalized. It should include the first name of the preferred customer and an inside address. You will create a form letter using WordPerfect's Merge feature to personalize each credit card letter.

As a second project, you have been asked to prepare a summary of gross sales for the four metropolitan stores. You will create a table of this data using WordPerfect.

The Merge Feature

Load Windows. Load the WordPerfect program. Display the Button Bar. Open the file CREDIT.

This is the same as the credit card letter you saved as LETTER4 in Lab 2. Notice that the date in the letter is the same as the system date. Each time this letter is opened or printed, the date will display the system date. This is because of the date code you entered in the document.

You need to change the credit card letter so that each letter sent to a preferred customer is more personal. The credit card letter will include the preferred customer's first name in the salutation and his or her full name and address as the inside address. To do this you will use the Merge feature of WordPerfect for Windows.

The Merge feature will combine a list of names and addresses that are contained in one file with a form letter in another file. The names and addresses are entered (merged) into the form letter in the blank spaces provided. The result is a personalized form letter.

Merge usually requires the use of two files: a **primary file** and a **secondary file**. The primary file contains the basic form letter. It directs the merge process through the use of **merge codes**. The merge codes control what information is used from the secondary file and where it is entered in the document in the primary file. The credit card letter will be modified to be the primary file.

The secondary file, sometimes called an **address file**, contains the information needed to complete the form letter in the primary file. It will contain the preferred customer's name and address data. Each piece of information in the secondary file is called a **field**. For example, the customer's first name is a field of data, the customer's last name is a field of data, the street address is another field of data, the city a fourth field of data, and so forth. All the fields of data that are needed to complete the primary document are called a **record**.

The secondary file you will create will contain the following fields of information for each record: First Name, Last Name, Street Address, City, State, and Zipcode. WordPerfect takes the field information from the secondary file and combines or merges it into the primary file.

First you will modify the credit card letter to accept information from the secondary file. Then you will create the secondary file, which will hold the preferred customers' names and addresses to be entered into the primary file.

Entering Merge Codes in the Primary File

The credit card letter needs to be modified to allow entry of the name and address information for each preferred customer from the secondary file. The inside address will hold the following three lines of information:

First Name Last Name
Street Address
City, State   Zipcode

The first line of the inside address, which will hold the preferred customer's full name, will be entered as line 5 of the credit card letter.

Move to: blank line above salutation (Ln 1.67" Pos 1")

How will WordPerfect know to enter the customer's name from the secondary file at this location in the primary file? WordPerfect uses the merge codes to do this. They direct the program to accept information from the secondary file at the specified location in the primary file. To display the menu of merge codes, you use the Tools/Merge or CTRL + F12 command.

Choose: Tools/Merge
➢ CTRL + F12

Your screen should be similar to Figure 3-1.

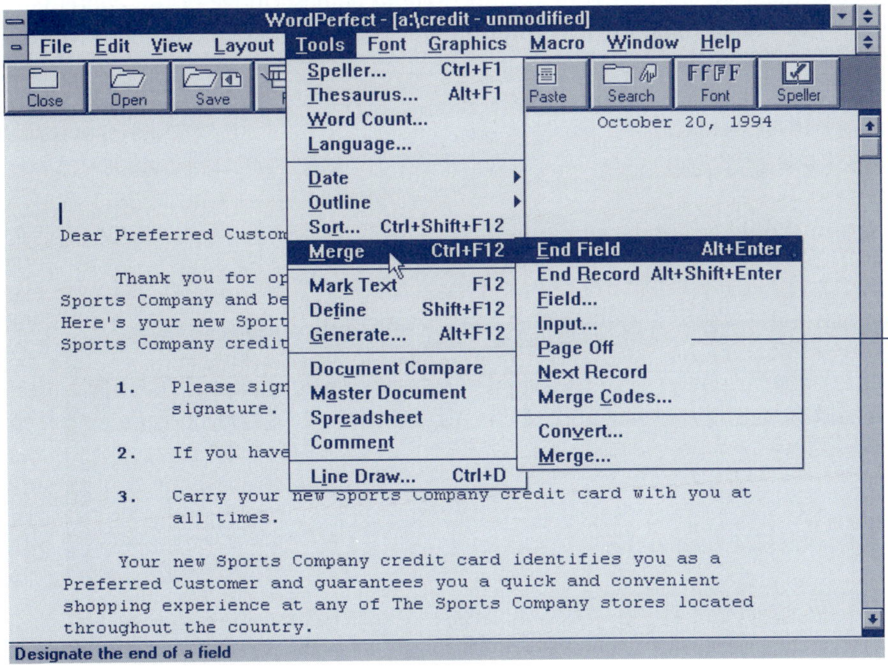

Merge menu

FIGURE 3-1

The Merge cascade menu options have the following meanings:

End Field	Signals the end of a field in a secondary file
End Record	Marks the end of a record in the secondary file
Field	Identifies the field to be inserted from the secondary document into the primary document
Input	Stops the merge and waits for keyboard input
Page Off	Instructs WordPerfect not to place page breaks after each primary file
Next Record	Instructs WordPerfect to move to the next secondary file record during the merge
Merge Codes	Displays a list box of merge codes
Convert	Converts old merge codes into the new merge format
Merge	Prompts for the name of the primary and secondary files and creates a merged file

A Field merge code needs to be entered in the primary file for each field of data you want copied from the secondary file. The location of the Field merge code directs WordPerfect where to enter the data. The insertion point is positioned on the line where the preferred customer's first name will appear as the first line of the inside address. The first field you will identify then is the first name field.

Choose: Field

The Insert Merge Code dialog box is displayed. The name you want to assign to the merge code must be entered. A field name should be descriptive of the contents of the field. It can be a single word or multiple words up to 80 characters. You will use the field name "First Name."

Type: **First Name**
Choose: OK

Your screen should be similar to Figure 3-2.

FIGURE 3-2

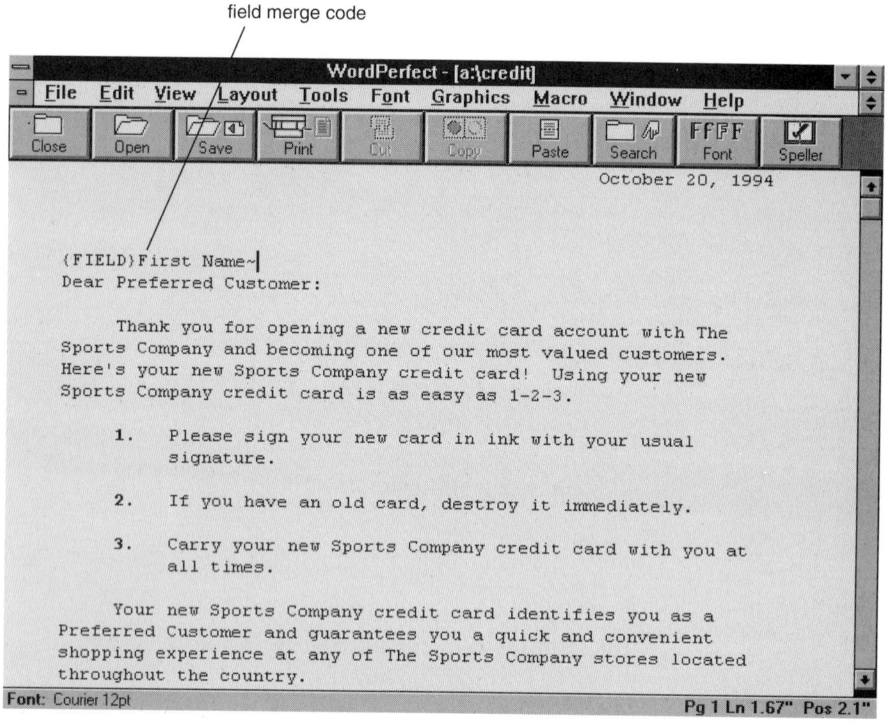

The field merge code, {FIELD}, followed by the name you assigned the field is displayed at the insertion point location. The ~ (tilde) at the end of the field name tells WordPerfect where the field name ends. When the command to merge the documents is used, the information for the preferred customer's first name from the secondary merge file will be entered at this location in the primary file.

The next field that needs to be entered is the preferred customer's last name. To enter a blank space between the first name and the last name,

Press: Spacebar

To the enter the last name field,

Choose: Tools/Merge/Field

In response to the field name prompt,

Type: **Last Name**
Choose: OK

The next line of the inside address will contain the street address. To create and move to the next line,

Press: (↵)

To enter the field merge code for the street address using the shortcut,

Press: (CTRL) + (F12)
Choose: Field
Type: **Address**
Choose: OK

The third merge field code is displayed in the credit card letter.

The next line of the inside address will display three fields of data from the secondary file: city, state, and zipcode. They will be identified by the field names City, State, and Zip.

Press: (↵)

To enter the merge code for the next field of data,

Choose: Tools/Merge/Field
➢ (CTRL) + (F12), Field
Type: **City**
Choose: OK

To separate the city field from the next field with a comma and a space,

Type: **,**
Press: Spacebar

The state field will be entered on the same line as the city field.

Choose: Tools/Merge/Field
➢ (CTRL) + (F12), Field
Type: **State**
Choose: OK

To separate the state field from the next field, zipcode,

Press: Spacebar (2 times)
Choose: Tools/Merge/Field
➢ (CTRL) + (F12), Field
Type: **Zip**
Choose: OK

To enter a blank line between the inside address and the salutation,

Press: ⏎

The last field of information that needs to be entered in the primary file is the preferred customer's first name in the salutation. First the words "Preferred Customer" need to be deleted.

Move to: "P" of "Preferred" (Ln 2.33" Pos 1.5")

Select and delete the text "Preferred Customer" (do not include the :). To enter the merge code for the first name into the salutation,

Choose: Tools/Merge/Field
➢ CTRL + F12, Field

A field name can be used more than one time in the primary document. For example, the first name field can be used again in the letter without assigning it a new field name. To enter the first name in the salutation,

Type: **First Name**
Choose: OK

Your screen should be similar to Figure 3-3.

FIGURE 3-3

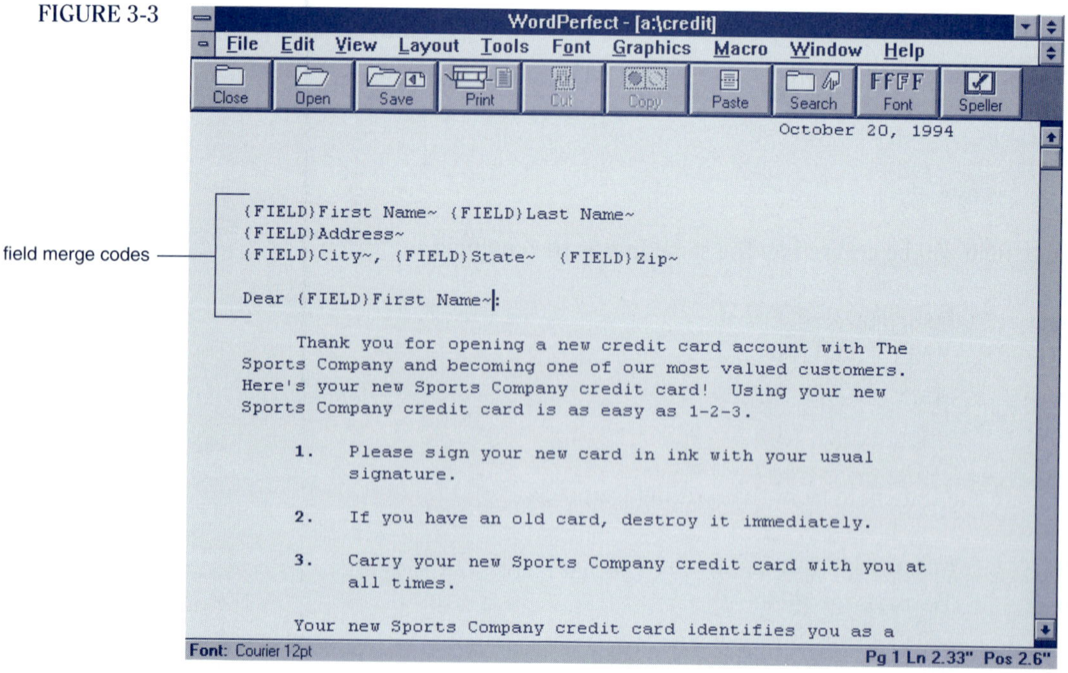

You have completed entering all the merge codes that are needed to personalize the credit card letter. Check your codes. If you have made an error, you can edit the merge codes just like any other text entry.

Once all the merge codes that are needed in the primary file are correctly entered, the file must be saved. To save the primary file as CREDIT.PF (the extension .PF identifies the file as a primary file) and clear the screen in preparation for creating the secondary file,

Choose:	File/Save As
➣	(F3)
Press:	(→)
Type:	**.PF**
Choose:	Save
Choose:	File/Close
➣	(CTRL) + (F4) or Close button

Creating the Secondary File

A blank WordPerfect screen is ready to be used to enter the fields and records for the secondary file. The secondary file will hold the six fields of data about each preferred customer. The six fields of data for each preferred customer form a record of information.

The primary file calls for the following six fields of data for each record:

Field Number	Field Name
Field 1	First Name
Field 2	Last Name
Field 3	Address
Field 4	City
Field 5	State
Field 6	Zip

When entering the data for the secondary file, the following rules must be observed:

- At the beginning of the document, enter a special merge code which identifies the names of each field used in the primary file.
- Mark the end of a field of data with an {END FIELD} merge code.
- Mark the end of a record with an {END RECORD} merge code.
- Enter each field of data in the same sequence for all records and include the same type of information.
- Enter the same number of fields in each record. Not all the fields in the secondary file need to be used in the primary file.

First you need to enter the special merge code that identifies the field names.

Choose:	Tools/Merge/Merge Codes
➣	(CTRL) + (F12), Merge Codes

Your screen should be similar to Figure 3-4.

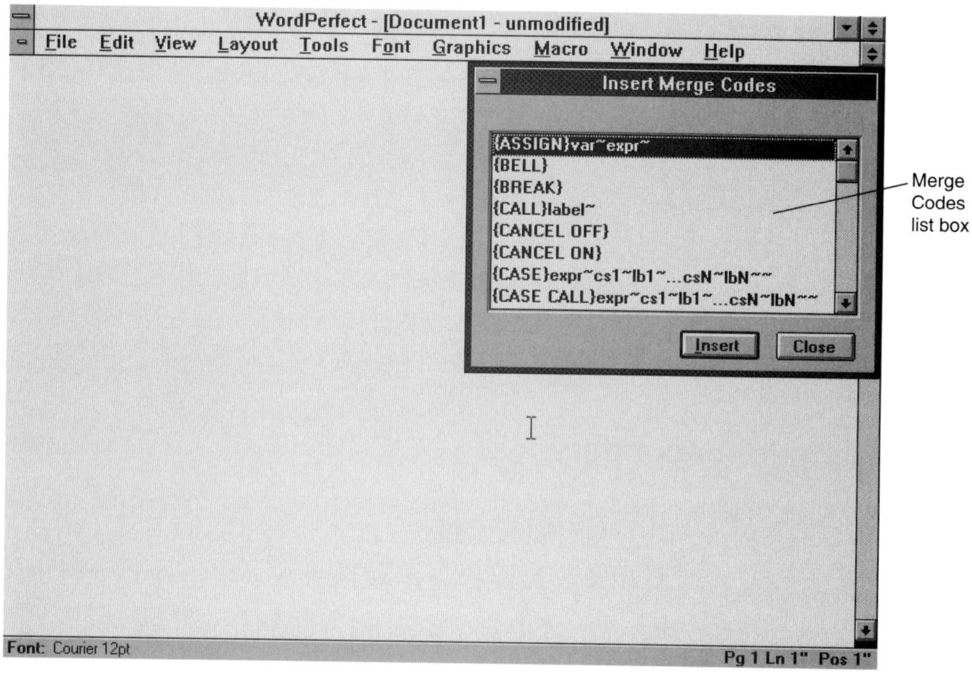

FIGURE 3-4

The Insert Merge Code list box is displayed. The merge codes are listed in alphabetical order. The Field Names merge code specifies the names and order of fields in the secondary file.

Using ⬇ or the scroll bar, scroll the list box and select {FIELD NAMES} name1..nameN~~. To insert it,

Choose: Insert

The Merge Field Name(s) dialog box is displayed. The format line shows you how this command should be entered. This is the command **syntax**. The command name is enclosed in braces and followed by the name of the first field and ending with a tilde (~) symbol. Each following field name is entered until the last field name. Two tilde symbols follow the last field name. The tilde symbols are entered for you by WordPerfect. WordPerfect identifies the number of the field you are entering, and since this is the first field name, 1 is displayed.

You need to enter the field name of the first field. The field name must be entered exactly as you typed it in the primary file. In the Field Name text box,

Type: **First Name**
Choose: Add

The field name is entered into the list box. To add the second field, Last Name, the text box needs to be reselected. To select the text box,

Click on the text box.

Press: (SHIFT) + (TAB) (2 times)

The field name First Name should be highlighted.

Type: **L**

Notice that the field number displayed has changed to 2.

Type: **ast Name**
Choose: Add

Continue to select the text box and define the remaining four field names (Address, City, State, and Zip). To indicate you have completed defining the field names,

Choose: OK

To close the Insert Merge Codes dialog box,

Choose: Close

Your screen should be similar to Figure 3-5.

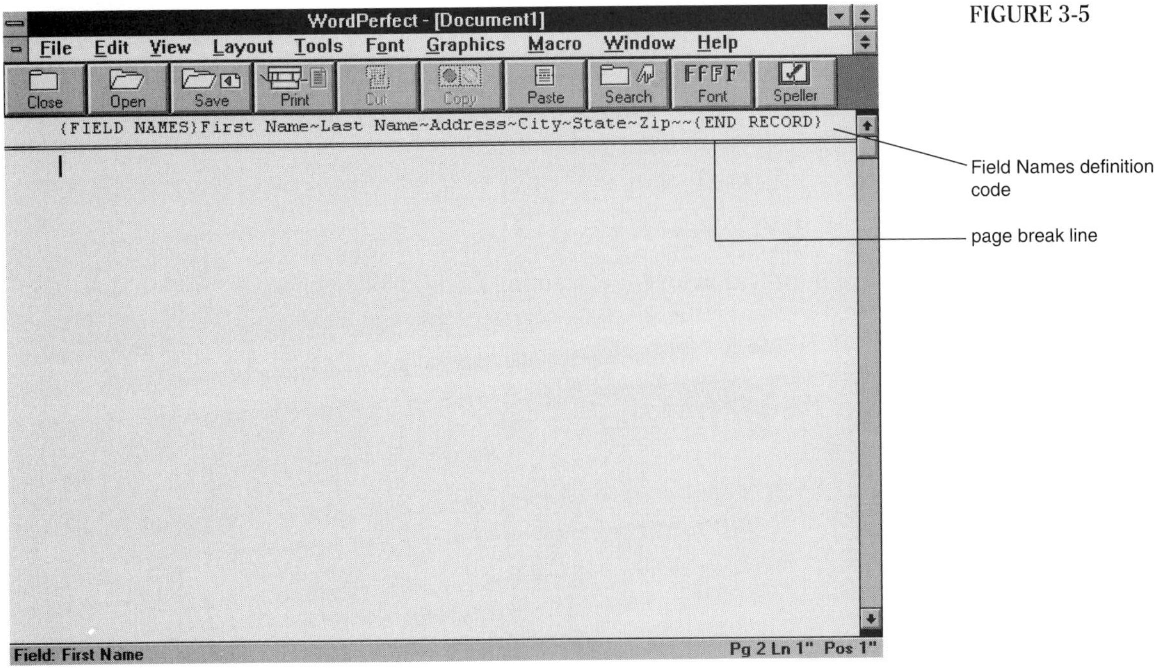

FIGURE 3-5

The {FIELD NAMES} definition code is displayed on the first line of the screen. The name of each field as you typed it followed by a tilde is displayed. The code ends with an extra tilde and an {END RECORD} merge code. WordPerfect automatically adds the {END RECORD} code because it treats the {FIELD NAMES} merge code as a special record in the secondary file. It also adds a **hard page break** line to separate this record from the other records you will be entering into the document next. This makes the file easier to read.

You can edit the field name definition code as you would edit any other text. If you add or delete a field name, make sure that each field name ends with a tilde symbol.

Now you are ready to enter the data for the first record. The first record begins immediately below the Field Names record. Your insertion point should be on the first line of page 2. Notice that the status line displays "Field: First Name." This tells you that WordPerfect is ready for you to enter the first field of data, the preferred customer's first name.

Type: **Anthony** (do not press ↵)

To tell the program that this is the end of the first field of data, you enter the merge code {END FIELD}.

Choose: Tools/Merge/End Field
➢ ALT + ↵

The {END FIELD} code is entered after the first field, and the insertion point moves down one line. WordPerfect displays "Field: Last Name" in the status line to tell you it expects you to enter the data for this field next.

Type: **Manahan**
Choose: Tools/Merge/End Field
➢ ALT + ↵

To enter the address data,

Type: **2931 E. Campus Drive**
Choose: Tools/Merge/End Field
➢ ALT + ↵

Enter the information for the remaining fields as follows:

Type: **Mesa**
Choose: Tools/Merge/End Field
➢ ALT + ↵

Type: **AZ**
Choose: Tools/Merge/End Field
➢ ALT + ↵

Type: 85202
Choose: Tools/Merge/End Field
➢ ALT + ↵

The six fields of information corresponding to the six field merge codes used in the primary file's inside address and salutation are complete for the first record in the secondary file.

To separate this record from the next record and to indicate a page break between documents, the {END RECORD} merge code is used. To enter this code,

Choose: Tools/Merge/End Record
➢ ALT + SHIFT + ↵

Your screen should be similar to Figure 3-6.

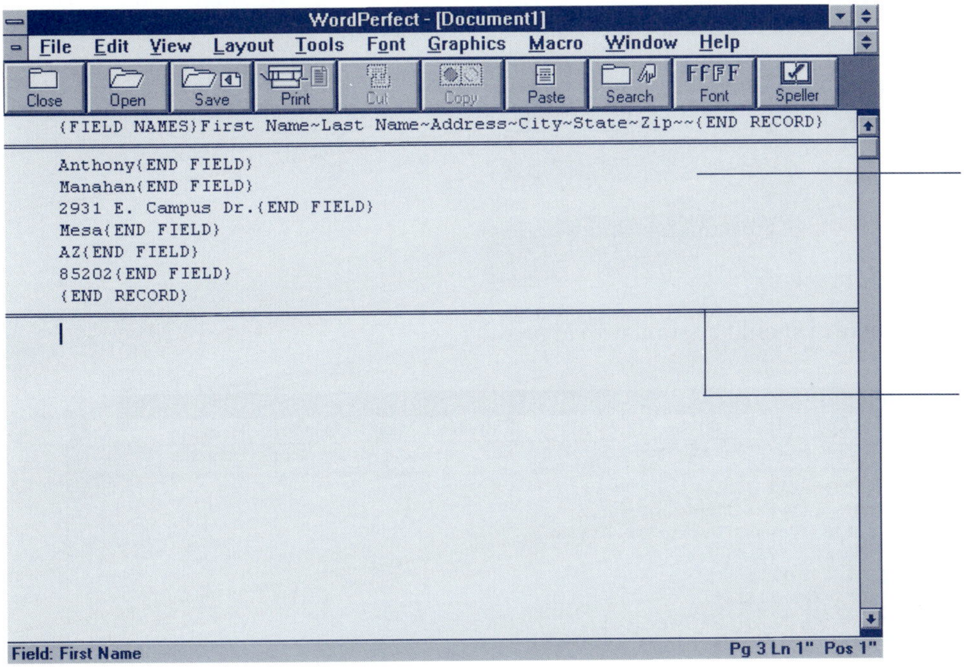

FIGURE 3-6

An {END RECORD} code is entered on the line, and the insertion point moves to the next line in the file. WordPerfect automatically enters a hard page break line to separate this record from the next. This tells the program to begin a new page following the page break regardless of the amount of text on the page.

Never separate fields or records with an extra hard carriage return. Also do not insert spaces following the last word in a field and an {END RECORD} merge code.

Enter the field information for the second record as follows:

Type: Corey
Choose: Tools/Merge/End Field
➢ ALT + ↵

Type: **Owens**
Choose: Tools/Merge/End Field
➢ ALT + ↵

Type: **3857 W. University Ave.**
Choose: Tools/Merge/End Field
➢ ALT + ↵

Type: **Tempe**
Choose: Tools/Merge/End Field
➢ ALT + ↵

Type: **AZ**
Choose: Tools/Merge/End Field
➢ ALT + ↵

Type: **85285**
Choose: Tools/Merge/End Field
➢ ALT + ↵

Choose: Tools/Merge/End Record
➢ ALT + SHIFT + ↵

Your screen should be similar to Figure 3-7.

FIGURE 3-7

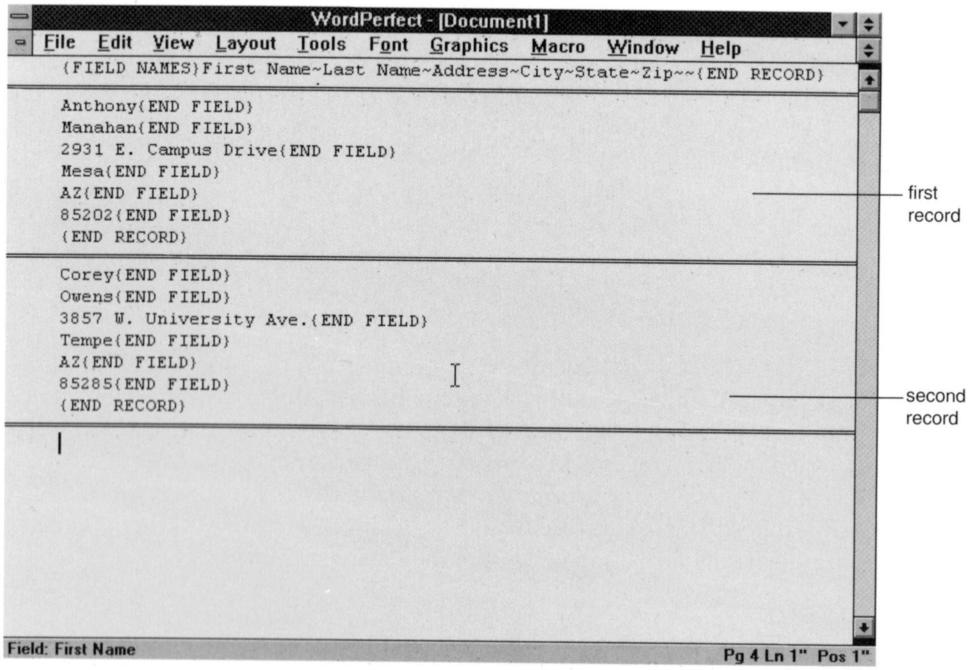

Enter your name and address as the third record in the secondary file.

Check your screen and make any corrections as needed (use regular editing methods). Make sure each field of data ends with an {END FIELD} code and that each record ends with an {END RECORD} code. If you do not have the information needed to complete a field, you can leave it blank, but the line must contain an {END FIELD} code.

The number of records you enter into the secondary file is limited only by your disk space.

Now you are ready to save the secondary file and clear the screen in preparation for merging the primary file with the secondary file.

Use the File/Save command and save the file on your data disk using the filename CREDIT.SF (the file extension .SF identifies this file as a secondary file). Close the file.

Merging the Primary and Secondary Files

Now that you have created and saved the primary and secondary files, you are ready to combine them to create the new personalized credit card letter. During this process a third file is created. The original primary and secondary files are not altered or affected in any way. The third file is the result of the merging of the primary and secondary files. It is very important to have a new document window open before merging files.

Choose: Tools/Merge/Merge
➢ CTRL + F12, Merge

The Merge dialog box is displayed. In this box you must enter the path and name of the primary and secondary files. In response to the prompt to enter the name of the primary file,

Type: **CREDIT.PF**
Press: TAB

Next, to enter the name of the secondary file,

Type: **CREDIT.SF**
Choose: OK

The two files are loaded into memory, and the status line displays the message "- Merging -." At the completion of the merge, the document containing the three letters is displayed on the screen. To move to the top of the document,

Press: CTRL + HOME

Your screen should be similar to Figure 3-8.

letter created by merge

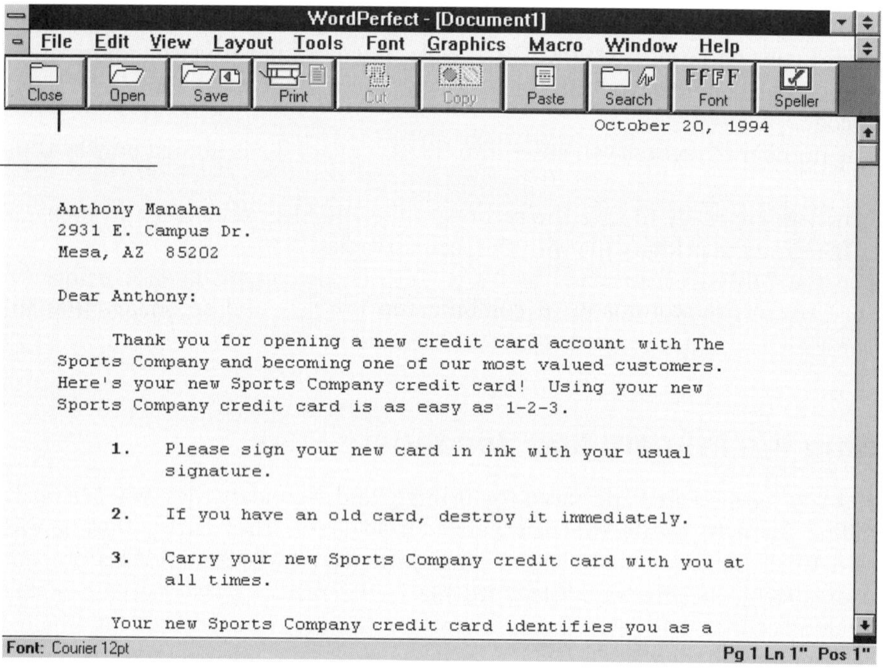

FIGURE 3-8

The personalized letter to Anthony Manahan is displayed. The fields of data from the secondary file have been entered into the primary file at the location of the merge codes.

To see the letter using the data for the second record,

Press: ALT + PGDN

Finally, to see the letter containing your name and address information,

Press: ALT + PGDN

Now each time you need to send credit card letters, all you need to do is to create the preferred customer secondary merge file and issue the Merge command. Because the Date command was used, the date will automatically reflect the date the letter was created.

Save the current document of three personalized credit card letters as CREDIT.MRG.

The letters can be printed like any other document. Print the letter containing your name and address information only. Remember to select the appropriate printer for your system first.

To leave the document and clear the screen,

Choose: File/Close

➢ CTRL + F4 or Close button

To review, the steps in creating a customized form letter are:

1. Create the primary file. Enter field merge codes in the document to tell WordPerfect where and what fields of information to use from the secondary file. Save the document as the primary file.
2. Create the secondary file. It will contain the special record that identifies the field names used in the primary file, along with the variable data or information needed to complete the primary file for each record. Each field of data must end with an {END FIELD} code. Each record must end with an {END RECORD} code. As many records as disk space will allow can be entered in this file.
3. Use the Merge command to combine the primary and secondary files to create a customized document for each record in the secondary file.

Creating a Table

Your next project is to prepare a summary of gross sales for the four metropolitan area stores for the past three years. You have located the data and feel the best way to present the data is in a **table**. A table consists of **rows**, which run horizontally, and **columns**, which run vertically. The intersection of a row and column creates a **cell** in which you can enter data or other information.

The table you want to create will display the data for the three years in the columns. The rows will display the data for the four stores and a total. Your completed table will be similar to Figure 3-9.

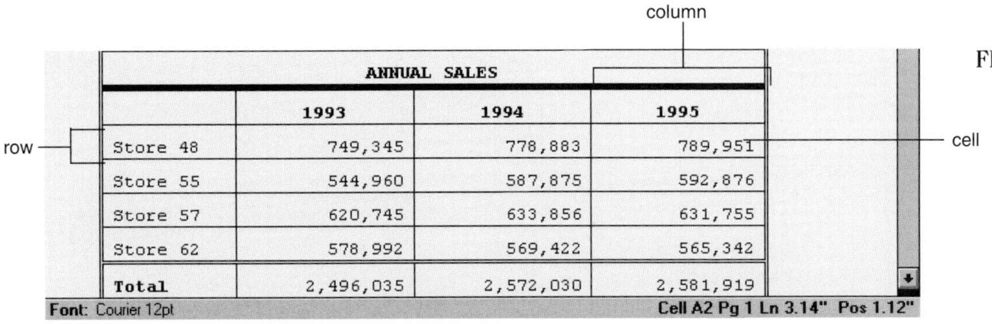

ANNUAL SALES			
	1993	1994	1995
Store 48	749,345	778,883	789,951
Store 55	544,960	587,875	592,876
Store 57	620,745	633,856	631,755
Store 62	578,992	569,422	565,342
Total	2,496,035	2,572,030	2,581,919

FIGURE 3-9

You have already started a memo to accompany the table and want to display the table below the memo. To see the memo, open the file SALESTBL. Display the Ruler. Enter your name and the current date in the appropriate space in the memo introduction.

You want the table to be displayed two lines below the last line of the memo.

Move to: Ln 2.67"

The Layout/Tables command will quickly create the structure of a table for you. The shortcut for this command is (CTRL) + (F9).

Choose: Layout/Tables/Create

➢ (CTRL) + (F9), Create

The Create Table dialog box is displayed. In this box you need to specify the number of columns and rows you want the table to have. The table you will create contains four columns of data and six rows (this includes row and column labels). To enter 4 for the number of columns and 6 for the number of rows,

Type:	**4**
Press:	TAB
Type:	**6**
Choose:	OK

Mouse shortcut: Press and hold down the [▦] Table button on the ruler bar (see Figure 3-10). The table-sizing grid is displayed. The grid is used to define the table size by dragging the mouse over the grid until the number of rows and columns you want in the table are highlighted. The selected table size appears in the table box. As soon as you release the mouse button, the table is drawn.

Your screen should be similar to Figure 3-10.

FIGURE 3-10

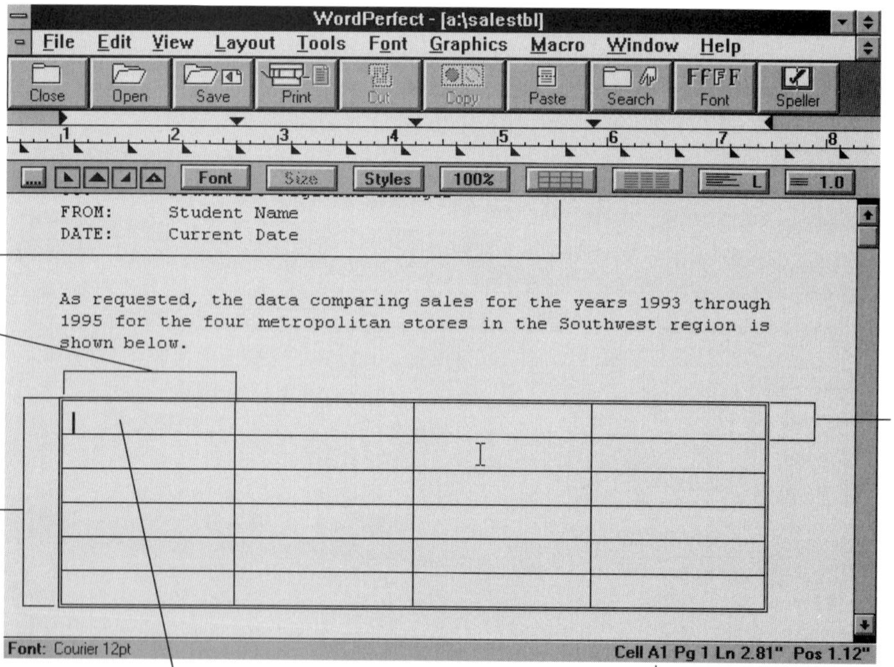

Table button

column

4 X 6 table

row

cell A1

cell address

A table consisting of four columns and six rows is drawn at the location of the insertion point in the document. The outside edge of the table consists of a double solid line. Each cell was created from a single solid line and contains a single line space where you can enter data. This is the default table style.

The insertion point is in the upper-left corner cell of the table. This cell is called cell A1. A1 is the **cell address**. Cells are labeled alphabetically from left to right and numerically from top to bottom. When the insertion point is in a table cell, the status line displays the cell address.

You can move from one cell to another by using the arrow keys or (TAB) and (SHIFT) + (TAB) if you are using the keyboard. If you are using a mouse, click on the cell you want to move when the mouse pointer is an I-beam. If the pointer is an arrow and you click on a cell, the entire cell is highlighted, indicating it is selected. You will learn about this feature shortly. To clear the highlight, click on any other cell when the pointer is an I-beam. If you press (↵) while in a cell, a new line is created in the cells of that row. To delete a line, simply delete the [HRt] code.

Move to: cell B1

The status line shows the new location of the insertion point as cell B1.

Entering Text in a Table

Now you are ready to enter the column labels for the table. Column B will display data for the year 1993. To enter this label,

Type: **1993**

In a similar manner, move to cells C1 and D1 and enter the labels 1994 and 1995.

Next you will enter the labels for the rows in column A.

Move to: A2
Type: **Store 48**

In a similar manner enter the following labels in the cells specified.

Cell	Label
A3	**Store 55**
A4	**Store 57**
A5	**Store 62**
A6	**Total**

Now that the labels have been entered, finish filling in the table by entering the data for the three years for the four stores using the following information:

	1993	1994	1995
Store 48	**749,345**	**778,883**	**789,951**
Store 55	**544,960**	**587,875**	**592,876**
Store 57	**620,745**	**633,856**	**631,755**
Store 62	**578,992**	**569,422**	**565,342**

Your screen should be similar to Figure 3-11.

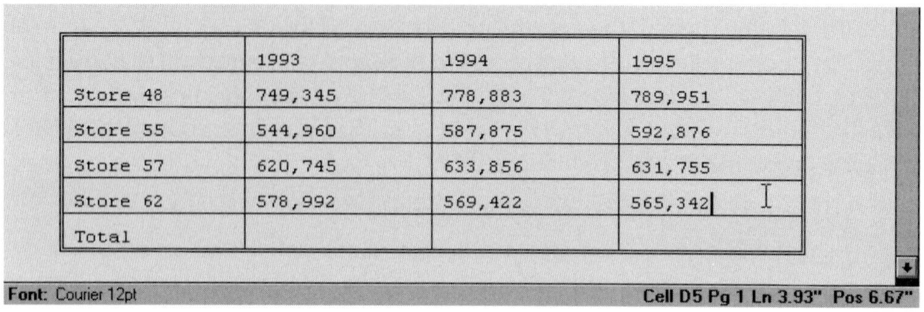

	1993	1994	1995
Store 48	749,345	778,883	789,951
Store 55	544,960	587,875	592,876
Store 57	620,745	633,856	631,755
Store 62	578,992	569,422	565,342
Total			

FIGURE 3-11

Entering a Formula

Now you are ready to enter the data for the totals. Rather than adding the values for each column of data and entering them in the Total row, you can enter a formula to make this calculation for you. To enter the formula to sum the values in the 1993 column of data,

Move to: B6
Choose: Layout/Tables/Formula
➢ (CTRL) + (F9), Formula

The Tables Formula dialog box is displayed. In the Formula text box you need to enter the formula. Formulas are composed of cell addresses and **operators**. Operators include symbols, such as + and –, which define the type of calculation to be made using the value in the cell. To sum the values in the 1993 column of data, the formula would be B2+B3+B4+B5. However, WordPerfect has several shortcut formulas, called **functions**, that tell the program what to do with a column of numbers. The subtotal (+) function adds the numbers directly above the function. The total function (=) adds the subtotals directly above it, and the grand total function (*) adds the totals directly above it. To add numbers in the column,

Type: +
Choose: OK

Your screen should be similar to Figure 3-12.

FIGURE 3-12

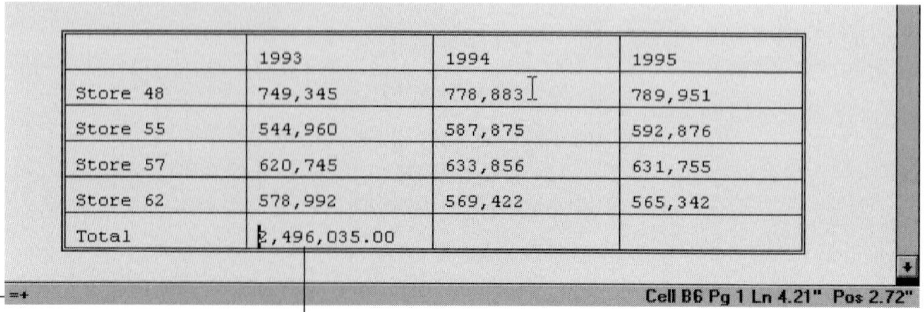

	1993	1994	1995
Store 48	749,345	778,883	789,951
Store 55	544,960	587,875	592,876
Store 57	620,745	633,856	631,755
Store 62	578,992	569,422	565,342
Total	2,496,035.00		

formula

calculated value

The calculated value is displayed in cell B6 and the function is displayed on the left end of the status bar. By default, however, the value is displayed with two decimal places. Since the data in the table does not include decimals, you want to change the display of the calculated value to zero decimal places. Additionally, the function included the values that serve as year column headings in the column of numbers to be totaled, making the total incorrect. You need to tell WordPerfect to ignore the cell containing the year when calculating the formula. To do this, you will delete the formula from the cell, select the cell to exclude from the calculation, specify the new decimal setting, and reenter the formula.

Selecting Cells

You can delete each character individually from the cell using (Bksp) or (DEL), or you can select the entire cell and delete its contents. The procedure you use varies if you are using a mouse or a keyboard. (If you have a mouse, do *not* follow the instructions in the Keyboard section.)

To select text in a table, you can use the standard convention of dragging the mouse across the desired cells, or you can use a special feature of tables called the selection arrow feature. To use the selection arrow feature, position the I-beam to the left or top border of the cell. It changes to an ⇧ if pointing to the top border and a ⇨ if pointing to the left border. When it changes to an arrow, you can select the cells by dragging or by clicking the mouse button. One click selects a single cell. Double-clicking selects the row or column the cell is in depending on whether the selection arrow is pointing left (row) or up (column). You can select all cells in the table by clicking three times on any cell. To clear a highlight, click on any other cell when the mouse pointer is an I-beam or click anywhere outside the table.

Select: cell B6

Cell B6 is highlighted.

To select text in a table, you use the standard keyboard method of selecting text. One shortcut is to press (SHIFT) + (F8). This method both turns on Select mode and selects the contents of the current cell. You can then continue to expand your selection by holding down (SHIFT) and pressing the appropriate directional keys. To clear a highlight, release (SHIFT) and move to any other cell.

Press: (SHIFT) + (F8)

Cell B6 is highlighted.

Your screen should be similar to Figure 3-13.

FIGURE 3-13

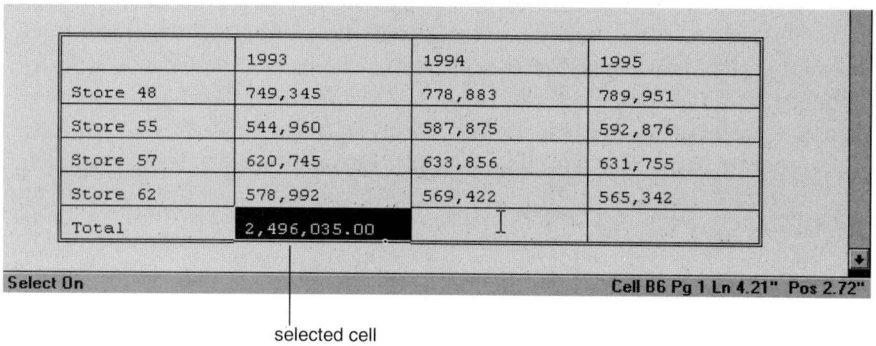

	1993	1994	1995
Store 48	749,345	778,883	789,951
Store 55	544,960	587,875	592,876
Store 57	620,745	633,856	631,755
Store 62	578,992	569,422	565,342
Total	2,496,035.00		

To clear the contents of the cell,

Press: DEL

Setting Cell Display

Now you are ready to change the default decimal display format. The command to do this is in the Layout/Tables/Column menu. Since you will also want to change the display for columns C and D, you will select the three cells in the columns first.

Select: cells B6, C6, and D6
Choose: Layout/Tables/Column
➢ CTRL + F9, Column

The Format Column dialog box displays the default appearance and size settings for columns. The Digits text box displays 2 as the current number of decimal places. To change this setting to 0,

Select: Digits

You can either type the new setting in the text box, or you can scroll the box to increase or decrease the number. To scroll the box, click on the up or down arrow symbols or press the ↑ or ↓ keys. Using either method, change the decimal setting to 0.

Choose: OK

Copying a Formula

Before reentering the formula, you need to tell WordPerfect to exclude the values in cells B1, C1, and D1 from the calculation of the total values. To do this,

Select: cells B1, C1, and D1
Choose: Layout/Tables/Cell
➢ CTRL + F9, Cell

The Format Cell dialog box allow you to change the display of text in the table. From the Cell Attributes section of the dialog box,

Select: Ignore Cell When Calculating
Choose: OK

Next you need to enter the formula in cell B6 again.

Move to: B6
Choose: Layout/Tables/Formula
➢ (CTRL) + (F9), Formula

In the Formula text box,

Type: **+**
Choose: OK

The calculated value is displayed with zero decimal places and does not include the year heading in the calculation. The same formula needs to be entered in cells C6 and D6.

Choose: Layout/Tables/Formula
➢ (CTRL) + (F9), Formula

Rather than enter the formula in each cell, you can copy the formula from cell B6 to cells C6 and D6. In the Copy Formula box, you can type the cell address where you want to copy the formula to. Alternatively you can choose Down or Right and specify the number of times you want WordPerfect to copy a formula below or to the right of the current cell. To copy to the right two cells,

Select: **R**ight
Type: **2**
Choose: OK

Your screen should be similar to Figure 3-14.

FIGURE 3-14

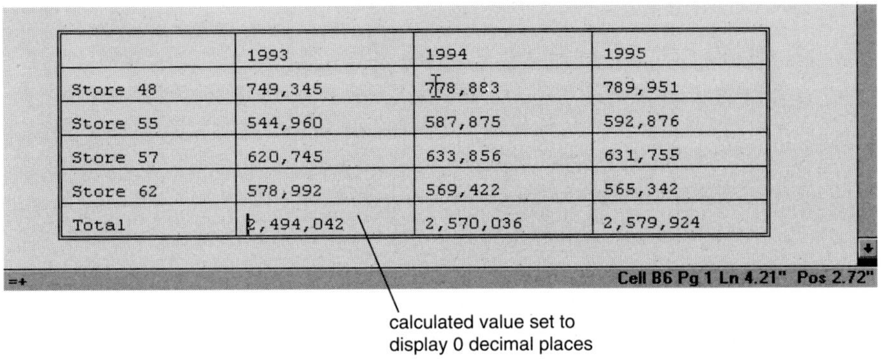

	1993	1994	1995
Store 48	749,345	778,883	789,951
Store 55	544,960	587,875	592,876
Store 57	620,745	633,856	631,755
Store 62	578,992	569,422	565,342
Total	2,494,042	2,570,036	2,579,924

The formula has been copied from cell B6 to cells C6 and D6. The formulas correctly calculate the sums for the new column locations. The calculated values are all displayed with zero decimal places.

Bolding and Centering Table Text

Now that all the data is entered, you want to improve the appearance of the table. First you want the year labels to be centered in the cell space and to be printed bold.

Select: cells B1, C1, and D1
Choose: Layout/Tables/Cell
➢ (CTRL) + (F9), Cell

The Format Cell dialog box displays the current cell display settings. To bold the text in the selected cells from the Appearance group,

Select: Bold

The Bold option in the Appearance group displays an X to show it is selected.

The Justification box is used to set the alignment of a label in the cell. This type of box displays a pop-up menu when selected. If you are using a mouse, drag the selection cursor to the option of your choice to select it. If you are using a keyboard, press Spacebar to display the menu, then use the ↑ or ↓ keys to select the option you want. Select Center from the Justification box.

Choose: OK

Clear the highlight.

Your screen should be similar to Figure 3-15.

FIGURE 3-15

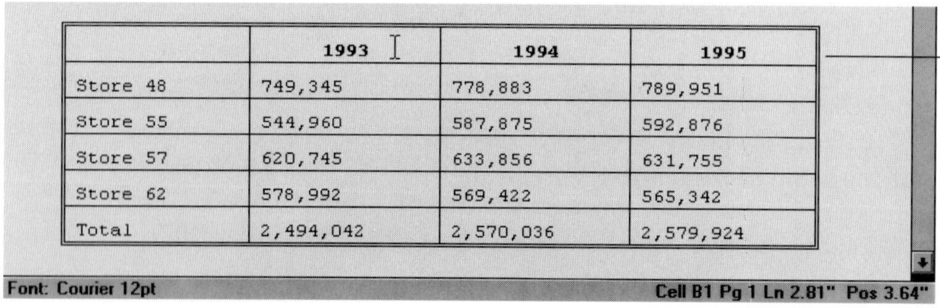

	1993	1994	1995
Store 48	749,345	778,883	789,951
Store 55	544,960	587,875	592,876
Store 57	620,745	633,856	631,755
Store 62	578,992	569,422	565,342
Total	2,494,042	2,570,036	2,579,924

The column heads are centered and bold.

In the same manner, bold the label "Total" in cell A6.

Next you feel the numeric data in the table would look better if it were right-aligned in the cell space. To change the justification of the data in these cells,

Select: cells B2 through D6

You can use the Justification button [≡ L] on the ruler bar (see Figure 3-17) to quickly change the alignment of the labels in the selected cells.

Choose: [≡ L] Justification

Select: Right

The button displays the justification setting for the selected cell. It should now appear as [≡ R] to show that the selected cells are right-aligned.

Choose: Layout/Tables/Cell

➢ (CTRL) + (F9), Cell

Select Right from the Justification box.

Choose: OK

Clear the highlight.

Your screen should be similar to Figure 3-16.

FIGURE 3-16

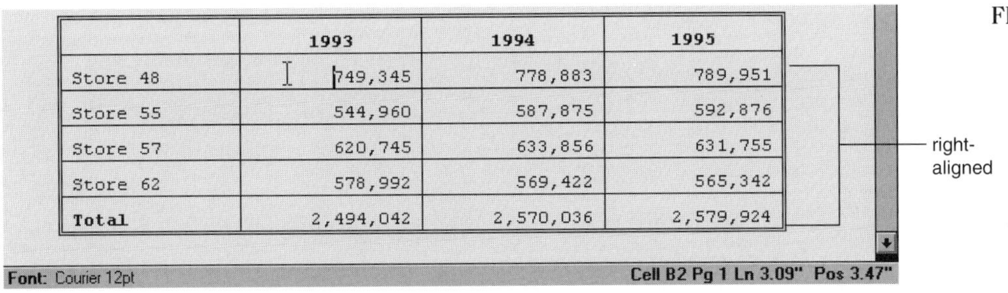

	1993	1994	1995
Store 48	749,345	778,883	789,951
Store 55	544,960	587,875	592,876
Store 57	620,745	633,856	631,755
Store 62	578,992	569,422	565,342
Total	2,494,042	2,570,036	2,579,924

Changing the Column Width

Next you want to decrease the width of column A.

Move to: cell A1

The procedure to change the width of a column varies if you are using a mouse or the keyboard. If you are using a mouse, do *not* perform the steps in the Keyboard section below.

Notice in the margin line of the Ruler (see Figure 3-17) that the column settings are represented by table column markers (▼). The table marker symbol is only displayed when the insertion point is positioned in the table. The column settings can be changed by dragging the column markers to a new location on the ruler. If you drag a marker, the markers to the right of it also move, adjusting the widths appropriately. If you hold down (SHIFT) and drag a column table marker, only that marker moves. If you hold down CTRL and drag a table column marker, the table markers to the right also move, but they retain their original widths. To use this last method,

Press CTRL and drag the table column marker that divides column A and B to the left along the Ruler until it lines up with the 2.25" setting. (Refer to the table split indicator in the status line for position reference.)

Choose: Layout/Tables/Column/Column Width

The current column width setting for column A is displayed. Enter the new column width setting of 1.25" in the text box.

Choose: OK

Your screen should be similar to Figure 3-17.

FIGURE 3-17

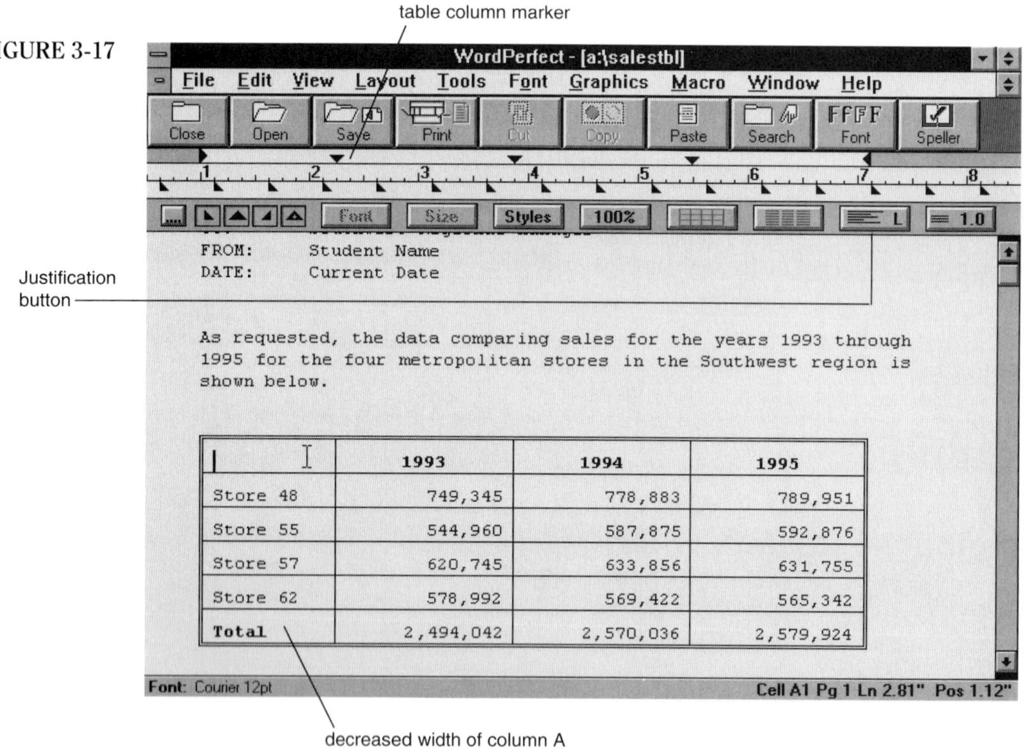

Column A has decreased to the specified width and columns B, C, and D have maintained their original size. The overall table size has decreased slightly.

Changing the Table Line Style

The next change you will make will emphasize the break between the store data and the Total row. To do this you will change the border or line style around the cells.

Each cell in a table has four borders, and each border can be assigned a different line style. The default style is to set the borders of those cells making up the outside edge of the table as double lines. Interior cells have single line borders.

Select: cells A6 through D6
Choose: Layout/Tables/Lines
➢ CTRL + F9, Lines

The Table Lines dialog box displays the line settings for the selected cells. You want to change the top line style from single to double.

From the Top pop-up list, select Double.

Choose: OK

Clear the highlight.

Your screen should be similar to Figure 3-18.

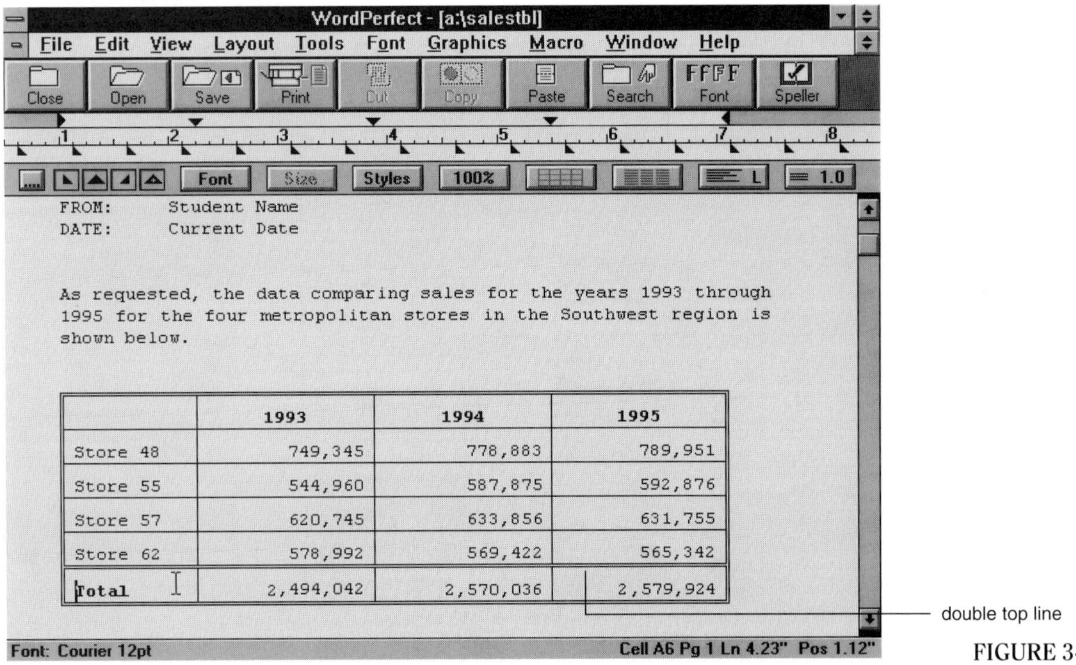

FIGURE 3-18

A double line separates the Total row from the rows of data above it.

Inserting a Row

After looking at the table, you decide it may look better if it included a table heading. To do this you need to insert a blank row at the top of the table.

Move to: A1
Choose: Layout/Tables/Insert/Rows/OK
➢ CTRL + F9, Insert Rows, OK

Notice that the inserted row has double lines all around it. This is because when a row is inserted at the top of the table, it uses the default line style for the outside edge of the table. Row 2, which was previously the top row, still has the double-line top border. You will change the top line border of row 2 shortly.

Since this new row will display a table heading, you do not need the column dividers. To clear the row of the column dividers,

Select: cells A1 through D1
Choose: Layout/Tables/Join
➢ (CTRL) + (F9), Join

Your screen should be similar to Figure 3-19.

inserted and joined

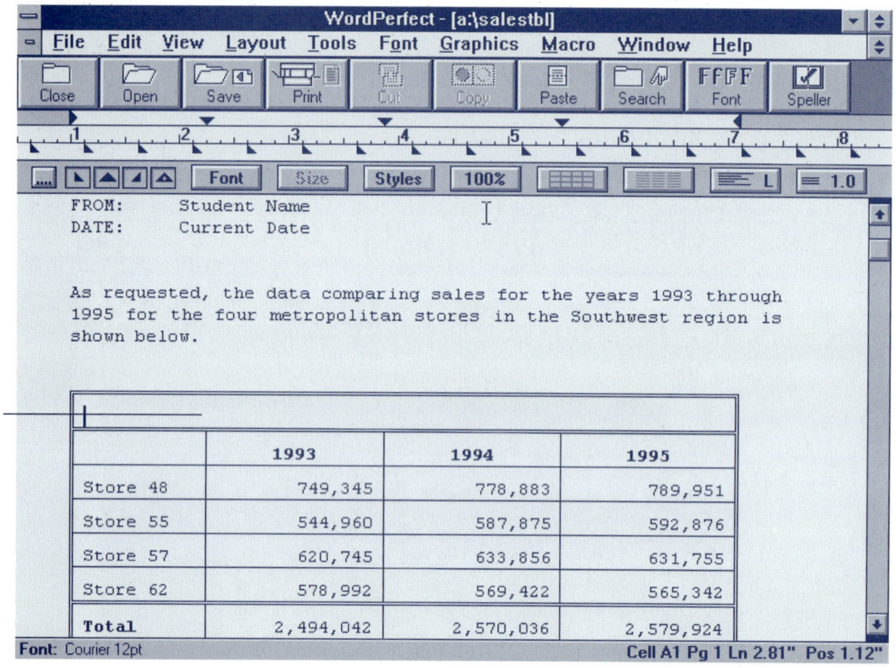

FIGURE 3-19

The three column dividers are eliminated, and the top row is now one cell. Now you are ready to add the text for the heading. Before you enter the heading, you will enter the codes to center and bold text in the cell.

Choose: Layout/Tables/Cell
➢ (CTRL) + (F9), Cell

Select Bold from the Appearance group and Center from the Justification pop-up list.

Choose: OK

The insertion point is positioned in the center of the cell space.

Press: (CAPS LOCK)
Type: **ANNUAL SALES**
Press: (CAPS LOCK)

The text appears centered and bold in the cell space. Finally, you want to change the line between rows 1 and 2 from a double line to a thick line to offset the title from the table.

Select: cells A2 through D2
Choose: Layout/Table/Lines/Top/Thick/OK
➢ CTRL + F9, Lines, Top, Thick, OK

Clear the highlight. Your screen should be similar to Figure 3-20.

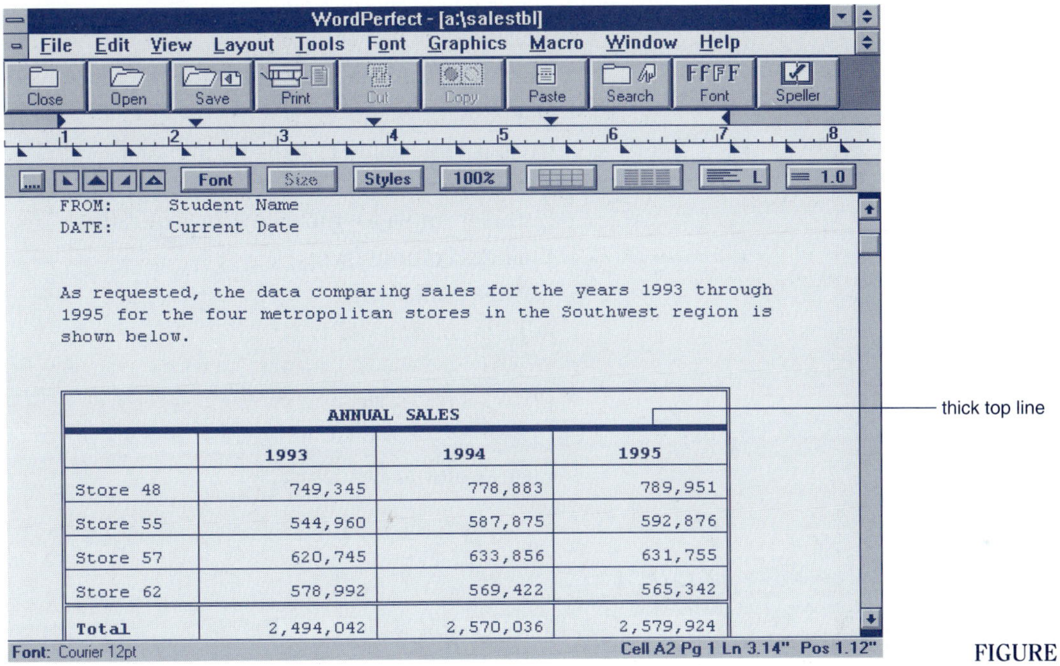

FIGURE 3-20

You have completed the table. Save and replace the file as SALESTBL. Print the document (select the appropriate printer). Turn off the display of the Ruler and Button Bar. Exit WordPerfect and Windows.

Key Terms

primary file	table
secondary file	row
merge code	column
address file	cell
field	cell address
record	operator
syntax	function
hard page break	

Command Summary

Command	Shortcut	Button Bar	Action
Tools/Merge	CTRL + F12		Opens Merge menu
Tools/Merge/Field			Inserts code for a merge field
Tools/Merge/Merge Codes			Opens Insert Merge Code list box
Tools/Merge/End Field	ALT + ↵		Marks end of merge field
Tools/Merge/End Record	ALT + SHIFT + ↵		Marks end of merge record
Tools/Merge/Merge			Merges primary and secondary files
Layout/Tables	CTRL + F9		Opens Table menu
Layout/Tables/Create		[table button]	Creates table using specified number of rows and columns
Layout/Tables/Formula			Enters formula to calculate values in cells
Layout/Tables/Column			Changes column format
Layout/Tables/Cell			Changes cell format
Layout/Tables/Column/Column Width			Adjusts column width
Layout/Tables/Lines			Changes line style
Layout/Tables/Insert/Rows			Inserts new rows
Layout/Tables/Join			Clears column dividers

LAB REVIEW

Matching

1. CTRL + F9	_____	**a.**	field name merge code
2. address file	_____	**b.**	enters {END FIELD} code to show end of field in secondary file
3. B2	_____	**c.**	intersection of a row and a column in a table
4. {FIELD}<name>~	_____	**d.**	shortcut for the Layout/Tables command
5. record	_____	**e.**	the secondary file
6. CTRL + F12	_____	**f.**	marks the end of a record in a secondary file
7. ALT + ↵	_____	**g.**	in a table, the cell located at column B, row 2
8. Layout/Tables /Join	_____	**h.**	all the fields of data that are needed to complete the primary file
9. {END RECORD}	_____	**i.**	shortcut for the Tools/Merge command
10. cell	_____	**j.**	removes column dividers in a table

Practice Exercises

1. To complete this problem, you must first have created the letter THANKS in Practice Exercise 3 in Lab 2. You will change the letter into a form letter and create a secondary file.

a. Using field names of your choice, create a secondary file. Each record will contain eight fields of data. Enter the following three records:

(1) Mr. James Snider
Recruiting Coordinator
Major Marketing Systems
953 E. Westwood Ave.
Parkside
CO
54829
Mr. Snider

(2) Ms. Karen Miller
Western Operations Manager
Apple Computers
183 Karman Ave.
Irvine
CA
93023
Ms. Miller

(3) Your first and last name
Your major
Your school
School address
City
State
Zipcode
Your last name

b. Save the secondary file as THANKS.SF.

c. Modify the letter THANKS to accept the eight fields of information. Save the primary file as THANKS.PF.

d. Merge the primary and secondary files. Print the three letters.

2. As the owner of The Home Remodeling Center, you want to create a table to compare the costs of some common remodeling jobs and the amount of money that can be recovered from the remodeling costs when the home is sold.

a. Create a table of ten rows and four columns and enter the data below.

Project	**Original Cost**	**Resale Value**	**Percent Lost at Resale**
Add 6 x 8 2nd bathroom	9,500	9,000	6%
Minor kitchen remodeling	8,000	7,200	10%
Major kitchen remodeling	19,800	17,600	11%
Convert attic to bedroom	18,500	15,600	16%
Bathroom remodeling	7,300	5,700	21%
16 x 20 deck-bench-railings	6,800	4,800	29%
Add 12 x 16 sun room	18,900	13,500	29%
16 new windows, double-paned	6,300	4,300	31%
Aluminum siding, gutters, trim	8,100	5,200	36%

b. Change the column widths of columns B, C, and D to a width of 1.25".

c. Insert a new row above the table. Clear the column dividers in the new row. Center and bold the title, REMODELING JOBS, in the new row.

d. Create a thick line under the title to offset the title row from the table.

e. Enter your name and the current date in the document.

f. Save the table as REMODEL. Print the table.

3. As President of the Fund Raising Committee, you have created the following letter to raise money for a research project on the Canyon Tree Frog.

a. Enter the form letter shown below using the following field names.

Field 1	Member's Name
Field 2	Street
Field 3	City
Field 4	State
Field 5	Zipcode
Field 6	Member's first name

Current Date

Field 1
Field 2
Field 3, Field 4 Field 5

Dear Field 6,

Have you ever wanted to be invisible? To sit in plain view and watch everyone else—and not be seen? That's very nearly what the tiny Canyon Tree Frog does.

Not much is known about this tiny frog. The Center for Animal Research is planning to study the Canyon Tree Frog in its natural environment and we need your help.

You can help us in one of two ways: as a volunteer spotter or by making a donation to help defer the costs of calculating the data as it is analyzed.

We appreciate any help you may be able to give. The enclosed booklet describes the project and how you can help. Please call me at (602) 756-1235 if you have any questions.

Sincerely,

(Your Name)

b. Save the file as FROGS.PF.

c. Create a secondary file using the data shown below for the records.

(1) Mr. John Woodson
892 W. Collage Dr.
Claremont
MN
03743
John

(2) Ms. Karen Cole
182 South St.
Newport
NM
04238
Karen

(3) Mr. Kevin Heatwole
83 W. Broadway Rd.
Claremont
NM
03743
Kevin

(4) Your first and last name
Street
City
State
Zipcode
Your first name

d. Save the secondary file as FROGS.SF.

e. Merge the primary and secondary files. Print the letters.

4. As the manager of a large advertising firm, each month you send memos to all the department heads announcing the monthly staff meeting. The three fields of data are the employee's name, department, and assignment.

a. Create the following memo using field names of your choice.

To: Field 1, Field 2
From: Your name
Date: Current date

The monthly staff meeting is scheduled for Monday, May 17, 1994 at 8:00. We have many new exciting projects and I look forward to hearing all your ideas.

The agenda for the meeting will be as follows:

Marketing Report	8:00
Financial Report	8:15
Old Business	8:30
Presentation of New Ads	9:00
Discussion of Ads	9:30
Break	10:30
New Projects Discussion	10:45
Lunch	12:00
Individual Group Meetings	1:00

Field 3

b. Save the primary file as MEMO.PF.

c. Create the secondary file using the data shown below for each of the records.

(1) Mr. James Walker
Marketing Manager
You are assigned to the group meeting with the Marketing and Advertising Directors.

(2) Ms. Susan Butler
Advertising Manager
You are assigned to the group meeting with the Creative Art Designers.

(3) Mr. Keith O'Shea
Financial Manager
You are assigned to the group meeting with the Budget Directors.

d. Save the secondary file as MEMO.SF

e. Merge the primary and secondary files. Print the memos.

5. Have you ever wondered what happens to all that film you use? Well, 16 percent of it ends up in the trash. You will create a table to show the top 10 reasons why your film may not be printed.

a. Create a table from the data below.

Under Exposure	32%
Improper Storage	13%
Fluorescents	12%
Blank Roll	10%
Over Exposure	8%
Film Advance	8%
Flash Synch	7%
Tungsten Light	5%
Object on Lens	3%
Out of Focus	2%

b. Change the column width of column A so that the words do not wrap to a second line. Center the data in column B.

c. Insert a new row above the table to hold the column labels. Insert descriptive labels for the table data.

d. Insert another new row above the table. Clear the column dividers in the new row. Center and bold the title, "The Top 10 Disasters," in the new row.

e. Create a thick line under the title to offset the title row from the table.

f. Enter your name and the current date in the document.

g. Save the table as FILM. Print the table.

6. To complete this problem you must first have completed Practice Exercise 6 in Lab 2. Modify the cover letter to a form letter format. Change the body of the letter to include the name of the company you interviewed with. Create a secondary file of three records that includes the name, address, and company name. Merge the two files. Print the three letters.

LAB

4 Creating a Report and a Newsletter

CASE STUDY

The Southwest Regional Manager is very pleased with your work so far and has asked you to help with the design and development of the first monthly newsletter. Specifically you have been asked to develop several topics to be used as articles in the newsletter, and to propose a sample newsletter design.

Competencies

In this lab you will learn how to:

1. Change letter case.
2. Generate a table of contents.
3. Enter and edit footnotes.
4. Specify page numbering.
5. Prevent widows and orphans.
6. Use block protection.
7. Change fonts.
8. Create graphic lines.
9. Define columns.
10. Add graphics to documents.

Changing Case

Load Windows and the WordPerfect program. Display the Button Bar. You have already researched several topics for the newsletter and would like to present the information to the manager before creating final copy to use in the newsletter.

Open the file RESEARCH. The first page of the document is a memo you have started to the manager.

Enter your name following "FROM:" and the current date following "DATE:" in the memo.

Your first article begins at the top of page 2. The category for this article is "Health and Fitness." The article title, "How to be a Weekend Warrior," is displayed below the category. You want to change the category heading to uppercase characters. Rather than retype the text, you can select it and quickly convert it to uppercase characters.

Move to: "H" in "Health" (Pg 2 Ln 1" Pos 1")

Select the category heading (through Pos 2.8").

Choose: Edit/Convert Case/Uppercase

Your screen should be similar to Figure 4-1.

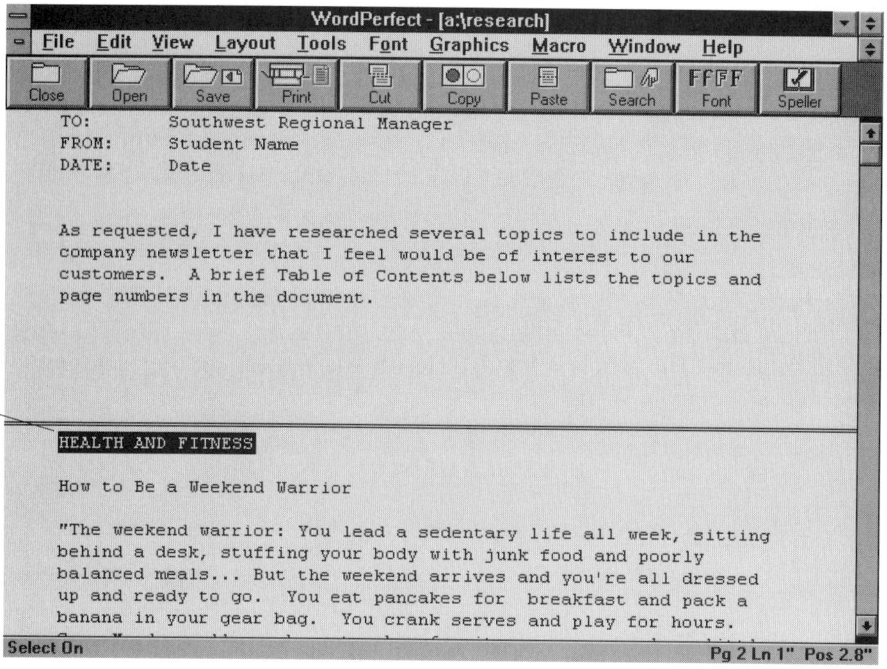

converted to uppercase

FIGURE 4-1

The selected text is changed to all uppercase characters. You want to do the same thing to the heading "Equipment Update" on page 5. Move to the top of page 5, select the text "Equipment Update," (Ln 1.83), and convert it to uppercase.

Press: CTRL + HOME

Creating a Table of Contents

Next you want to add a brief list or table of contents of the topics and the pages where they are located in the memo. First you will enter a heading centered above the table of contents.

Move to: Pg 1 Ln 2.83"

To center text on a line,

Choose: Layout/Line/Center
Shortcut: SHIFT + F7

The insertion point moves to the middle of the line. As you type the text, it will be centered on the line.

Type: TABLE OF CONTENTS

Next you need to create a table of contents for the memo. A table of contents can be generated automatically by WordPerfect from text within the document. There are three steps to creating a table of contents:

Step 1	Mark the text to be used in the table of contents.
Step 2	Specify the location and numbering format of the table.
Step 3	Generate or create the table.

Step 1: Marking Text for the Table of Contents

The Tools/Mark Text (F12) command marks the text to be used in the table of contents. Before choosing the command, you must first select the text to be used in the table of contents. The article category "Health and Fitness" at the beginning of page 2 is the first heading you will select.

Select: Health and Fitness (Pg 2 Ln 1" Pos 1" through 2.8")

Next, to tell WordPerfect that the selected text is to be used in a table of contents, it must be marked.

Choose: Tools/Mark Text
➢ (F12)

As you can see from the Mark Text menu, text can also be marked to create a list, an index, a cross reference, or a table of authorities (ToA). The Table of Contents option will mark a block for use in a table of contents by placing a [Mark:ToC] code at the beginning of the selected text and an [End Mark:ToC] code at the end of the selected text.

Choose: Table of Contents

The Mark Table of Contents dialog box is displayed. In this box you specify the level of the heading to be used in the table when it is generated. A table of contents can have up to five levels of heads. The selection of the level of heads determines how the table of contents will look. A level one head is the main head. A blank line is placed before all first-level headings. The level two through five subheads are subordinate to the level one head. Each level of subhead is indented below the higher level subhead. For example:

This Is a Level One Head.
    This Is a Level Two Subhead.
    This Is Another Level Two Subhead.
        This Is a Level Three Subhead.

This Is a Level One Head.
    This Is a Level Two Subhead.

You want the selected text to appear as a first-level heading, so you do not need to change the default setting that is displayed. To complete the command,

Choose: OK

You are returned to the document. The heading has been marked to be used as a first level head in a table of contents. To see the codes, open Reveal Codes (ALT + F3).

Your screen should be similar to Figure 4-2.

FIGURE 4-2

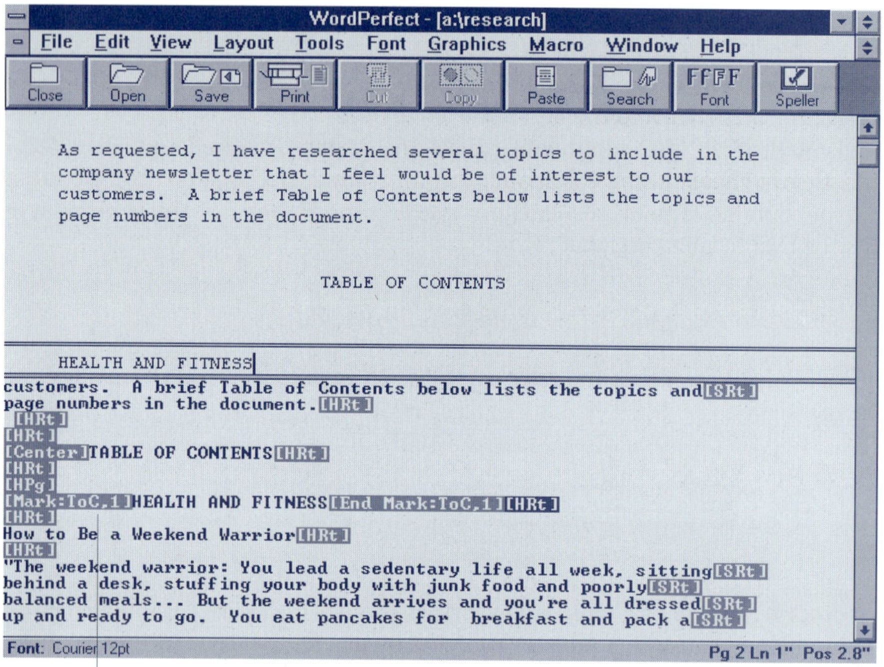

level 1 table of contents code

The Mark Text codes are displayed surrounding the text to be used in the table of contents. The number in the code indicates it is a first-level heading. Clear Reveal Codes (ALT + F3).

The second heading to be marked is the article title, "How to Be a Weekend Warrior," on Pg 2 Ln 1.33". Select this text.

Then, to mark the text as a second-level head in the table of contents,

Choose: Tools/Mar**k** Text/Table of **C**ontents

➢ F12, Table of **C**ontents

This head will be a level two head. You can type the number in the text box or click the up incrementing button to increase the number. Using one of these methods, change the level to 2.

Choose: OK

This heading is marked with the same codes, except for the level number within the code. If you needed to delete a table of contents heading, you would simply delete the code surrounding the text.

Mark the remaining headings in the document using the levels shown below:

Heading	**Location**	**Level**
A Balanced Diet	Pg 2 Ln 4.33"	Level 3
Daily Aerobic Exercise	Pg 3 Ln 2.17"	Level 3
What Fluids Are Best?	Pg 4 Ln 1.83"	Level 2
EQUIPMENT UPDATE	Pg 5 Ln 1.83"	Level 1
Stationary Bikes	Pg 5 Ln 2.17"	Level 2

When you are done, return to the top of the document.

Step 2: Define Table of Contents Location

The second step is to define the location of the table of contents and the numbering format. You want the table to be displayed several lines below the heading TABLE OF CONTENTS. To place the insertion point where you want the table of contents to begin,

Move to: Pg 1 Ln 3.17"

The Tools/Define command ((SHIFT) + (F12)) is used to define the table format.

Choose: Tools>Define
➢ (SHIFT) + (F12)

The cascading menu lists the four types of listings that can be defined.

Choose: Table of Contents

Your screen should be similar to Figure 4-3.

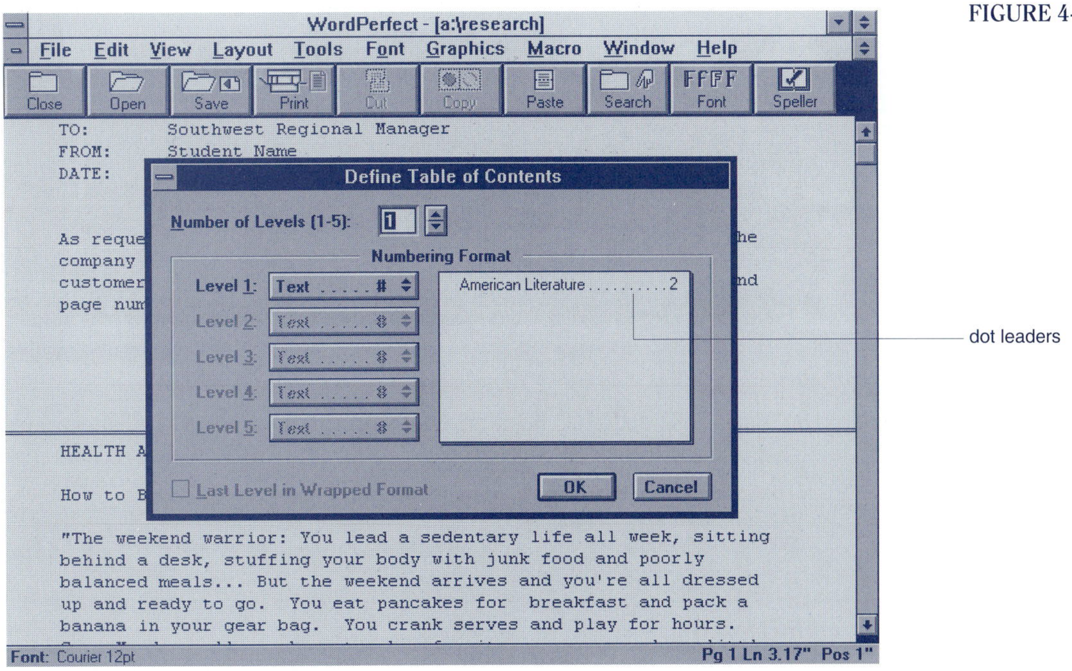

FIGURE 4-3

The Define Table of Contents dialog box is displayed. The first option, "Number of Levels," displays the default setting of 1 as the number of levels used in the table of contents. Since you defined three levels in your table of contents, change this setting to 3.

In correspondence to your selection, the first three levels in the Numbering Format box appear bright while levels 4 and 5 are dimmed. The Numbering Format box is used to define the page number style for each level. The default will display the page numbers flush with the right margin with a series of dots, called **dot leaders**, between the heading and the page number. The right side of the Numbers Format box displays a sample of how the table of contents will appear when generated using the selected style. Each Numbering Format pop-up list contains a menu of other styles you can select.

You feel that the default settings look fine and will not make any changes. To complete the command,

Choose: OK

You are returned to the document. To see the codes, open Reveal Codes.

Your screen should be similar to Figure 4-4.

FIGURE 4-4

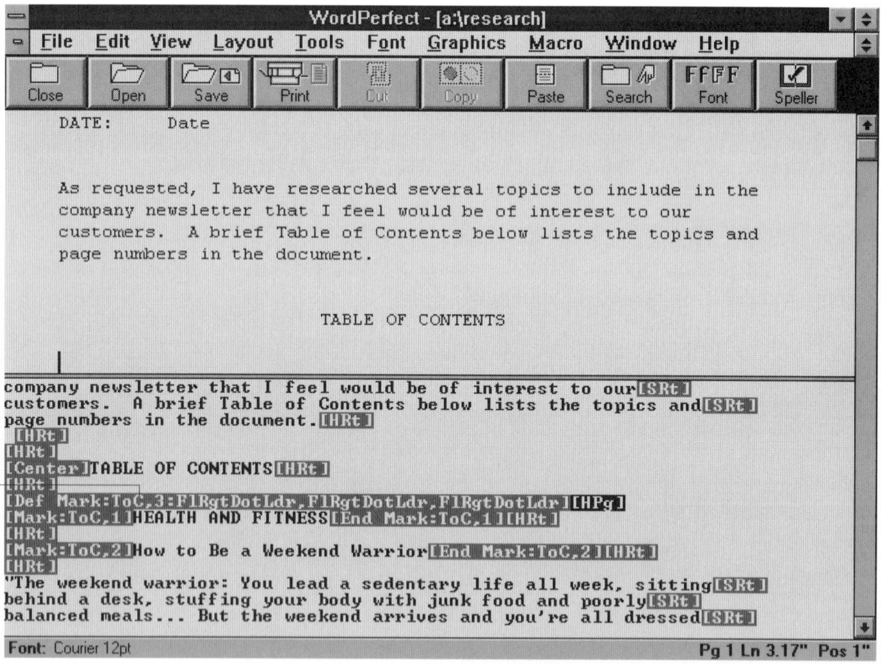

table of contents definition code

The code [Def Mark:ToC] code has been entered into the document at this location. This code also includes the settings you specified to control the table of contents style. Clear Reveal Codes.

Step 3: Generate the Table of Contents

Finally, you are ready for WordPerfect to do a little work. Once all the headings are marked and the table of contents definitions completed, the table of contents can be generated. It will be displayed at the location marked by the code.

Choose: Tools/Generate

➢ (ALT) + (F12)

A Generate warning box advises you that any existing tables will be updated with the new settings you have specified. Since there are no other tables created in this document, you can accept the default response of Yes.

Choose: Yes

The "Generate" message displayed in the status line tells you that generation has started. The "Pass:" and "Page:" indicators help you keep track of its progress. When complete, the table of contents should be displayed.

Your screen should be similar to Figure 4-5.

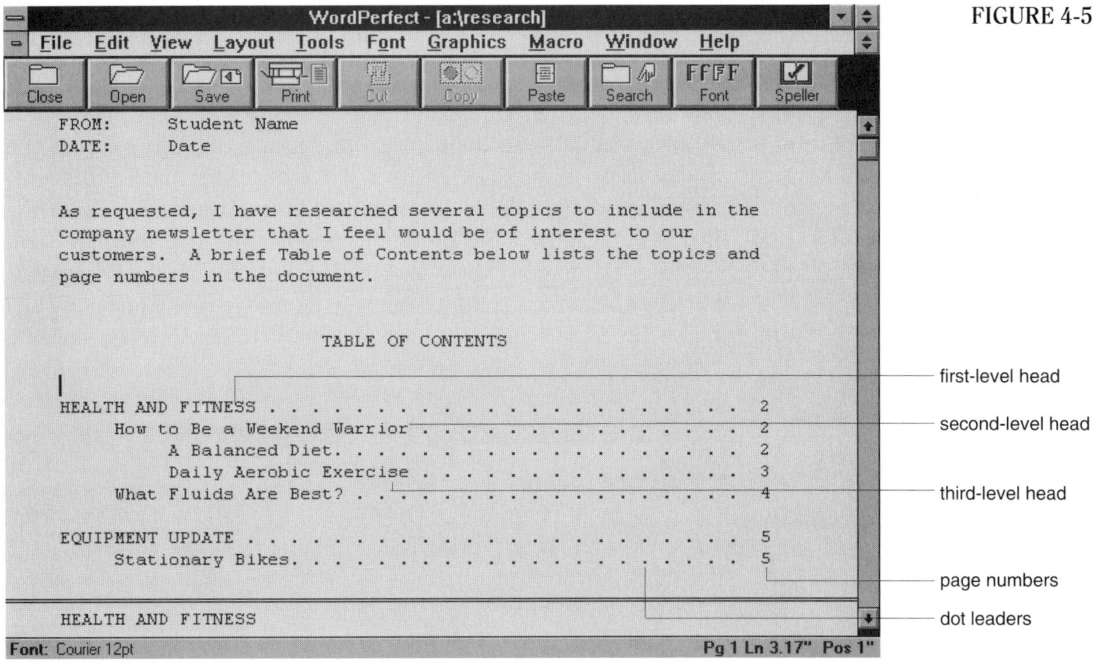

FIGURE 4-5

The table of contents for the memo is displayed. A blank line separates the first-level heads. The level two heads appear indented under the level one heads, and the level three heads indented under the level two heads. The page numbers are displayed flush with the right margin. A series of dot leaders separates the heads from the page numbers.

Creating Footnotes

Next you need to add several **footnotes** (source references placed at the bottom of the page) to the document. The Layout/Footnote/Create command will automatically number and place footnotes properly at the bottom of the page. The first reference that needs to be footnoted is on page 2.

Press: ALT + PGDN

The first paragraph consists of a quotation whose source needs to be documented in a footnote. Before using the Footnote command, the insertion point must be positioned in the text where the footnote number is to be inserted. To move to the end of the quotation (after the quotation marks),

Move to: end of the quote (Pg 2 Ln 2.67" Pos 6.4")
Choose: Layout/Footnote/Create

The document window has been replaced with the Footnote window. This is a special editing window used to enter the text for the footnote. The number 1 displayed in the Footnote window shows that this is the first footnote to be entered in the document.

To enter a space after the number and before the text of the footnote,

Press: Spacebar

When entering a footnote, you can use the same commands and features as in the normal document window. The menus can be used while entering text in this window. Any commands that are not available are dimmed. You will use the Underline command to underline the magazine title, Tennis, when entering this footnote. You can use the menu Font/Underline command or the shortcut CTRL - U. Whichever you use, turn the feature on before entering the text to be underlined and then turn it off by pressing CTRL - U before typing the comma, just as you do when bolding text.

Type: **Julie Anthony, "Are You a Nutrition Flunkie?" Tennis, May 1992, p. 89.** (do not press ↵)

Your screen should be similar to Figure 4-6.

FIGURE 4-6

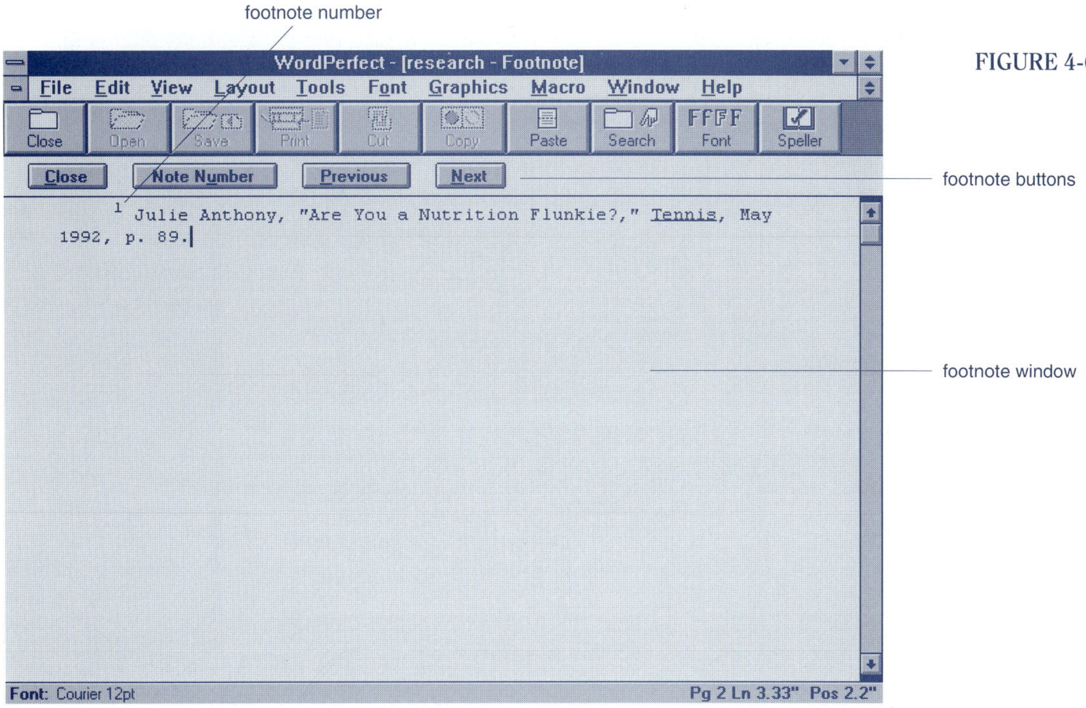

The four buttons located below the Button Bar are used to exit and move to other footnotes. The Close button saves the footnote and returns you to the document window. The Note Number button allows you to assign a different number to the footnote. The Previous and Next buttons let you view and edit other existing footnotes. If you have a mouse, simply click on the button to choose it. If you are using the keyboard, press ALT and the underlined letter to choose the button.

To return to the document,

Choose: Close

The footnote number, 1, is entered in the text at the location of the insertion point. The footnote itself is not displayed in the window. When the page or entire document is printed, the footnote will be automatically printed on the bottom of the page containing the footnote number. However, you can preview how the footnote will look using the File/Print Preview command.

Choose: File/Print Preview

➢ SHIFT + F5

Your screen should be similar to Figure 4-7.

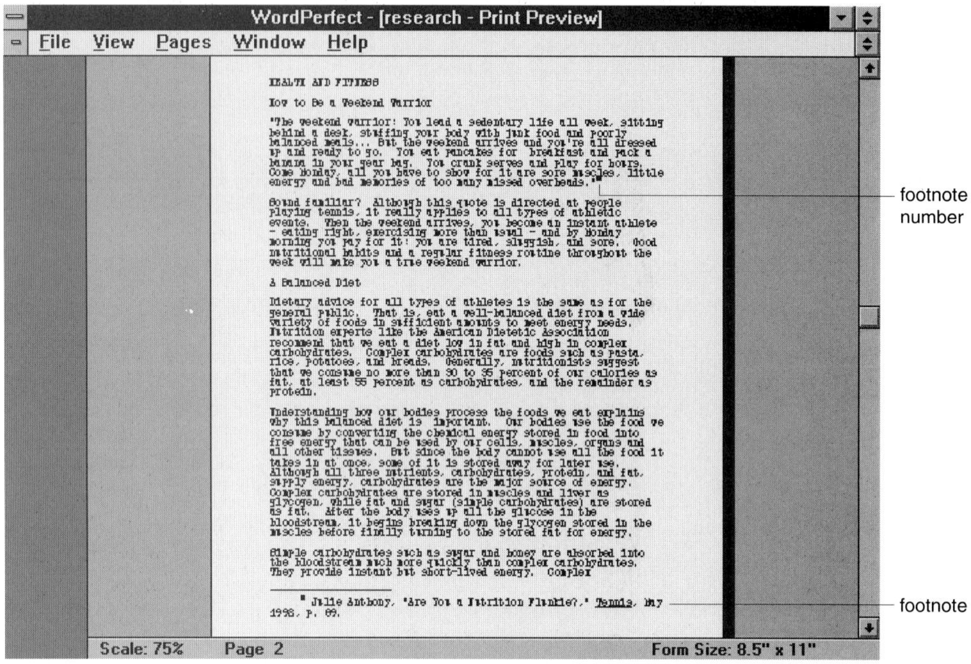

FIGURE 4-7

The Print Preview window displays how the current page will appear when printed.

Note: If your screen does not display the full page, choose Zoom Out from the View menu to set the scale to 75 percent. This command reduces the scale by 25 percent each time it is used.

The footnote is displayed at the bottom of the page. Some of the text at the bottom of the page was moved to the top of the next page to make space for the footnote. To return to the document window,

Choose:	File/Close
➢	(CTRL) + (F4)
or	
Double-click:	Preview window control menu box

The second footnote will provide the source for a quote located on page 3.

Move to:	end of quote on page 3 (Pg 3 Ln 5.5" Pos 3.4")
Choose:	Layout/Footnote/Create

Notice that the footnote number in the Footnote window is 2. To enter the text for the second footnote,

Press:	Spacebar
Type:	**Covert Baily, The New Fit or Fat, Houghton Mifflin Company, Boston, p. 161.**
Choose:	Close

The second footnote is entered in the document. Each time you add a footnote, WordPerfect adjusts the text in the document to allow space at the bottom of the page for the footnote.

Now you realize that you forgot to enter a footnote earlier in the text, on page 2.

Move to: end of paragraph 3 (Pg 2 Ln 6.17" Pos 1.8")

The insertion point should be positioned following the period after the word "protein" on the last line of the third paragraph.

Choose: Layout/Footnote/Create

Notice that this footnote is number 2. WordPerfect automatically adjusted the footnote numbers when the new footnote was inserted.

Press: Spacebar
Type: **Doug Henderson, "Nutrition and the Athlete," FDA Consumer, May 1987, p. 18.**
Choose: Close

The new footnote has been inserted into the text and the footnotes have been renumbered automatically.

Editing a Footnote

Next you realize that you forgot to enter the date in the footnote text for the third footnote. The Edit option in the Footnote menu lets you change the information in an existing footnote. To edit a footnote, you can be anywhere within the document. To edit footnote 3,

Choose: Layout/Footnote/Edit

The Edit Footnote dialog box is displayed. In this box you enter the number of the footnote that you want to edit. If the number 3 is not displayed in this box,

Type: **3**

To complete the command,

Choose: OK

The text for footnote 3 is displayed in the Footnote window. To add the date before the page number of the footnote,

Move to: "p" of "p." (Ln 6.67" Pos 1.8")
Type: **1991,**
Press: Spacebar

Now you are finished entering footnotes. Before closing the Footnote window, however, you want to check the other two footnotes.

Choose: Previous

Footnote 2 is displayed. If you see any errors, correct them.

In the same way, view footnote 1 and correct if necessary. When you are done, close the Footnote window.

Numbering Pages

Next you want to add page numbers to the document. Although page numbers are displayed in the status line, they do not appear on the printed document unless you enter the appropriate command. You enter the code to create page numbering on the page where you want page numbering to begin. Generally this is the beginning of the document. To move to the top of page 1,

Press: CTRL + HOME

The Layout/Page (ALT + F9) Numbering command is used to specify page numbering.

Choose: Layout/Page
➣ ALT + F9

The Page Format menu is displayed. The options on this menu affect entire pages. The Numbering command lets you select the type of numbers you want and where you want them placed on the page.

Choose: Numbering

In the Define Page Number area of the Page Numbering dialog box, you specify where the page number is to be placed on the page. The default setting, No Page Numbering, is displayed in the Position list box. You want to display the page numbers at the bottom center of each page. If you are using the keyboard, press Spacebar to open and close the Position menu. Do not press ↵ after selecting the option or you will close the dialog box. If you are using the mouse, open the Position menu by clicking on the list box, then drag the highlight to the option to select it.

Choose: Position/Bottom Center

Your screen should be similar to Figure 4-8.

FIGURE 4-8

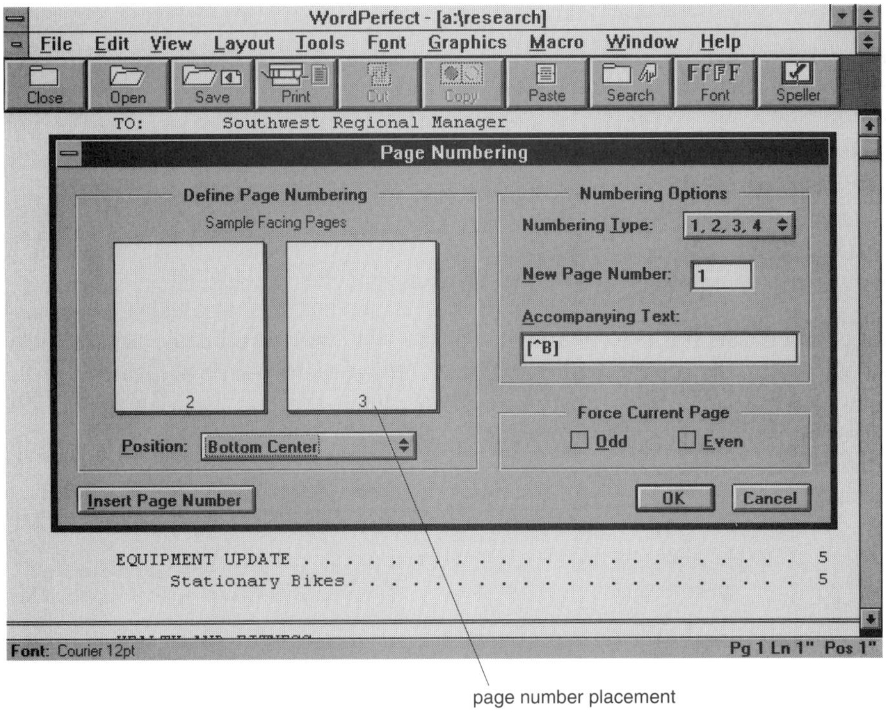

Now the sample pages show how this selection will appear. The right side of the dialog box contains the Numbering Options group. In this group you can select the page number type (Arabic is the default), specify if you want to begin numbering with a number other than 1, and add additional text to the page number. The defaults for this group are satisfactory. To complete the command,

Choose: OK

The page numbers will not appear on the screen. However, when you preview or print the document, the page numbers will appear on the margin of the location specified. If new pages are inserted or others deleted, WordPerfect will automatically renumber the pages.

Suppressing Page Numbers

Next you realize that you really do not want the table of contents page number to show. You can turn off the page numbering for specified pages using the Suppress command on the Layout/Page menu. This command does not alter the page numbering sequence of the document. To do this, the insertion point must be positioned anywhere on the page to be unnumbered. Since the insertion point is already on page 1,

Choose: Layout/Page/Suppress

The options in the Suppress dialog box let you suppress headers, footers, and page numbers. To suppress page numbers,

Choose: Page Numbers/OK

Use the Reveal Codes screen to look at the codes inserted at this location in your document. It should display [Pg Numbering:Bottom Center][Suppress:PgNum]. Exit the Reveal Codes screen.

Preventing Widows and Orphans

Generally, when you print a document, you do not want one line of a paragraph printed by itself at the top or bottom of a page. When the first line of a paragraph is the last line on a page, it is called an **orphan**. When the last line of a paragraph appears at the top of a new page, it is called a **widow**.

To see an example of this,

Move to: top of page 3
Press: ↑

The last line from the last paragraph on page 2 appears at the top of page 3. This is an orphan. To prevent this type of problem from occurring, the Widow/Orphan Protection feature is used.

The Widow/Orphan Protection command should be entered at the beginning of the document so that all the text following the code will be affected. To move back to the beginning of the document and to use this command,

Press: CTRL + HOME
Choose: Layout/Page/Widow/Orphan
➢ ALT + F9, Widow/Orphan

The feature is now on. To see the effect in the document,

Move to: top of page 3

Your screen should be similar to Figure 4-9.

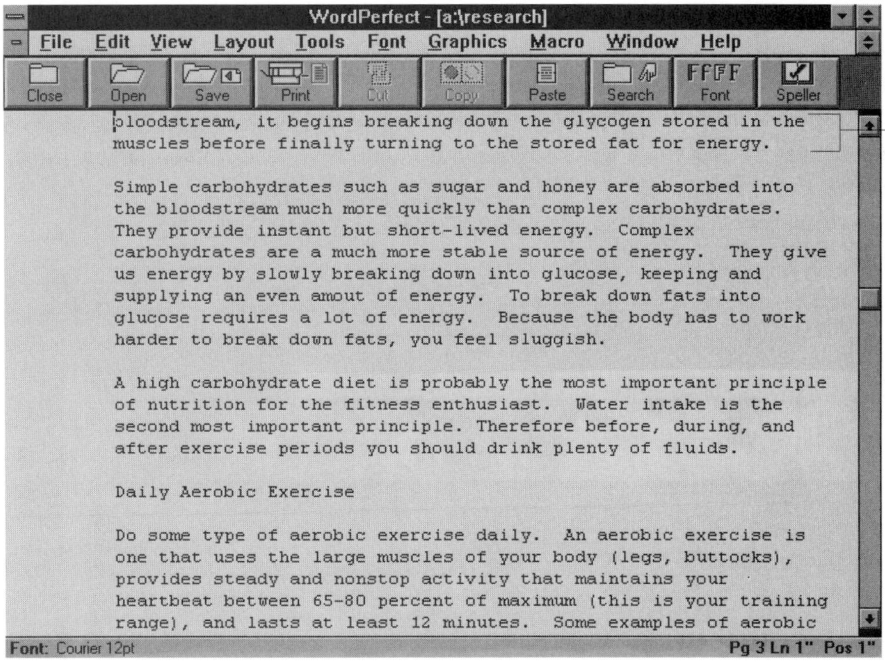

FIGURE 4-9

To solve the orphan problem, WordPerfect forced the last line from the previous page to the beginning of the next page. Now there are two lines at the top of page 3.

Using Block Protection

As you continue to check the document, you see another problem at the top of page 4.

Move to: top of page 4

Notice that the second item of a list of items begins at the top of this page. Item number 1 is at the bottom of the previous page. To see this text,

Press: ↑ (5 times)

You want to keep the lead-in sentence to this list and the first item together on a page as they are. However, you feel it would look better if the first two lines of the second item were also on the same page.

Text that should remain together on one page, such as a table or a long quote, is often divided over two pages because WordPerfect automatically calculates the length of each page and inserts a **soft page break** when needed without discrimination as to the text. To control where a page ends, you could simply enter a hard page break by pressing CTRL + ↵ to make WordPerfect begin a new page. However, if you continue to edit the document by adding and deleting text that affects the length of the document, the location of the hard page break may no longer be appropriate. Then you would need to delete the hard page break code and reenter it at the new location. This is time consuming.

The Block Protect command on the Layout/Page menu can be used to keep a specified block of text together on a page. Before using block protection, the text must be selected. Select the text beginning on Pg 3 Ln 8.17" through Pg 4 Ln 1.33". You want the the lead-in sentence, item 1, and the first two lines of item 2 to be together on a page.

Choose: Layout/Page/Block Protect
Shortcut: (ALT) + (F9), Block Protect

Clear the highlight.

Your screen should be similar to Figure 4-10.

FIGURE 4-10

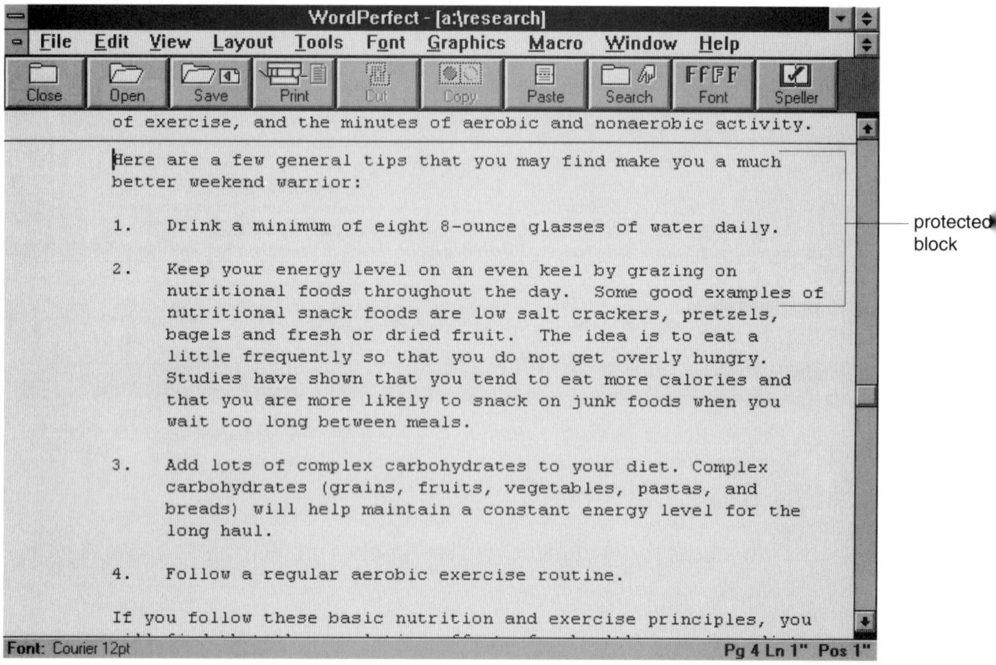

In order to keep the selected block of text together, all the selected text has moved to the top of page 4.

You are now ready to print the document. Select the appropriate printer for your computer system. Your text will be reformatted to the capabilities of your printer. Print the entire document. Save the edited document as REPORT. Close the file.

You presented your suggested articles to your manager, who found the topics interesting. The manager suggested, however, that several of the articles were too long and that it would be better not to include any information that requires footnotes. Following your manager's suggestions, you revised the articles and saved them in a file called ARTICLES. Now you are ready to create a sample newsletter using the revised articles.

Changing Fonts

The first thing you want to do is to enter the title for the newsletter at the top of the first page. The title will display the name of the newsletter, "The Sports Company Update," and issue identification information such as the date of publication and volume number. You will create the newsletter in a new file. To display a new blank document window,

Choose: File/New
➢ (SHIFT) + (F4)

Because you just selected your own printer, you will need to change the selected printer back to the Workbook Printer so that you will have the same font and graphic choices as needed in this section of the lab. Select the Workbook Printer (File/Select Printer).

The newsletter title will be bold and centered on the page. It will also be in a different font and larger type size. Before typing the title, you will enter the codes to make these changes. To center the text,

Choose: Layout/Line/Center
➢ (SHIFT) + (F7)

The insertion point is positioned in the center of the line.

Next you want to change the font to a different type, a larger size, and bold. Type sizes are measured in points, abbreviated "pt." Regular text is usually 10pt or 12pt.

Choose: Font/Font/Helvetica 18pt/Bold/OK
➢ (F9) or [FFFF Font] Font button, Helvetica 18pt, Bold, OK

To enter the first line of the newsletter title,

Type: **The Sports Company**

The rest of the newsletter name, UPDATE, will be on the next line.

Press: (↵)

You want it to be the same type style but a larger type size. To change the font to 24pt,

Choose: Font/Font/Helvetica 24pt/OK
➢ (F9) Font button, Helvetica 24pt, OK

or

Click: [FFFF Font], Helvetica 24pt, OK

You do not need to respecify bold because the text you are entering is within the Bold on/off codes. To center the text on the line and enter the title,

Press: (SHIFT) + (F7)
Type: **UPDATE**

Your screen should be similar to Figure 4-11.

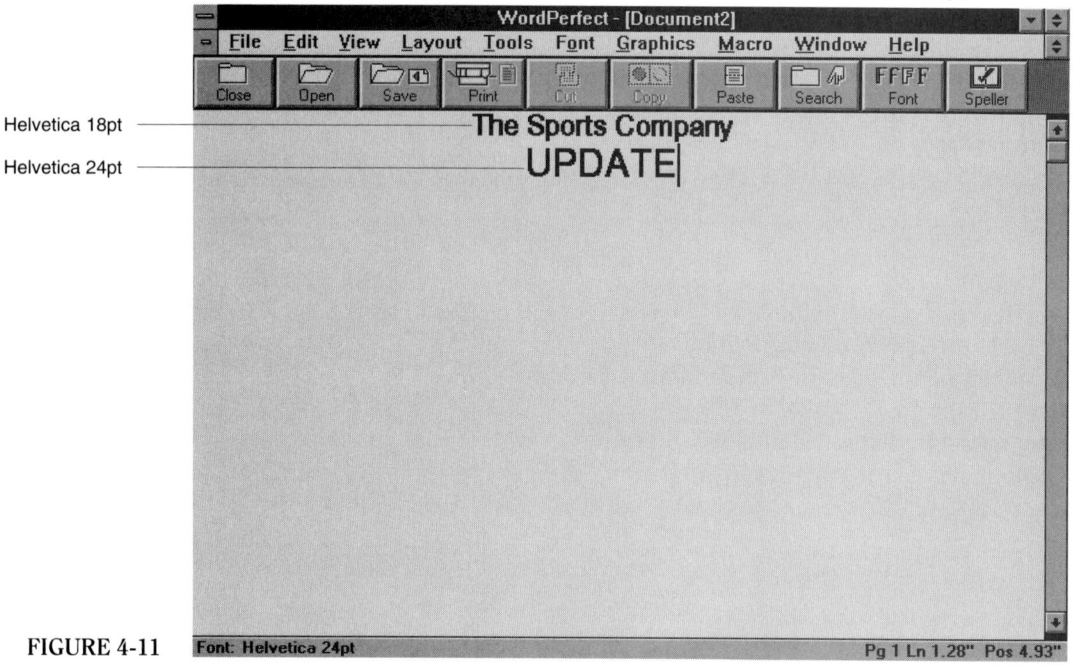

FIGURE 4-11

The next line in the newsletter title will be in a smaller type size, three lines below the main title. You will change the font size before entering the blank lines so that the blank lines will not be sized for 24pt characters. To change the font and enter the text,

Choose:	Font/Font/Times Roman 12pt, OK
➢	(F9), Times Roman 12pt, OK
or	
Click:	FFFF Font, Times Roman 12pt, OK
Press:	(↵) (2 times)
Press:	(SHIFT) + (F7)
Type:	**A Publication for Customers of The Sports Company**
Press:	(↵) (3 times)

Creating Graphic Lines

Finally the identification information needs to be entered. This information will be displayed inside two horizontal lines. This is done using the Graphics/Line/Horizontal ((CTRL) + (F11)) command. To create the top line,

Choose:	Graphics/Line/Horizontal
➢	(CTRL) + (F11)

Your screen should be similar to Figure 4-12.

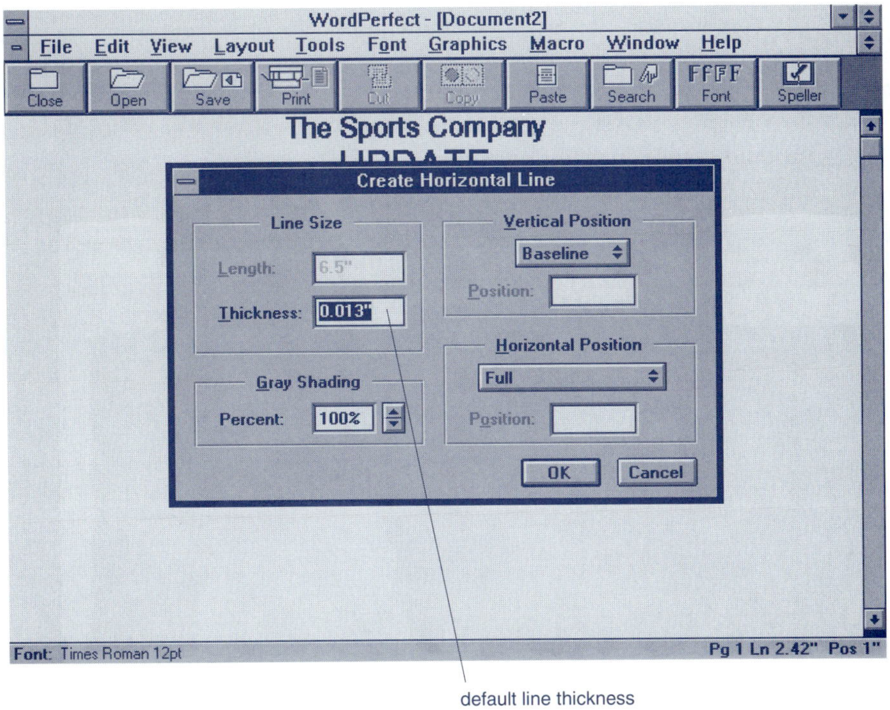

FIGURE 4-12

The Create Horizontal Line dialog box is displayed. It is used to control the placement and size of the line. The default settings for a horizontal line will create a thin (.013") horizontal line the full width of the page. You will use the default settings for the top line.

Choose: OK

A thin solid line is created the full width of the page. To move below the line and enter the date of publication,

Press: (Enter)
Type: **FALL 1995**

The volume information will be displayed flush right on the line. To enter this information,

Press: (ALT) + (F7)
Type: **VOLUME I**
Press: (Enter)

Now you are ready to create the bottom line.

Choose: Graphics/Line/Horizontal
➢ (CTRL) + (F11)

You want this line to be heavier than the upper line. To increase the thickness to .05", in the Thickness box,

Type: **.05**
Choose: OK

Your screen should be similar to Figure 4-13.

FIGURE 4-13

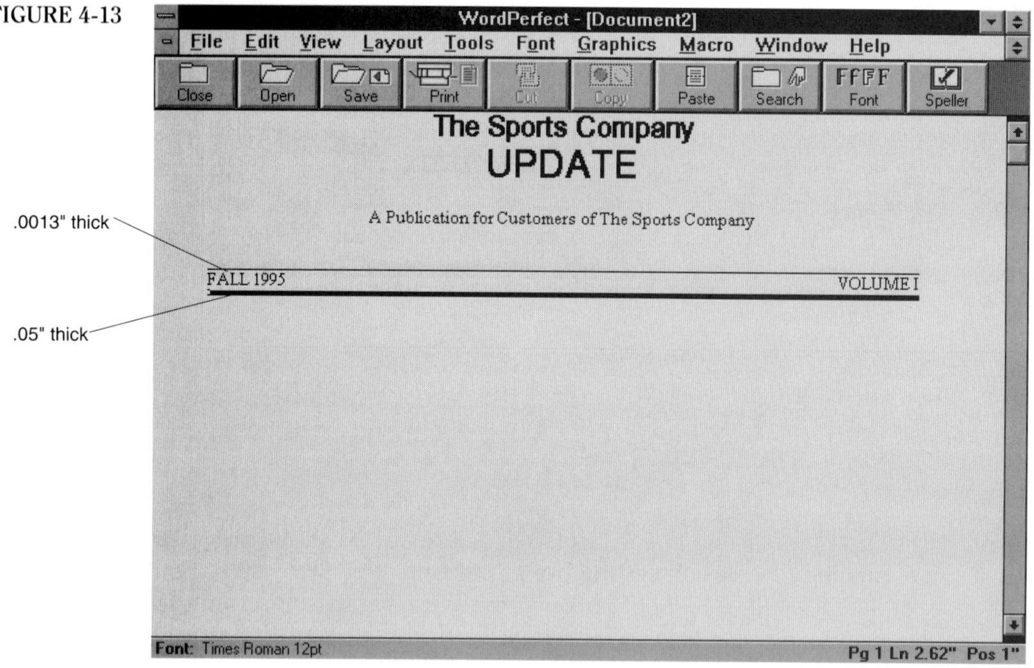

A heavy horizontal line is drawn.

Finally, to turn off the bold setting,

Press: (CTRL) + **B**

Defining Columns

Now you are ready to add the text for the newsletter below the newsletter title. It will begin two lines below the title.

Press: (↵) (2 times)

The insertion point should be on Pg 1 Ln 2.87". If it is not, move it there.

The text for the newsletter is in a file on your data disk. The File/Retrieve command will retrieve an existing file into the active document at the location of the insertion point.

Choose: File/Retrieve

From the Retrieve File dialog box you need to specify the name of the file you want to add to the current document. From the Files list box,

Select: ARTICLES
Choose: Retrieve

To confirm that you want to insert the specified file into the current document,

Choose: Yes

Your screen should be similar to Figure 4-14.

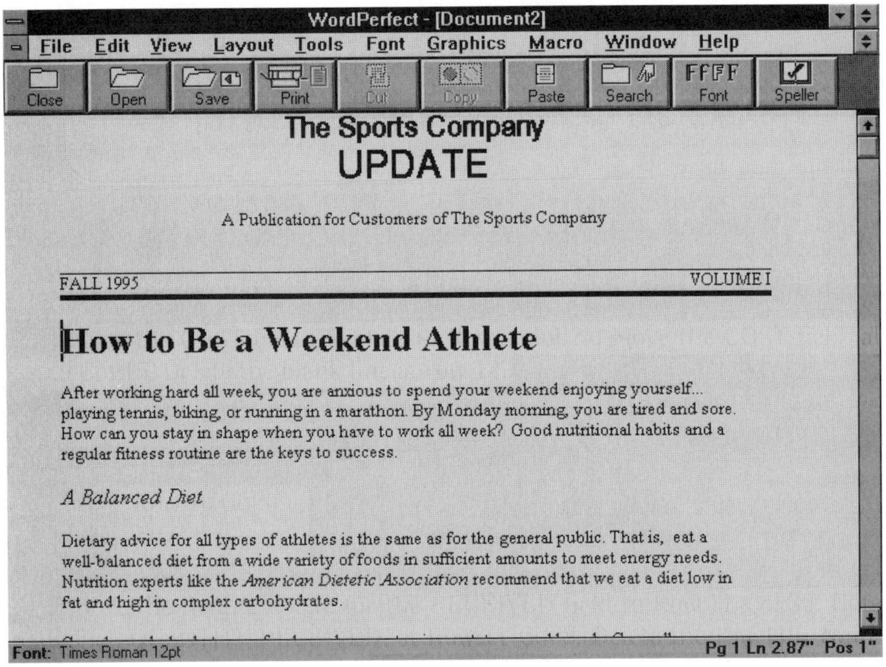

FIGURE 4-14

The text for several of the articles to be used in the newsletter is inserted below the newsletter title. Following your manager's suggestions, you shortened several of the articles and removed any text that required footnotes. You also added a brief article on how to train for an upcoming biking event and a list of several upcoming event dates.

You have also set the font size for the main heading for the articles to Times Roman 24pt, for subheads to Times Roman 14pt, and for the main text to Times Roman 12pt. The text is also left-justified.

Scroll through the text to view the contents of the articles. When you are done, return to the top of the document.

You want the articles in the newsletter to be displayed in column format. The Layout/Columns (ALT + SHIFT + F9) command lets you easily set the text format of a document to columns.

The Ruler contains several mouse buttons you can use as menu shortcuts when working with columns. Display the Ruler.

As with many WordPerfect commands, a code is entered into the document to control the display of the text. The location of the code indicates the point in the document at which the command will take effect. You want the column format to begin after the first paragraph of the first article. The insertion point needs to be positioned anywhere in the line of text where you want the format to begin.

Move to: anywhere in the subhead "A Balanced Diet" (Ln 4.39")

To create columns, you must first define the column settings. The column definition includes selecting the type of column, spacing between columns, and the number of columns. To do this,

Choose: Layout/Columns/Define
➢ (ALT) + (SHIFT) + (F9), Define

Your screen should be similar to Figure 4-15.

FIGURE 4-15

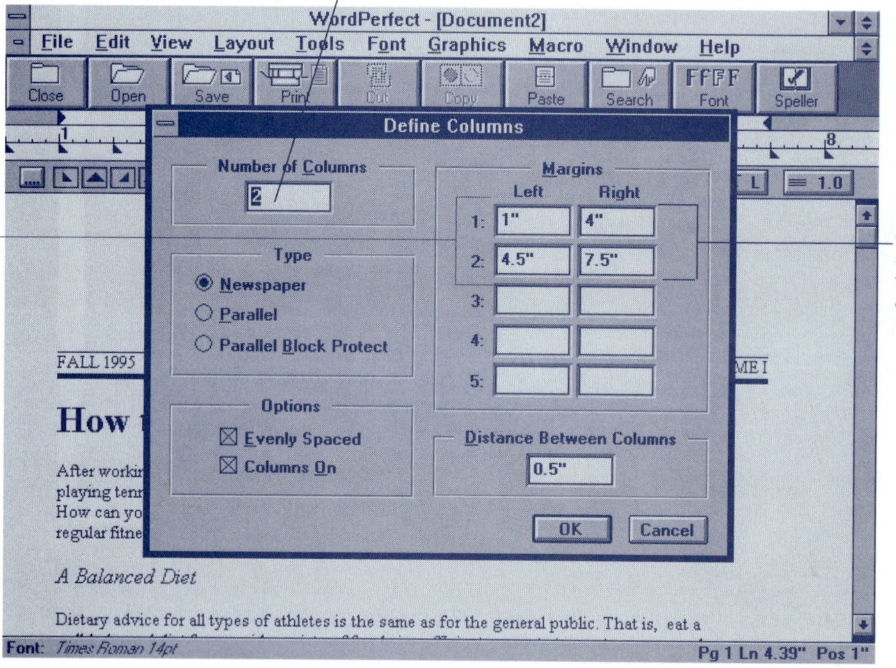

The Define Columns dialog box is displayed. The Number of Columns text box lets you specify how many columns of text you want across the width of the page. The default number of two columns is acceptable, so you do not need to change this setting.

The three types of columns that can be created are displayed in the Type group: Newspaper, Parallel, and Parallel Block Protect. In **newspaper columns**, text runs vertically up and down the page through the columns. In **parallel columns**, text runs horizontally across the page, such as in a table or a script. One of the columns may spill over to the next page while the other does not. The third option, Parallel Block Protect, is the same as parallel columns except that text is protected from being split between two pages. The newsletter will use newspaper style columns. Again, this is the default setting.

Based on the number of columns you specify, WordPerfect automatically calculates the left and right margins for the columns. The default settings are displayed in the Margins group. The first column will begin at the left default margin of 1 inch and end at 4 inches. The second column will begin at 4.5 inches and end at the right default margin setting of 7.5 inches.

The next group, Distance Between Columns, lets you specify how much space you want between the columns. The default setting is 0.5 inches and is also appropriate. The last two options in the dialog box are also on by default. They specify that the columns are evenly spaced on the page and that the column definition you specified will be turned on immediately. To complete the definition,

Choose: OK

Your screen should be similar to Figure 4-16.

FIGURE 4-16

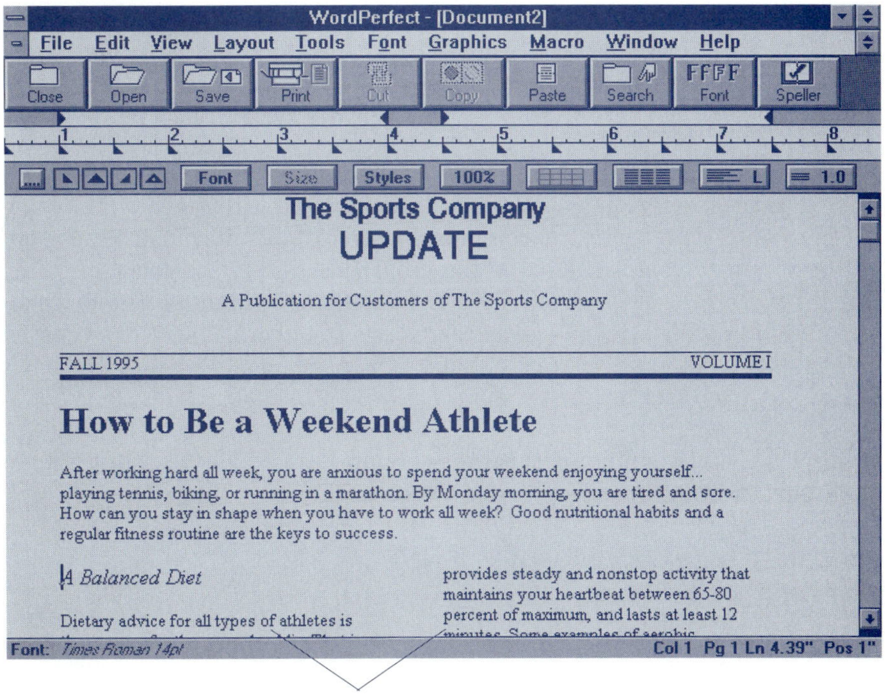

newspaper style, two-column format

The text is displayed as two columns. A column definition code, [Col Def], was entered into the document at the beginning of the line containing the insertion point. A second code, [Col on], was also entered. It directs the program to display the document using the defined column settings.

To move around the columns, click anywhere in the text if you are using the mouse. If you are using the keyboard, the same keys you use in normal text display are used to move within a column. However, to move from one column to another, use the Edit/Go To/Position command. You can also move to the next or previous column using the ALT + → or ALT + ←.

Scroll the two pages of the newsletter to see how the two-column layout looks. When you are done, scroll the screen so that the page break between pages 1 and 2 is in the middle of the document window.

The heading for the second article begins at the bottom of the first page. You want the second article to begin at the top of the second page. Additionally, you want the second page to be in three-column format rather than two.

Before you can define the column settings for the second page, you must turn off the display of the first column definition at the location in the document where you want it to end. This is called redefining columns. If you do not turn off the first column definition, the first column definition changes to the second column definition. For example, if the insertion point is located in a two-column text area, and you define a three-column setting, the three-column definition replaces the two-column definition, and the style changes to three columns throughout.

You want the two-column format to end at the bottom of the article on page 1.

Move to: end of column 2 on page 1 (Col 2 Pg 1 Ln 8.47" Pos 6.19")

The display of columns is turned off by selecting the Columns Off option in the Layout/Columns menu.

Choose: **L**ayout/**C**olumns/Columns **O**ff
➢ ALT + SHIFT + F9, Columns Off

A [Col Off] code is placed in the document at the location of the insertion point to control the display. The text following the code is displayed with no columns while the text before the code remains two columns. Be careful when turning columns on or off. If the command is not entered in the proper location in the document, any text located between the on and off codes is formatted in columns. The original column definition settings remain in effect in the document unless the code is deleted or another column definition is entered.

The heading and text for the second article now begins on page 2. Delete the blank line at the top of page 2.

To display the remaining text in three-column format, you need to create a second column definition. To define three columns beginning at the top of page 2,

Move to: anywhere in the head "Going for the Goal" (Pg 2 Ln 1")

The button on the ruler bar allows you to specify up to five columns using the default column definitions.

Click: Columns button

The menu is displayed as long as you hold down the mouse button. The options in this menu let you turn columns on and off and specify the number of columns you want displayed. To choose an option, drag the mouse down the menu until the option you want is highlighted. As soon as you release the mouse button, the selected option is executed.

Choose: 3 Columns

Choose: Layout/Columns/Define/Number of Columns/3/OK
➢ ALT + SHIFT + F9, Define, 3, OK

Your screen should be similar to Figure 4-17.

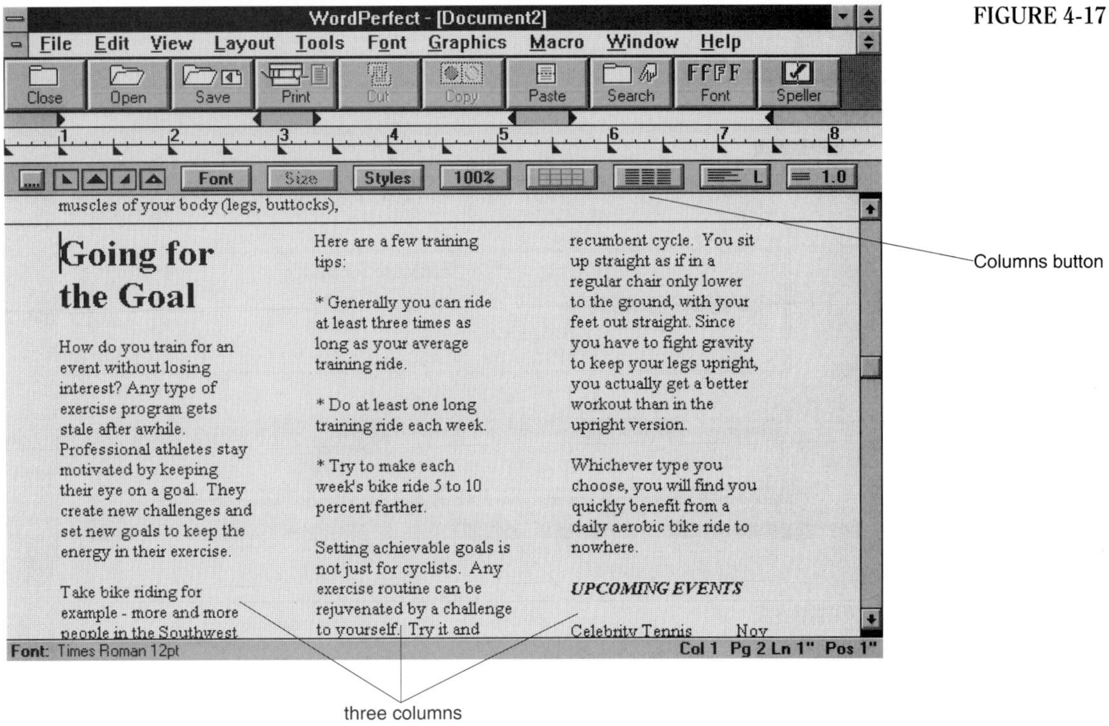

FIGURE 4-17

The text following the new column definition code is displayed as three newspaper style columns.

Using Hyphenation

Scroll the document to the bottom of the page.

You notice now that the columns are narrower, that many of the lines have very uneven right margins. On lines of text where there are several short words, the wrapping of text to the next line is not a problem. However, on lines that contain long words, the long word is wrapped to the next line, leaving a large gap on the previous line. Hyphenating a long word at the end of a line will help solve this problem.

To turn on the hyphenation feature beginning at the top of the newsletter,

Press: CTRL + HOME
Choose: Layout/Line/Hyphenation
➢ SHIFT + F9, Hyphenation

The Line Hyphenation dialog box displays the default hyphenation settings. These look satisfactory. To turn on this feature,

Choose: Hyphenation On/OK

To see how hyphenation has affected the document, using ⓓ,

Move to: second line of second paragraph (Pg 1 Ln 6.75")

Your screen should be similar to Figure 4-18.

FIGURE 4-18

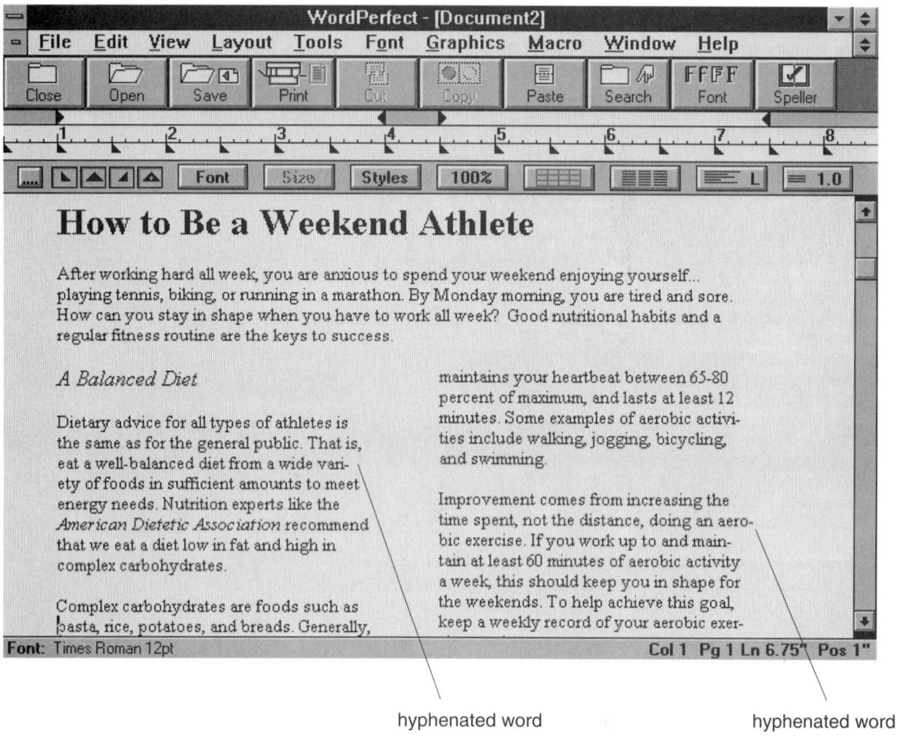

WordPerfect has examined each line and determined where to hyphenate a word if possible. Hyphenating the newsletter has made the column margins much less uneven.

Adding Graphics

Next you want to add two graphic boxes to the newsletter. The first will be a picture of foods that will complement the text in the first article. This type of graphic box is called a **figure box** because it contains a graphic image, chart, or diagram. You would like the box to appear near the second paragraph in the section, "A Balanced Diet." The insertion point should already be positioned in the second paragraph. If it is not, move to Pg 1 Ln 6.75".

Almost any graphic from another software package can be added to a WordPerfect document. You will add a graphic contained in a file on your data disk.

To retrieve a figure,

Choose: **G**raphics/**F**igure/**R**etrieve
➢ (F11)

In the Retrieve Figure text box of the dialog box you specify the name of the graphic file you want to retrieve, just like you would select a document file. Change the directory to the drive containing your data disk.

Select: HARVEST.WPG
Choose: **R**etrieve

Your screen should be similar to Figure 4-19.

FIGURE 4-19

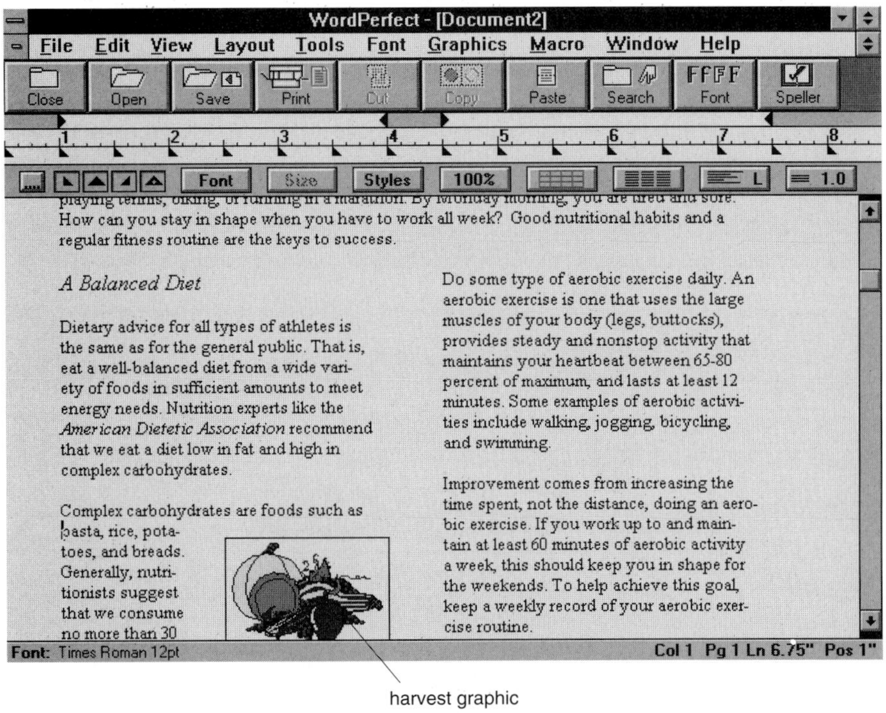

The harvest graphic is displayed at the right margin of the column where the insertion point is located. The text is reformatted around the figure. Each graphic figure you add to a document is assigned a number, and the program inserts a graphic box number code in the document. To see the code, open the Reveal Codes window. The code [Fig Box;1;harvest.wpg;] is displayed. Close the Reveal Codes window.

Once a graphic is retrieved, you can manipulate it in many ways. For example, you can change its size and position in the text, add captions, and change or remove the border style. You want to reposition the figure so that it is displayed at the top left side of the paragraph.

Instead of using the Graphics menu in the menu bar to make this change, you will use the short Graphics menu. To display the menu,

Point to the graphic and click the right mouse button.

The short Graphics menu is opened. It contains three commonly used menu options that are also available on the Graphics/Figure menu. The option that allows you to change the position of the box is Box Position.

Choose: Box Position

To change the position of a graphic box,

Choose: Graphics/Figure/Position

The first Box Position and Size dialog box is displayed. You need to enter the number of the figure you want to change.

Type: 1
Choose: OK

Your screen should be similar to Figure 4-20.

FIGURE 4-20

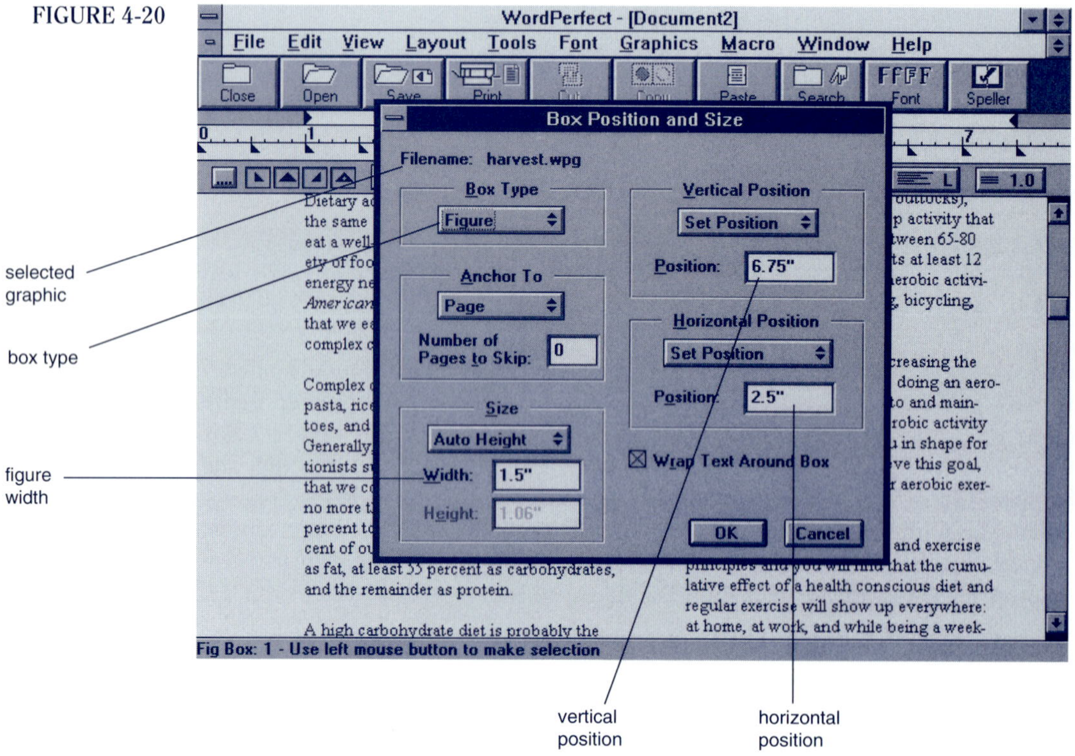

The Box Position and Size dialog box is displayed. The filename for the selected graphic is displayed at the top of the box. The other settings in this box identify the default settings for the box.

The box type is a Figure box. The default width in the figure Size box is one half the width of the column (1.5"). The height is determined by the contents of the box. The Vertical Position box shows that the figure box is 6.75" from the top of the page. This setting was determined by the location of the insertion point when the box was created. The Horizontal Position box shows that the figure box is 2.5" from the left margin. This aligns the right side of the box with the right margin of the column. The vertical and horizontal position settings are default settings based upon the setting in the Anchor To box, Page. This setting anchors the box to a particular location on the page. If you add or delete text, the figure does not move on the page. You would like to change this setting to Paragraph. Then if text is added or deleted, the box moves with the paragraph. To change the anchor setting from the Anchor To pop-up list,

Choose: Paragraph

Notice that the horizontal position setting has changed to Margin, Left, and the vertical option is dimmed, showing that it is not available. These are the default settings for a figure that is anchored to a paragraph. It automatically places the figure at the beginning of the paragraph, aligned flush with the left margin. To see how this setting looks,

Choose: OK

Your screen should be similar to Figure 4-21.

FIGURE 4-21

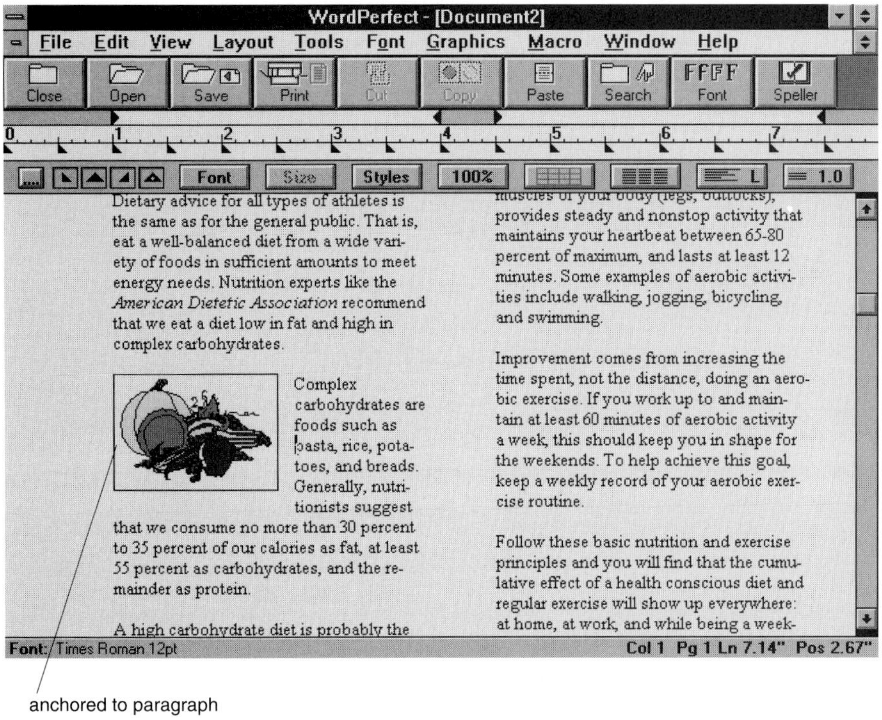

The harvest graphic anchors to the upper left corner of the paragraph. The text is rehyphenated as necessary and wraps on the right and below the graphic. Now the graphic will always be attached to this paragraph of text no matter what changes are made to surrounding text.

To see how the addition of this figure affects the layout of text on this page, using ⓥ scroll to the bottom of the first column. The heading for the next section, "Daily Aerobic Exercise," is on the last line of the first column. To force this heading to the top of the second column,

Move to: beginning of the heading (Ln 9.66" Pos 1")
Press: (↵)

The two subheads now appear at the top of each column.

The second figure you want to include in the newsletter is a graphic of a bike. You want the figure displayed near the second paragraph of the second article.

Press: (ALT) + (PGDN)
Move to: beginning of second paragraph (Col 1 Pg 2 Ln 4.25")

The insertion point should be positioned at the beginning of the second paragraph. Add the graphic file BIKE.WPG (on your data disk) to the document.

Notice the figure is quite small. This is because half the width of a three-column format is less than 1 inch. You feel the graphic would look better if it were the full width of the column. You also want to anchor this graphic to the paragraph. To do this,

Choose: Graphics/Figure/Position/2/OK
or
Press: (SHIFT) and double-click on the bike graphic

From the Box Position and Size dialog box, select Paragraph from the Anchor To pop-up list.

To change the default horizontal position of the figure from Margin, Left to the full width of the column, from the Horizontal Position pop-up list,

Choose: Margin, Full
Choose: OK

Your screen should be similar to Figure 4-22.

FIGURE 4-22

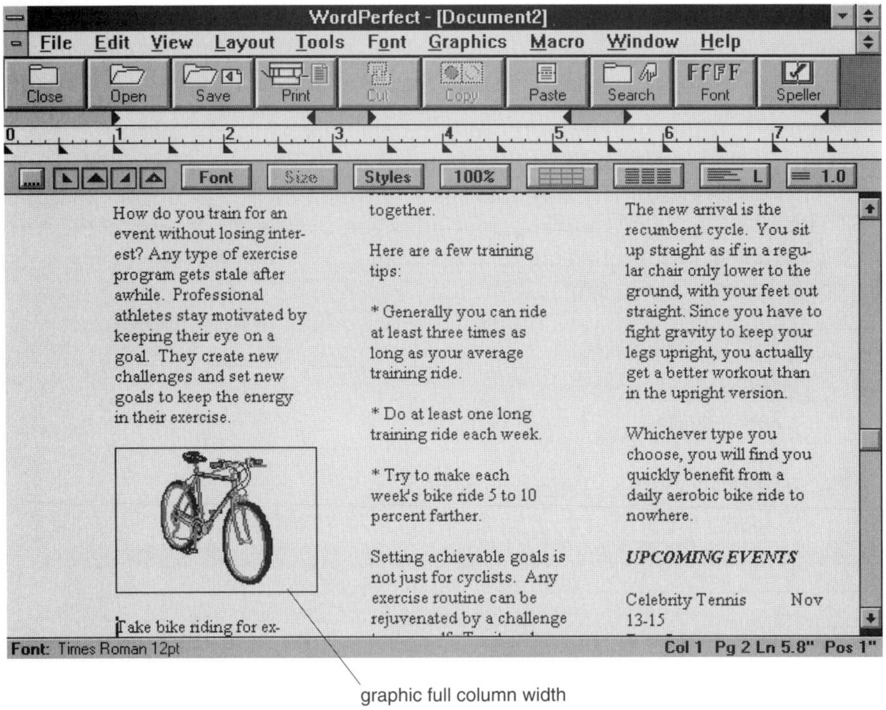

The bike graphic is anchored to the paragraph. It is displayed above the paragraph and fills the area between the left and right margins of the column.

Adding a Text Box

The next item you want to add to the newsletter is a box to display the list of upcoming events. This type of box is called a **text box**. The information you want to display in this box is located at the bottom of column 3 on page 2. You will cut this text from the document and store it in the Clipboard. Then you will paste the text into the text box after you have created it.

Move to: the heading "Upcoming Events" (Col 3 Pg 2 Ln 5.27")

Select the text to the end of column 3.

Choose: Edit/Cut
➢ (SHIFT) + (DEL) or Cut button

The selected text is removed from the document and stored in Clipboard.

Next you will create the text box and then paste the stored text in the box. Then you will move the text box to the location you want it in the newsletter. It is easiest to create a text box at the beginning of a document, before any codes, and then size and move it to another location.

Press: CTRL + HOME
Choose: Graphics/Text Box/Create
➢ ALT + F11

The Text Box editor window is displayed. The title bar displays the filename and the text box number. In this window you can enter the text you want displayed in the box. You can use formatting and editing features when typing the text. By default the width of the box is half the available space between the left and right margins (4.25" is half of 8.5"). Then the program allows for margin space inside the box, making the actual space for entering text less than 4.25". The ruler bar displays the actual space you have for entering text.

Rather than type in text, you will paste the text stored in the Clipboard.

Choose: Edit/Paste
➢ SHIFT + INS or Paste button

Your screen should be similar to Figure 4-23.

FIGURE 4-23

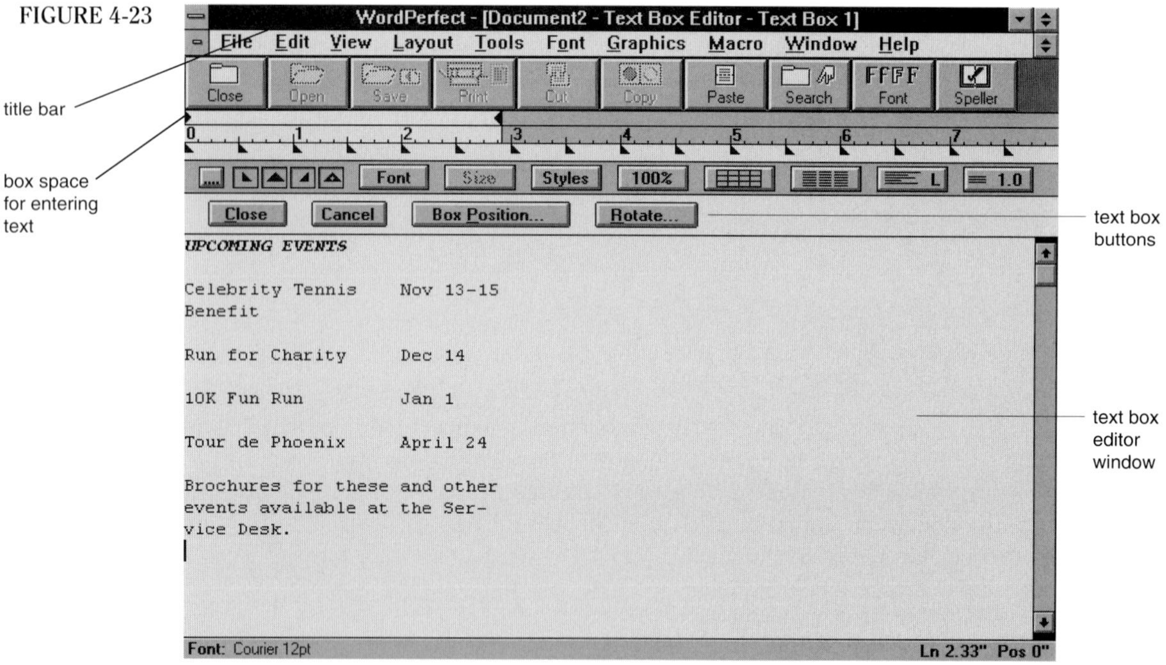

The text is copied into the text box window. It is formatted to fit within the available box width. You feel the default box size may be too large. If you reduce the type size of the text in the box, then you can reduce the overall size of the box.

Select the text below the heading and change the font to Times Roman 10pt and bold. Clear the highlight.

Now that the text size is smaller, you can reduce the box size. To open the Box Position and Size dialog box, the Box Position button is used (click on it or press ALT + P).

Choose: Box Position

The default width and height are displayed in the Size box. To enter a specific size, from the Size pop-up list,

Choose: Set Both

Enter the width of 2.5" and height of 2.7".

Choose: OK

Adjust the dates in the box (use TAB) so that they line up beneath each other.

Now you are ready to see how the text box looks in the document. To close the Text box editor window, the Close button is used (click on it or press ALT + C).

Choose: Close

Your screen should be similar to Figure 4-24.

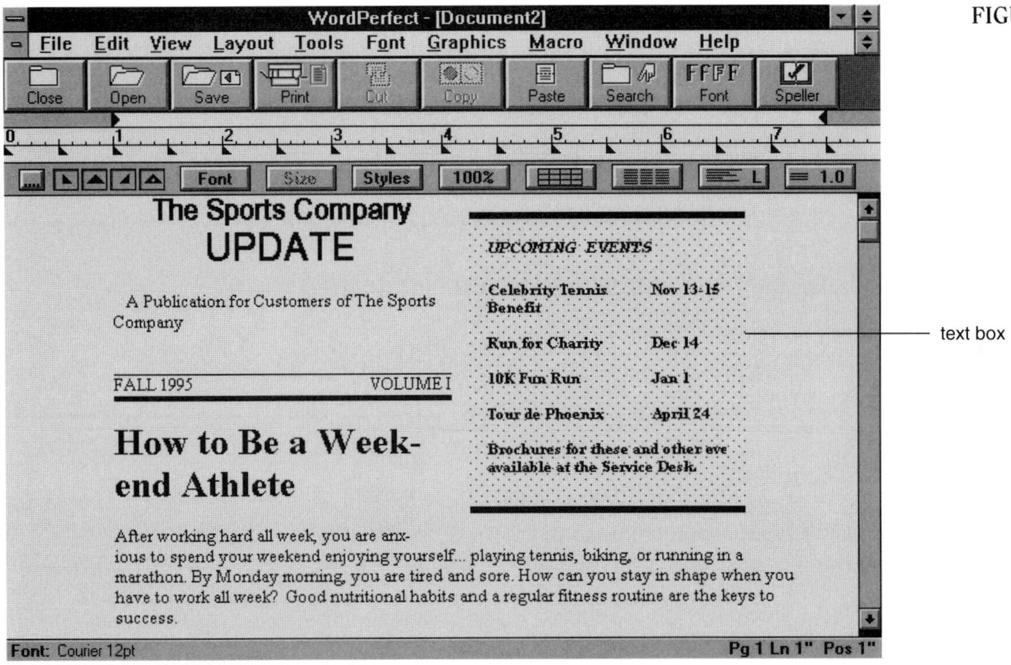

FIGURE 4-24

The text box is displayed flush with the right margin of the document, opposite the insertion point. The surrounding text wraps on the left side of the box. The text box has a shaded background and thick top and bottom border style. These are the default text box style settings.

Now you will move the box to the top of column 3 on page 2. You can do this using either the mouse or the keyboard.

Any graphic box can be easily moved and sized by selecting it. To select the text graphics box,

Click on the text box.

When a box is selected, it is surrounded by small squares called **sizing handles**, and the mouse pointer changes to a four-pointed arrow (✥) when positioned in the selected box. When this arrow is displayed, you can move the entire box by dragging it to another location. You can also change the size of the box by pointing to a sizing handle (the pointer changes to a double-headed arrow, ↕) and dragging the handle. The box will increase or decrease in size in the direction you are dragging, and the contents of the box will adjust appropriately.

You want to move the text box to the top of column 3 on page 2. To move a box, first position the mouse pointer inside the box so that it appears as a four-pointed arrow.

Position the pointer in the box.

Next you drag the mouse. As you do, an outline of the box shows its position. When you release the button, the box is repositioned at the new location.

Drag the box to the top of column 3 on page 2 (do not release the mouse button.)

The top of the box outline should be even with the top line of the column, and the right edge of the box should align with the right margin of the column. (Line up the right box edge with position 7.5" on the Ruler.)

When the box is correctly positioned, release the mouse button.

The box should be positioned as in Figure 4-25. If it is not, reposition the box again by dragging it until it is displayed at the top of column 3 on page 2.

To deselect a box, click anywhere outside the box.

Deselect the box.

To move the text box,

Choose: Graphics/Text Box/Position/1/OK

Notice that the box is anchored to a page. Because you were on page 1 when you created the box, it is anchored to page 1. To change the setting to anchor it to the next page, you need to tell the program to skip one page.

Choose: Number of pages to Skip
Type: 1

You also need to specify that you want the box positioned at the top of the page. To do this,

Choose: Vertical/Top

Finally, you want the horizontal position of the box to be 5 inches from the left margin.

Choose: Position
Type: 5

These settings specify that the text box will be displayed at the top of page 2, 5 inches from the left margin.

Choose: OK

To see the box in its new location,

Press: (ALT) + (PGDN)

Your screen should be similar to Figure 4-25.

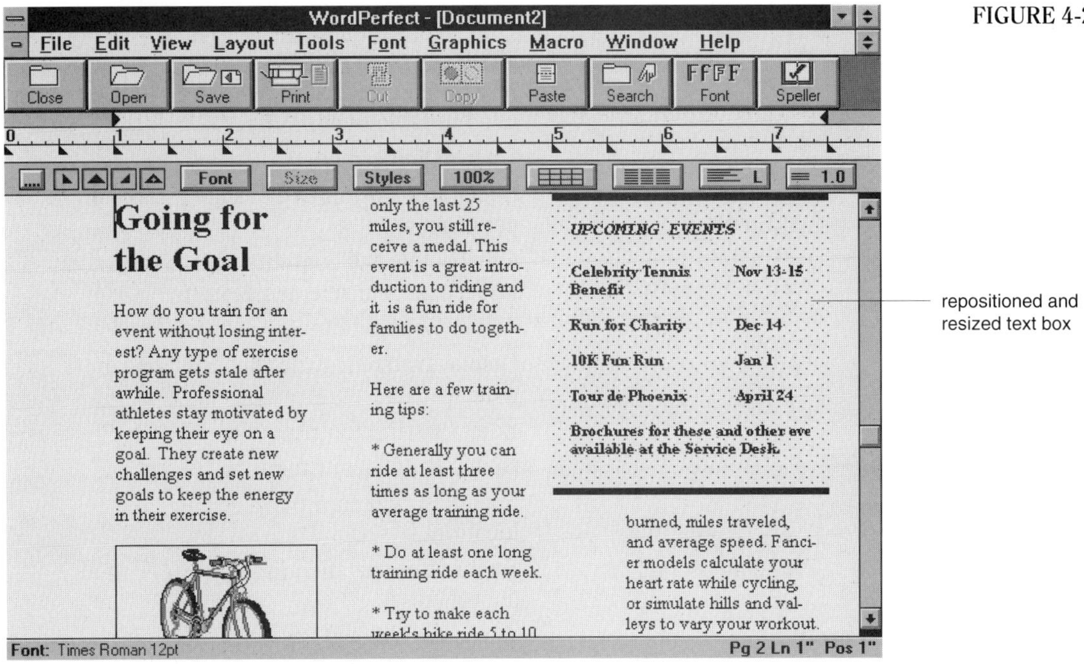

FIGURE 4-25

The box is positioned correctly.

Move to the bottom of page 2, column 3 and enter your name. Save the formatted newsletter as FALLNEWS.

If your instructor wants you to print the newsletter, select the appropriate printer for your computer system first (File/Select Printer). The text is reformatted to the font and graphic capabilities of your printer. Scroll through the document to see the changes that were made. Adjust the text wherever necessary to produce a newsletter as similar as possible to the one you created in this lab. You may also need to adjust the text in the text box and the size of the box. If text overlaps on the screen, you need to change to a smaller size font. Preview, then print the newsletter. Resave the document.

Close the Button Bar and the Ruler. Close the file REPORT. Exit WordPerfect and Windows.

Key Terms

dot leaders	newspaper column
footnote	parallel column
widow	figure box
orphan	text box
soft page break	sizing handles

Command Summary

Command	Shortcut	Button Bar	Action
Edit/Convert Case/Uppercase			Changes selected text to uppercase
Layout/Line/Center	SHIFT + F7		Centers line of text between left and right margins
Tools/Mark Text	F12		Opens Mark Text menu
Tools/Mark Text/Table of Contents			Marks selected text to be used in table of contents
Tools/Define	SHIFT + F12		Opens Define menu
Tools/Define/Table of Contents			Specifies location and design of table of contents
Tools/Generate	ALT + F12		Creates table of contents using marked references and selected design
Layout/Footnote/Create			Adds footnote to text
File/Print Preview			Displays current page as it will appear when printed
Layout/Footnote/Edit			Edits existing footnote
Layout/Page	ALT + F9		Opens Page layout menu
Layout/Page/Numbering/Position			Specifies page number location
Layout/Page/Suppress			Suppresses specified items from printed document
Layout/Page/Widow/Orphan			Turns on Widow/Orphan protection
Layout/Page/Block Protect			Turns on block protection for selected text
File/New	SHIFT + F4		Displays new document window
Font/Font	F9		Changes appearance of characters on printed page
Graphics/Line/Horizontal	CTRL + F11		Creates horizontal line
File/Retrieve			Retrieves an existing file into current document
Layout/Columns	ALT + SHIFT + F9		Opens Layout Columns menu
Layout/Columns/Define			Specifies number, type, and size of columns
Layout/Columns/Columns Off			Turns off columns
Layout/Line/Hyphenation			Specifies hyphenation settings
Graphics/Figure/Retrieve	F11		Retrieves a graphic figure into document
Graphics/Figure/Position			Specifies position, size, and anchor options for a figure box
Graphics/Text Box/Create	ALT + F11		Adds a text box to document

LAB REVIEW

Matching

1. (F12)	_____	**a.**	stops display of headers, footers, and page numbers
2. (SHIFT) + (F9)	_____	**b.**	creates table of contents
3. widow	_____	**c.**	shortcut for Layout/Line command
4. Anchor To /Paragraph	_____	**d.**	shortcut for Tools/Mark Text command
5. Layout/Page /Suppress	_____	**e.**	source references displayed at the bottom of a page
6. [Def Mark:ToC]	_____	**f.**	shortcut for Layout/Page command
7. (CTRL) - U	_____	**g.**	text left at bottom of page
8. footnotes	_____	**h.**	underlines text
9. (ALT) + (F9)	_____	**i.**	definition code for table of contents
10. Tools/Generate	_____	**j.**	attaches a graphic box to a paragraph

Practice Exercises

1. Open the file FLUIDS. This is one of the articles from the research used in the lab. You will use this article to create the third page of the newsletter you created in this lab. (Use the Workbook Printer if yours does not have the required fonts.)

- **a.** Change the font and increase the size of the article title to Helvetica 14pt.
- **b.** Change the line justification to left.
- **c.** Turn hyphenation on.
- **d.** Define two newspaper columns with .7" between the columns.
- **e.** Cut the last paragraph and the four bullet items that follow it (guidelines from the American Dietetic Association) and store them in the Clipboard.
- **f.** Create a graphic text box using the text in the Clipboard. Change the font of the text box to Times Roman 10pt.
- **g.** Size the text box width to the full width of column 2.
- **h.** Place the box at the end of the second column. The text box should be centered in the column.
- **i.** Enter your name and the current date at the end of the second column.
- **j.** Save the third page of the newsletter as FLUIDS1. Select your printer. Preview the document and adjust if necessary. Print the document.

2. Open the file WATER. This file contains the body of a report on water exercises.

- **a.** Center and convert the main title to uppercase letters. Change the font to Helvetica 18pt.
- **b.** Display the page numbers at the bottom center of each page. Enter the new page number 1 on page 2. Suppress the page number on the table of contents.
- **c.** Change the following headings to Helvetica 14pt:

  Warm-up Stretches

  Aerobic Warm-up Exercises

  Conditioning Activities

  Cool-down Activities

  Toning
- **d.** Mark the five previous headings as level one table of contents headings. Mark the following three headings as level two headings:

  Circuit Training

  Interval Training

  Fartlek Training
- **e.** Turn on widow and orphan protection.
- **f.** Block protect the examples in the text.
- **g.** Place the following footnote at the end of the Aerobic Warm-up Exercises paragraph:

  McEnvoy, Joseph, <u>Fitness Swimming: Lifetime Programs</u>, Princeton: Princeton Book Company Publishers, 1985.

  Place the following footnote at the end of the of the report:

  President's Council on Physical Fitness and Sports, <u>AquaDynamics: Physical Conditioning Through Water Exercise</u>, Booklet, Washington, DC: Government Printing Office, 1-33, 1981.
- **h.** Generate the table of contents.
- **i.** Save the file as WATEREXC. Print the report.

3. Open the file COMPUTER. You will complete the layout of this report on children and computers. (Use the Workbook Printer if yours does not have the required fonts.)

- **a.** Bold and change the following titles to all uppercase:

  Computers make learning fun
  Future kids
  Software for kids
- **b.** Italicize the following names:

  By Andy Rathbone
  By Gary S. Dannenbaum

c. Bold the following text:
Computers at home
Computers in the classroom
Reader Rabbit 2
Oregon Trail
Where in the World is Carmen Sandiego?
New Math Blaster
Kidworks

d. Add two pages above the body of the report. On the first new page center the title "Children and Computers." Bold the title and change the font to Helvetica 18pt.

e. Center your name and the current date on separate lines one line below the main title. Change the font for your name and the date to Helvetica 14pt.

f. Center the title page. (Use Help for information on this feature.)

g. Center the title "Table of Contents" on the second new page.

h. Insert page numbers at the bottom right corners of the pages. Suppress the page number on the title page and table of contents.

i. Define and generate a two-level table of contents from the titles in the body of the report.

j. Turn on the widow and orphan feature.

k. Save the report as KIDSCOMP. Print the report.

4. You will create an update to be mailed to The Sports Company stores' preferred customers. (Use the Workbook Printer if yours does not have the required fonts.)

a. Center the following three-line title:
The Southwestern Discount Store
Sales Update
For Customers of the Southwestern Discount Stores

b. Change the font of the first line to Helvetica Italic 18pt. Change the font size of the second line to Helvetica 14pt. Enter a blank line between the second and third title lines.

c. Retrieve the graphic figure BKGRND-2.WPG from your data disk. Place and size the figure left-justified next to the first two lines of the title. (The third title line should be below the graph.)

d. Create a thin horizontal line one line below the third title line. Left-justify the current date on the next line. Right-justify "VOLUME III." Create a thick horizontal line below the date.

e. Retrieve the file DISCOUNT. This file contains some new items for The Southwestern Discount Store Update. Bold the uppercase description of each item. Bold the Discount Store Price line for each item.

f. Create two newspaper columns below the first paragraph of text. Change the justification to left for the columns only and turn hyphenation on.

g. Change the font for the first paragraph to Helvetica 10pt.

h. Adjust the layout of the columns so that item E starts at the top of the second page.

- **i.** Cut to the Clipboard the paragraph that begins "Check our values" and the ordering information text that follows. Create a graphic text box with a width of 3.5" and height of 3.3" to hold the text.
- **j.** Move the graphic text box to the top of column 2 on page 2.
- **k.** Enter your name below the graphic text box. Save the update as SALES.
- **l.** Preview the update. Select your default printer. Print the update.

5. Write a paper. The paper can be a paper you have written in the past. It must be a minimum of five pages. You must demonstrate the following:

- **a.** Title page
  - **(1)** The title of the paper must be centered and bold.
  - **(2)** The title should be in a font size two sizes larger than the default font for your printer.
  - **(3)** Center your name and the current date (using the Date command) near the bottom of the title page.
  - **(4)** The entire title page should be centered top to bottom. (Use Help for information on this command.)
- **b.** Table of contents
  - **(1)** The heading on this page should be centered and bold.
  - **(2)** The table of contents should show three main headings as level one headings. The structure of your report will determine the number of level two heads. Use additional levels if the structure of your paper includes additional levels.
  - **(3)** The page numbers should appear right-justified. There should not be any dot leaders before the page numbers.
- **c.** Body of the report
  - **(1)** There must be a minimum of three pages of text.
  - **(2)** There should be at least two levels of headings.
  - **(3)** Enter a minimum of four footnotes.
- **d.** Report layout
  - **(1)** Place the page numbers on the top right corner of every page. Suppress the page numbers on the title page and table of contents.
  - **(2)** Turn on widow and orphan protection.
  - **(3)** Format the level one headings to be bold.
  - **(4)** Format the level two headings to be displayed in italics.
- **e.** Print the report.

6. Create a two-page newsletter on any subject that interests you. Include at least the following layout features:

- **a.** One page set to two columns. Set the other to three columns.
- **b.** Have the titles and important information displayed in larger font sizes or types. Bold and italicize at least one line of text.
- **c.** Create a line border at the top of the newsletter.
- **d.** Create a graphic text box.
- **e.** Save and print the newsletter.

Introduction

This project is designed to reinforce your knowledge of the word processing features used in the WordPerfect for Windows labs. You will also be expected to use the Help feature to learn more about advanced features available in WordPerfect for Windows.

Note: The file you will use in this project, TRENDS, has been saved with the WorkBook printer as the selected printer. The completed newsletter will display on two pages using the WorkBook printer settings. If you change to another printer before starting the project, it may not display on two pages because of printer setting variations. If you select another printer after completing the project, it may be necessary to change some of the settings you specified so that your completed newsletter is presentable.

Case

Marianne Virgili is the director of the Glenwood Springs Chamber Resort Association. Semiannually the Chamber produces a newsletter called *Trends* that reviews the latest economic indicators for Garfield County. It is sent to all Chamber members. She has compiled much of the data to be included in the next issue and has asked you to work on several of the articles.

Part I

a. Open the file TRENDS. This file contains some of the text that will be used in the newsletter.

b. The first paragraph contains many errors. Use the editing techniques you learned in the labs to correct the paragraph.

c. Spell-check the document.

d. Search for the word "TRENDS" throughout the document and change it to be displayed in italics. Locate all occurrences of incorrect capitalization for Glenwood Springs and replace them with the correct capitalization.

e. Delete the paragraph about school attendance in the "Population, Housing, and Construction" section. In the same section move the paragraph about commercial construction below the paragraph on residential construction.

f. Bold the headings throughout the document. Change the font type and enlarge the heading "Trend Indicators" one point size.

g. Save and replace your document. Print the document.

Part II

This issue of *Trends* will contain two tables. The first table will provide employment information for 1992 to 1993 for Garfield County. The second table will provide information on gross sales.

a. The employment information is shown below. Create a table from this data in a new document.

Job Category	**1992**	**1993**	**% Change 1992–1993**
Agr., For., Fish	141	174	23.4%
Mining	705	813	15.3%
Construction	856	1,171	36.8%
Manufacturing	284	327	15.1%
Trans., Comm., Util.	443	504	13.8%
Wholesale Trade	338	410	21.3%
Retail Trade	2,580	2,859	10.9%
Fin., Ins., Real Est.	522	601	15.1%
Services	2,679	2,767	3.3%
Government	2,234	2,328	4.2%
TOTAL			10.8%

b. Right-justify the entries in the three data columns, including the column heads.

c. Enter functions to sum the 1992 and 1993 columns of data and have the total displayed with zero decimal places.

d. Insert a new row above the table. Remove the column splits. Add the title, "Table 1: JOBS IN GARFIELD COUNTY." Center the title.

e. Enhance the appearance of the table by bolding the title and making the bottom line of row 1 heavy. Make the top line of row 2 none and the bottom line single.

f. Save the table as a separate document. Print the table.

The second table will display the percent of gross sales for the first half of 1994 for the five major cities in the county.

g. Open a new document file. Create a table from the following data.

City	**Sales**	**% of Total**
Glenwood Springs	165.7	61.0%
Parachute	2.3	0.8%
Silt	3.4	1.3%
Carbondale	19.3	7.1%
Rifle	34.7	12.8%
Remainder of County	46.1	17.0%
TOTAL 1st Half		

h. Enter functions to total the two columns of data.

i. Insert a new row above the table. Remove the column splits. Enter the title "Table 2: TOTAL GROSS SALES" on the first line, "JAN - JUNE 1994" on the second line, and "(In millions of dollars)" on the third line. Center the title lines.

j. Right-justify the data columns.

k. Enhance the appearance of the table by adding bold and changing the line appearances as you like.

l. Save the table as a separate document. Print the table.

Part III

You need to create the newsletter masthead next.

a. The masthead should display the following information:

Newsletter name:	TRENDS
Subheadings:	A Semiannual Review of Economic Indicators
	Glenwood Springs Chamber Resort Association
	Your Name
	Current Date

b. Use the following features when designing the masthead:

centered text
font and type sizes of your choice
italics
bold
lines of different weights

c. Save the masthead as a separate document file.

Part IV

Now you are ready to create the newsletter.

a. Add the text file TRENDS below the masthead. Change the text display to two columns. Make the newsletter margins .5 inch. Make the space between columns .25 inch.

b. Turn on hyphenation.

c. Retrieve each table into a separate table box and insert them in the newsletter near the reference to the table in the text. Adjust the size of the table so that it completely fills the column width. Adjust the type size of the text in the table and the size of the table columns until all the information in the table can be displayed in the table box. It may take you several tries before the table is completly displayed in the table box.

d. Display the last paragraph of text in a shaded text box.

e. Save the newsletter. If necessary, select another printer and adjust the newsletter layout (you may need to change font and type sizes, adjust columns, or change the placement of the tables). Print the newsletter.

SUMMARY

WordPerfect 5.1 for Windows

Glossary of Key Terms

Active: The document window containing the insertion point. It is the document that will be affected by your actions.

Address file: The secondary file used in a merge. It typically contains names and address data to be combined with the primary file document.

Bold: Printed text that appears darker than surrounding text as a result of printing over the text several times.

Buffer file: A temporary file used to store the last three deletions made to the document.

Button Bar: Graphic icons displayed below the menu bar that are used with the mouse as a shortcut for commands on the menu.

Cascading menu: A submenu of options that is displayed whenever a _ symbol appears next to the drop-down menu item.

Cell: In a table, the space created by the intersection of a row and column.

Cell address: The letter and number label assigned to each cell in a table.

Center: To position text on a line evenly between the margins.

Code: A hidden symbol entered in the text when a command that affects the format of the text, such as justification, margins, and boldfacing, is used.

Column: The vertical line in a table.

Context-sensitive: The Help feature that displays information directly related to the procedure you are trying to perform.

Dot leaders: A series of dots or other characters between the heading and the page number in the table of contents.

Edit: To correct or change the text or format of a document file.

Field: Each piece of data contained in a record of information in the secondary merge file for use in the merge process.

Figure box: A type of graphic box that is used to display a graphic figure.

Font: A specific typeface and point size.

Footnote: A note of reference in a document displayed at the bottom of the page where the reference occurs.

Formatting: Automatic readjustment of text on a line after the text has been changed so that the justification is reestablished.

Full justification: The text is aligned with both the left and right margins, producing even or straight margins on both the right and left sides of the document.

Function: A predefined formula that performs calculations on a column of data in a table.

Hard carriage return: Moves the cursor to the beginning of the next line or inserts a blank line into a text file when (↵) is pressed.

Hard page break: A page break entered by pressing (CTRL) + (↵). A new page will begin following a hard page break regardless of the amount of text on the page.

Insert mode: Allows new text to be entered in a document at the cursor location by moving all existing text to the right.

Line: The vertical position of the insertion point on the page, measured from the top of the page.

Merge codes: WordPerfect codes entered in the primary file that control what fields are used from the secondary file and where they are entered in the primary file.

Newspaper columns: Columns of text that are read down the page and wrap to the top of the next column on the same page, like a newspaper.

Operators: Symbols such as + and –, which define the type of calculation to be made.

Orphan: The first line of a paragraph that is printed as the last line of a page.

Page: The number of lines that can be printed on a single sheet of paper.

Parallel columns: Columns of text that run horizontally across a page, such as in a table or script.

Position: The location of the insertion point on the line.

Primary file: In a merge, the file that contains the form letter or master document that controls the merge process.

Record: All the fields of data in the secondary file that may be used to complete the primary file during the merge process.

Row: The horizontal line in a table.

Secondary file: In a merge, the file that contains name and address data to be combined with the primary file document.

Sizing handles: The squares surrounding a graphic figure box when it is selected.

Soft carriage return: Carriage return entered automatically by the word-wrap feature, which determines where a line of text should end.

Soft page break: A page break automatically entered by WordPerfect when the entire page is filled. The location of the page break changes automatically as text is added or deleted.

Status line: The bottom line of the document window, which displays the document number, page, line, and position of the insertion point in the document.

Syntax: The structure of a command.

Supplementary dictionary: A secondary dictionary used by the Speller consisting of words added by the user. Whenever the Speller does not locate the word in the main dictionary, it checks the supplemental dictionary.

Table: A grid of horizontal rows and vertical columns. The intersection of the rows and columns creates a cell in which you can enter text.

Text box: A type of graphic box that is used to display text.

Typeover mode: When activated by pressing the (INS) key, new text replaces the existing text by typing over it.

Widow: The last line of a paragraph that is printed as the first line of a new page.

Word wrap: Feature that automatically determines when to begin the next line of text. The user does not press (↵) at the end of a line unless it is the end of a paragraph or to insert a blank line.

Summary of Selected WordPerfect 5.1 for Windows Commands

Command	Shortcut	Button Bar	Action
File/New	SHIFT + F4		Displays new document window
File/Open	F4	Open	Opens selected file
File/Retrieve			Retrieves an existing file into current document
File/Close	CTRL + F4	Close	Closes file
File/Save	SHIFT + F3	Save	Saves file using same filename
File/Save As	F3		Saves file with new filename
File/Print	F5	Print	Prints file using selected printer
File/Print/Preview	SHIFT + F5		Displays current page as it will appear when printed
File/Exit	ALT + F4		Exits WordPerfect program
Edit/Undelete	ALT + SHIFT + Bksp		Restores deleted text
Edit/Cut	SHIFT + DEL	Cut	Cuts selected text
Edit/Copy	CTRL + INS	Copy	Copies selected text to Clipboard
Edit/Paste	SHIFT + INS	Paste	Pastes text from Clipboard
Edit/Select			Selects a complete sentence or paragraph
Edit/Convert Case/Uppercase			Changes selected text to uppercase
Edit/Search	F2		Locates specified text or codes
Edit/Search Next	SHIFT + F2		Looks for next occurrence of search text
Edit/Search Previous	ALT + F2		Looks for previous occurrence of search text
Edit/Replace	CTRL + F2		Searches for matching text and replaces it with new text
Edit/Go To	CTRL + G		Moves to specified page
View/Ruler	ALT + SHIFT + F3		Displays margin and tab settings
View/Reveal Codes	ALT + F3		Displays hidden codes on split screen
View/Button Bar			Displays Button Bar
Layout/Line	SHIFT + F9		Opens Layout/Line menu
Layout/Line/Tab Set			Specifies types and positions of tab stops
Layout/Line/Hyphenation			Specifies hyphenation settings
Layout/Line/Center	SHIFT + F7		Centers line of text between left and right margins
Layout/Line/Flush Right	ALT + F7		Aligns text flush with right margin
Layout/Paragraph/Indent	F7		Indents text to first tab stop until a hard carriage return is reached
Layout/Page	ALT + F9		Opens Page layout menu
Layout/Page/Numbering/Position			Specifies page number location
Layout/Page/Suppress			Suppresses specified items from printed document
Layout/Page/Widow/Orphan			Turns on Widow/Orphan protection
Layout/Page/Block Protect			Turns on block protection for selected text
Layout/Columns	ALT + SHIFT + F9		Opens Layout/Columns menu
Layout/Columns/Columns Off			Turns off columns
Layout/Columns/Define			Specifies number, type, and size of columns

Command	Shortcut	Button Bar	Action
Layout/Tables	CTRL + F9		Opens Table menu
Layout/Tables/Create		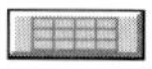	Creates a table using specified number of rows and columns
Layout/Tables/Join			Clears column dividers
Layout/Tables/Insert/Rows			Inserts new rows
Layout/Tables/Cell			Changes cell format
Layout/Tables/Column			Changes column format
Layout/Tables/Column/ Column Width			Adjusts column width
Layout/Tables/Lines			Changes line style
Layout/Tables/Formula			Enters a formula to calculate values in cells
Layout/Footnote/Create			Adds footnote to text
Layout/Footnote/Edit			Edits existing footnote
Layout/Justification/Left	CTRL + L	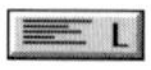	Aligns text on left margin
Layout/Justification/Right	CTRL + R		Aligns text on right margin
Layout/Justification/Center	CTRL + J		Centers text between margins
Layout/Justification/Full	CTRL + F		Aligns text on left and right margins
Layout/Margins	CTRL + F8		Changes left, right, top, and bottom margins
Tools/Speller	CTRL + F1		Turns on Speller application
Tools/Date/Text	CTRL + F5		Inserts current date as text
Tools/Date/Code	CTRL + SHIFT + F5		Inserts current date maintained by computer system as code
Tools/Date/Format			Changes how dates you insert will appear in the document
Tools/Merge	CTRL + F12		Opens Merge menu
Tools/Merge/End Field	ALT + ↵		Marks end of merge field
Tools/Merge/End Record	ALT + SHIFT + ↵		Marks end of merge record
Tools/Merge/Field			Inserts code for a merge field
Tools/Merge/Merge Codes			Opens Insert Merge Code list box
Tools/Merge/Merge			Merges primary and secondary files
Tools/Mark Text	F12		Opens Mark Text menu
Tools/Mark Text/ Table of Contents			Marks selected text to be used in TOC
Tools/Define	SHIFT + F12		Opens Define menu
Tools/Define/ Table of Contents			Specifies location and design of TOC
Tools/Generate	ALT + F12		Creates TOC using marked references and selected design
Font/Font	F9		Changes appearance of characters on printed page
Font/Bold	CTRL + B		Turns on bold
Font/Italics	CTRL + I		Turns on italics
Font/Underline	CTRL + U		Turns on underline

Command	Shortcut	Button Bar	Action
Graphics/**F**igure/**R**etrieve	F11		Retrieves a graphic figure into document
Graphics/**F**igure/**P**osition			Specifies position, size, and anchor options for a figure box
Graphics/Text **B**ox/**C**reate	ALT + F11		Adds a text box to document
Graphics/**L**ine/**H**orizontal	CTRL + F11		Creates horizontal line
Window/**T**ile			Displays windows in Tile style (without overlapping)
Window/#<filename>			Makes selected window active

Active document window, WP46
Address files. *See* Secondary files
Appending text, WP47
Applications window, WP8
Arrow keys, WP17

BKSP key, WP22-24
Block Protect command, WP126
Block protection, WP125-126
Blocks of text, WP5
Boldface text, WP5, WP62
  in tables, WP98
Borders in tables, WP100-101
Box Position and Size dialog box, WP138-140
Braces, in merge codes, WP84
Buffers, for deleted text, WP31
Button Bar:
  displaying, WP11-12
  turning off, WP36
Buttons:
  Minimize/Maximize, WP8
  in Speller, WP44
  Tab, WP59

Capitalization, checking, in Speller, WP45
Carriage returns:
  hard, WP30, WP56
  soft, WP56
Cascading menus, WP10
Case, changing, WP111-112
Cells, in tables:
  address for, WP92
  and formulas, WP94-98
  moving between, WP93
  selecting, WP95-96
  setting display format of, WP96
Centering text, WP5, WP69, WP112
  in tables, WP98-99
Characters:
  deleting, WP22-24
  inserting, WP24-26
Check list box, WP43
Clicking mouse to select text, WP28
Clipboard, and copying text, WP46-49
Closing files, WP33-34
Codes, hidden, WP30
  for columns, WP134
  for Date, WP53
  deleting, WP67-68
  displaying, WP55-57
  for margin settings, WP58
  for merge function, WP78-89
  for table of contents, WP113-114, WP116
Columns, in newsletters:
  defining, WP130-135
  newspaper style, WP132
  parallel style, WP132
Columns, in tables:
  changing width of, WP99-100
  defined, WP91
Commands:
  Block Protect, WP126
  Edit/Cut, WP49, WP141
  Edit/Go To, WP20
  Edit/Paste, WP50, WP142
  Edit/Replace, WP64
  Edit/Select, WP49
  File/Close, WP90
  File/Exit, WP36, WP70
  File/New, WP127
  File/Open, WP12-15
  File/Preference/Environment, WP6
  File/Print, WP35, WP70
  File/Print Preview, WP119-120
  File/Retrieve, WP130
  Font/Bold, WP62
  Graphics/Figure, WP137
  Graphics/Line, WP128
  Graphics/Text Box, WP142
  Layout/Columns, WP131
  Layout/Footnote, WP118-122
  Layout/Justification, WP68-69
  Layout/Line/Flush Right, WP54-55
  Layout/Line/Tab Set, WP59-61
  Layout/Margins, WP57-59
  Layout/Page, WP122-124
  Layout/Paragraph/Indent, WP62
  Layout/Tables, WP91-103

Commands (*continued*):
- Save, Save As, WP46, WP69-70
- Tools/Date, WP53
- Tools/Define, WP115
- Tools/Mark Text, WP113
- Tools/Merge, WP78
- View/Reveal Codes, WP55-57
- Window/Tile, WP47
- Zoom Out, WP120

Contents, table of, creating, WP112-117
Context-sensitive Help, WP21
Control-menu boxes, WP8
Convert merge code, WP79
Copying formulas in tables, WP96-98
Copying text:
- between documents, WP46-49
- defined, WP5
- shortcut keys for, WP47

Create Horizontal Line dialog box, WP129
Create Table dialog box, WP92
Cutting:
- defined, WP4, WP5
- shortcut for, WP47

Date, entering, WP52-54
Decimal places, in tables, WP96
Default settings, initial, WP9
Define Columns dialog box, WP132
Define Table of Contents dialog box, WP116
(DEL) key, WP22-24
Deleting:
- blank lines, WP30-31
- characters, WP22-24
- codes, WP67-68
- to end of line, WP27-28
- selected text, WP28-30
- undeleting, WP31-32
- words, WP26-27

Dialog boxes:
- Box Position and Size, WP138-140
- Create Horizontal Line, WP129
- Create Table, WP92
- Define Columns, WP132
- Define Table of Contents, WP116
- Format Column, WP96
- Insert Merge Code, WP80
- Line Hyphenation, WP136
- Margins, WP57-58
- Mark Table of Contents, WP113
- Merge, WP89

Dialog boxes (*continued*):
- Merge Field Name(s), WP84
- Open File, WP13
- Page Numbering, WP122-123
- Print, WP35-36, WP70
- Retrieve File, WP131
- Save As, WP46
- Search and Replace, WP65
- Select Printers, WP36
- Tab Set, WP60
- Table Lines, WP101
- using, WP13

Dictionary, for Speller, WP42
- supplementary, WP44

Displaying hidden codes, WP55-57
Document windows, WP8
- active, WP46
- moving around, WP15-17
- tiling, WP47

Documents:
- columns in, WP130-135
- copying text between, WP46-49
- creating, WP40-42
- defined, WP5
- editing, WP22-33
- graphics in, WP136-141
- hyphenation in, WP135-136
- merging to personalize, WP77-91
- moving through, WP18-22
- newsletter format for, WP127-145
- preventing widows/orphans in, WP124-125
- printing, WP35-36, WP70
- saving as new files, WP69-70
- text box in, WP141-145

Dot leaders, in tables of contents, WP116
Drop-down menus, WP9-11

Edit/Cut command, WP49, WP141
Edit/Go To command, WP20
Edit menu, WP64
Edit/Paste command, WP50, WP142
Edit/Replace command, WP64
Edit/Select command, WP49
Editing:
- defined, WP4, WP5
- deleting characters, WP22-24
- deleting to end of line, WP27-28
- deleting selected text, WP28-30
- deleting words, WP26-27
- field name definition codes, WP86

Editing (*continued*):
- footnotes, WP121-122
- inserting and deleting blank lines, WP30-31
- inserting characters, WP24-26
- searching and replacing text, WP64-66
- undeleting text, WP31-32

Ellipses, on menu commands, WP9-10
End Field merge code, WP79, WP86, WP89
End Record merge code, WP79, WP86, WP87, WP89
Entering commands, and menus, WP9-11
Exiting:
- files, WP70-80
- WordPerfect for Windows, WP36-37

Field merge code, WP79
Field Names definition code, WP85-86
Fields, in secondary files, WP78-89
Figure box, adding, WP136, WP139
File/Close command, WP90
File/Exit command, WP36, WP70
File Manager, WP8
File menu, WP9-11
File/New command, WP127
File/Open command, WP12-15
File/Preference/Environment command, WP6
File/Print command, WP35, WP70
File/Print Preview command, WP119-120
File/Retrieve command, WP130
Filenames, entering, WP13
Files:
- closing, WP33-34
- naming, WP46
- opening, WP12-15
- primary merge, WP78-83, WP89-91
- saving and replacing, WP34-35
- saving documents as new, WP69-70
- saving new, WP46
- secondary merge, WP78, WP83-91
- unmodified indicator, WP15

Flush right alignment, WP56
Font:
- changing, WP127-128
- current, WP8, WP9
- defined, WP5
- size of, WP36

Font/Bold command, WP62
Footers, suppressing, WP124
Footnotes:
- creating, WP118-121
- editing, WP121-122

Format Column dialog box, WP96
Formatting:
- dates, WP53
- defined, WP5

Formulas, in tables:
- copying, WP96-98
- entering, WP94-95

Functions, in tables, WP94

Go To text box, WP21
Grand total function, in tables, WP94
Graphic lines, creating, WP128-130
Graphics/Figure command, WP137
Graphics in text, WP136-141
Graphics/Line command, WP128
Graphics/Text Box command, WP142

Handles, sizing, on text boxes, WP144
Hard carriage return, WP30, WP56
Hard page breaks, in secondary files, WP86
Headers, suppressing, WP124
Headings, levels of, WP113
Help menu, WP10-11
- context-sensitive, WP21

Hidden codes, WP30
- for columns, WP134
- for Date, WP53
- deleting, WP67-68
- displaying, WP55-57
- for margin settings, WP58
- for merge function, WP78-89
- for table of contents, WP113-114, WP116

Hyphenation, controlling, WP135-136

I-beam, WP9
Icons on Button Bar, WP12
Indenting text, WP61-64
Input merge code, WP79
Insert Merge Code dialog box, WP80
Insert Merge Code list box, WP84
Insert mode, WP24-25
Inserting:
- blank lines, WP30
- characters, WP226
- defined, WP5
- rows in tables, WP101-103

Insertion point:
- moving, WP15-17
- moving to top of document, WP57

Justification menu, WP69
Justification of text:
- centered, WP69
- defined, WP5
- full, WP23, WP69
- left, WP69
- right, WP56, WP69
- setting, WP68-69
- in table cells, WP98-99

Keyboard:
- moving around document window with, WP16-17
- moving through document with, WP18-19

Keys:
- arrow, WP17
- BKSP, WP22-24
- DEL, WP22-24
- for editing, WP33
- for moving through documents, WP22
- NUM LOCK, WP16
- TAB, WP61

Layout/Columns command, WP131
Layout/Footnote command, WP118-122
Layout/Justification command, WP68-69
Layout/Line/Flush Right command, WP54-55
Layout/Line/Tab Set command, WP59-61
Layout/Margins command, WP57-59
Layout/Page command, WP122-124
Layout/Paragraph/Indent command, WP62
Layout/Tables command, WP91-103
Leaders, dot, in tables of contents, WP116
Left justification, WP69
Letters, personalizing. *See* Merging documents
Line Hyphenation dialog box, WP136
Line indicator, on screen, WP8, WP9
Lines:
- graphic, in newsletters, WP128-130
- increasing thickness of, WP130
- in tables, WP100-101, WP103

List boxes:
- Check, WP43
- Insert Merge Code, WP84

Margins, setting, WP57-59
Margins dialog box, WP57-58
Mark Table of Contents dialog box, WP113
Mark Text menu, WP113
Menu bar, WP8, WP9
Menus:
- cascading, WP10
- drop-down, WP9-10
- Edit, WP64
- File, WP9-11
- Help, WP10-11
- Justification, WP69
- Mark Text, WP113
- Merge, WP78
- Page Format, WP122
- View, WP120

Merge dialog box, WP89
Merge Field Name(s) dialog box, WP84
Merge menu, WP78
Merging documents, WP77-91
- codes for, WP78-89
- creating secondary file, WP83-89
- entering codes in primary file, WP78-83
- merging primary and secondary files, WP89-91

Minimize/Maximize buttons, WP8
Modes, Insert and Typeover, WP24-26
Mouse:
- clicking to select text, WP28
- moving around document window with, WP15
- moving through document with, WP18
- pointer, WP9

Naming files, WP46
Newsletters, creating, WP127-145
- adding a text box, WP141-145
- adding graphics to, WP136-141
- defining columns for, WP130-135
- graphic lines in, WP128-130

Newspaper-style columns, WP132
Next Record merge code, WP79
Numbering pages, WP122-124
Numeric keypad, WP16
NUM LOCK keys, WP16

Open File dialog box, WP13
Operators, in table formulas, WP94
Orphans, preventing, WP124-125

Page breaks:
- in secondary files, WP86
- soft, WP125

Page Format menu, WP122
Page Numbering dialog box, WP122-123
Page numbers:
- positioning on printed document, WP122-123
- on screen, WP8, WP9
- suppressing, WP123-124

Page Off merge code, WP79
Parallel style columns, WP132
Pasting text:
- defined, WP4, WP5
- into a new document, WP48, WP50
- shortcut keys for, WP47

Paths, entering, WP13
Position indicator, WP8, WP9
Primary files for merging:
- entering merge codes in, WP78-83
- merging with secondary files, WP89-91
- saving, WP83

Print dialog box, WP35-36, WP70
Print previewing, WP119-120
Printing documents, WP35-36, WP70
- offset to right or left, WP70
- and quality settings, WP70
- saving printer settings, WP37, WP70
- *See also* Merging documents

Quick Finder File Indexer, WP8

Ragged margins, WP68-69
Records, in secondary files, WP78-89
Reformatting, WP23
Replacing text, WP50-52
Retrieve File dialog box, WP131
Reveal Codes area of window, WP56, WP67
Right-aligned text, WP56, WP69
Rows, in tables:
- creating a new line in, WP93
- defined, WP91
- inserting, WP101-103

Ruler:
- and margin settings, WP59
- and tab settings, WP59-61
- turning on and off, WP58-59

Save and Save As commands, WP46, WP69-70
Save As dialog box, WP46
Saving:
- documents as new files, WP69-70
- new files, WP46
- primary merge files, WP83
- printer settings, WP37, WP70
- and replacing files, WP34-35
- secondary merge files, WP89

Screens:
- features of, WP8-9
- changing scale of, WP120

Scroll bar, using, DOS18, WP19
Scrolling through documents, WP18-19
Search and Replace dialog box, WP65
Searching and replacing text, WP64-66
Secondary files, for merging:
- creating, WP82-89
- merging with primary file, WP89-91
- saving, WP89

Select Printers dialog box, WP36
Selecting text, WP28-29
Selection cursor, WP9
Shortcut keys. *See* command name
Sizing handles, on text boxes, WP144
Soft carriage return, WP56
Soft page break, WP125
Spelling checker:
- defined, WP4, WP5
- icon for, WP8
- using, WP42-45

Status line, WP8, WP9
Subtotal function, in tables, WP94
Supplementary dictionary, WP44
Suppressing page numbers, WP123-124
Syntax, for merge codes, WP84
Syntax checker, WP4
System error message, WP13

(TAB) key, WP61
Tab Set dialog box, WP60
Table Lines dialog box, WP101
Table of contents, creating, WP112-117
Tables:
- bolding and centering text in, WP98-99
- changing column width in, WP99-100
- changing line style in, WP100-101, WP103
- copying formulas in, WP96-98,
- creating structure for, WP91-93
- entering formulas in, WP94-95
- entering text in, WP93-94

Tables (*continued*):
  inserting rows in, WP101-103
  selecting text in, WP95-96
  setting cell display in, WP96
Tabs, setting, WP59-61
Text:
  aligning with right margin, WP54-55
  bolding, WP5, WP62, WP98
  centering, WP5, WP69, WP98-99, WP112
  changing fonts in, WP127-128
  columns in, WP130-135
  copying between documents, WP46-49
  indenting, WP61-64
  justifying, WP68-69
  moving, WP49-50
  preventing bad breaks in, WP125-126
  replacing, WP50-52
  searching and replacing, WP64-66
  selecting, WP28-29
  in tables, entering, WP93-94
  undeleting, WP31-32
Text boxes, in documents, WP141-145
Text data, WP3, WP5
Thesaurus:
  defined, WP4, WP5
  icon for, WP8
Tilde (~) in merge codes, WP80, WP84
Tiling windows, WP47
Title bar, WP8
Tools/Date command, WP53
Tools/Define command, WP115
Tools/Mark Text command, WP113
Tools/Merge command, WP78
Total function, in tables, WP94
Typeover mode, WP25, WP50

Undeleting text, WP31-32
Unmodified indicator, WP15
Uppercase, changing to, WP111-112

View menu, WP120
View/Reveal Codes command, WP55-57

Widows, preventing, WP124-125
Window/Tile command, WP47
Windows:
  active, WP46
  document, WP8
  Help, WP10-11
  tiling, WP47
  zooming on, WP120
Word wrap, WP3, WP5, WP40, WP56
Word processing
  advantages of, WP3-4
  defined, WP3
WordPerfect for Windows:
  exiting, WP36-37
  loading, WP7
  program icons, WP8
Words:
  deleting, WP26-27
  moving between, WP17
WPWin Installation, WP8
WYSIWYG, WP4, WP5

Zoom Out command, WP120

NOTES

NOTES